MERCURY
RADIO ARTS

ALSO BY GLENN BECK

IT *IS* ABOUT ISLAM

GLENN BECK

THRESHOLD EDITIONS / MERCURY RADIO ARTS

New York   London   Toronto   Sydney   New Delhi

THRESHOLD EDITIONS/MERCURY RADIO ARTS
An Imprint of Simon & Schuster, Inc.
1230 Avenue of the Americas
New York, NY 10020

First Threshold Editions/Mercury Radio Arts
trade paperback edition August 2015

THRESHOLD EDITIONS and colophon are
trademarks of Simon & Schuster, Inc.

For information about special discounts for bulk purchases,
please contact Simon & Schuster Special Sales at
1-866-506-1949 or business@simonandschuster.com.

The Simon & Schuster Speakers Bureau can bring authors
to your live event. For more information or to book an event,
contact the Simon & Schuster Speakers Bureau at
1-866-248-3049 or visit our website at www.simonspeakers.com.

Interior design by Davina Mock

Manufactured in the United States of America

5   7   9   10   8   6

Library of Congress Cataloging-in-Publication Data is available.

ISBN 978-1-5011-2612-3
ISBN 978-1-5011-2613-0 (ebook)

To Bonhoeffer, King, Lincoln, and all those
who were brave enough to stand up to evil and risk losing
everything to speak the truth and save another man's life.

And to those giants who will stand again this time
and cast a new shadow of righteousness.

All lives matter.

Glenn Beck
Dallas, 2015

CONTENTS

CONTENTS

INTRODUCTION

Jefferson's Quran

One block from the U.S. Capitol sits the Library of Congress. Housing more than 160 million books, manuscripts, photographs, recordings, and maps, it's the largest library in the world. If you put its bookshelves together in a single line, they would extend 838 miles.

The current collection owes its start to one of America's greatest Founding Fathers. After the Library of Congress was burned to the ground by the British during the War of 1812, Thomas Jefferson, then in retirement at Monticello, offered once more to be of service to his young nation. Jefferson, who owned the nation's largest private collection of books—6,500 at the time—offered the entire lot to the newly rebuilt library "for whatever price found appropriate."

Jefferson was a voracious reader and a distinguished intellect. Along with hundreds of books that matched his varied interests was a well-worn two-volume set that he believed offered his nation a warning.

Jefferson had bought these volumes, bound in leather and

filled with yellowed pages that crackled when you turned them, forty years earlier when he'd been a young red-haired law student in Williamsburg. By then he'd already developed a reputation as a passionate debater in the service of justice—even if it meant challenging the laws of the Crown. In 1765, the young rabble-rouser had become known for his strident opposition to Parliament's passage of the Stamp Act, the latest in a series of unjust taxes imposed by the British on the colonies without representation.

As a student of the law, Jefferson was curious about laws of many kinds, including those that had a voice in exotic lands or claimed to carry the word of God. That is why, when he wandered into the offices of the *Virginia Gazette*, the local newspaper that doubled as a bookstore, one day in October 1765, Jefferson found the two-volume set so tantalizing. Printed in London by a British lawyer named George Sale, the books were one of the first English translations of the Quran. After paying sixteen shillings, Thomas Jefferson held in his hands the holy book of Islam. He kept them among his possessions for the following four decades.

When I first heard that one of our nation's Founding Fathers owned one of America's earliest copies of the Quran, I endeavored to do some research on it. I was curious as to why Jefferson, a man famously curious and cosmopolitan, but also skeptical of organized religion, had it in his possession.

We don't know exactly how closely Thomas Jefferson read the Quran he owned. We do know that he is the only Founding Father to have a basic understanding of Arabic. We do know that he promoted and championed the creation of an Oriental languages department at his alma mater, the College of William & Mary. And we do know that he would be the first American president to go to war with Islamic radicals.

It is clear, however, that Jefferson was, to put it mildly, suspicious of Islam. He compared the faith with Catholicism, and believed that neither had undergone a reformation. Both religions, he felt, suppressed rational thought and persecuted skeptics. When combined with the power of the state, religion would corrupt and stifle individual rights. Islam, to Jefferson's mind, provided a cautionary tale of what happened when a faith insisted on combining religious and political power into one.

As a member of the Virginia House of Delegates, Jefferson cited Islam as an example for why Virginia should not have an official religion. A state religion, he argued, would quash "free enquiry," as he recorded in his notes at the time. He knew Islam held little tolerance for other faiths.

But Jefferson was neither a bigot nor an Islamophobe. The irony of Jefferson's observations about Islam is that they were made in service of an argument that would ensure that Muslims— along with Jews, Christians, atheists, and adherents of every other faith—would have full citizenship as Virginians, and ultimately, as Americans.

The landmark legislation Jefferson championed, "A Bill for Establishing Religious Freedom," which served as a model for the United States Constitution a decade later, ensured that there was no official religion of state. Between 1776 and 1779, Jefferson drafted more than one hundred pieces of legislation, but he was most proud of number 82, which is referenced on his gravestone as "the Statute of Virginia for religious freedom." The fiercely controversial bill disestablished Christianity as the official religion of his state.

Jefferson's legislation was nothing short of revolutionary, a first in the history of the world: absolute freedom of religious conscience and permanent separation of church and state. And as evidenced by his copious notes, Jefferson's knowledge of the Quran and Islam had shaped his views of the importance of protecting religious liberty.

Jefferson believed that everyone should have the right to worship, or not to worship, as they choose. It was, unfortunately, not a view shared by the Muslims he eventually encountered.

In March 1786, after America had won its independence, Jefferson was serving as minister to France, shuttling between European capitals to secure commercial agreements. One of the thorniest challenges he had to confront was the growing power of the Barbary States, four North African territories that sponsored marauding pirates who were increasingly confiscating thousands of dollars in American shipping and enslaving hundreds of U.S. citizens in prisons across the Mediterranean.

In London, Jefferson and his fellow diplomat John Adams met with the ambassador from the pasha of Tripoli, a man named Abdul Rahman, to resolve the growing dispute. The war that existed between his nation and America, the ambassador explained, "was founded on the Laws of their Prophet." The capture of U.S. ships and people was a just and holy war, sanctioned by the Quran.

Jefferson and Adams took meticulous notes of the meeting. "It was written in their Koran," the two Americans noted, "that all nations who should not have acknowledged their authority were sinners, that it was their right and duty to make war upon them wherever they could be found, and to make slaves of all they could take as prisoners, and that every Musselman [Muslim] who should be slain in battle was sure to go to Paradise."

Jefferson needed only reference his own two-volume translation of the Quran to understand that everything in the ambassador's explanation of the Barbary States' "holy war" against America was accurate and faithful to Islam's holy book.

The Quran's Sura (or chapter) 9, verse 29, explains the Islamic duty to make war upon non-Muslims:

Fight against those who (1) believe not in Allah, (2) nor in the Last Day, (3) nor forbid that which has been forbidden by Allah and His Messenger, (4) and those who acknowledge not the religion of truth (i.e., Islam) among the people of the Scripture (Jews and Christians), until they pay the *Jizyah* with willing submission, and feel themselves subdued.*

Sura 47, verse 4 sanctions the taking of captives as spoils of war:

So, when you meet (in fight *Jihad* in Allah's Cause), those who disbelieve smite at their necks till when you have killed and wounded many of them, then bind a bond firmly (on them, i.e., take them as captives). Thereafter (is the time) either for generosity (i.e., free them without ransom), or ransom (according to what benefits Islam), until the war lays down its burden. Thus [you are ordered by Allah to continue in carrying out *Jihad* against the disbelievers till they embrace Islam (i.e., are saved from the punishment in the Hell-fire) or at least come under your protection], but if it had been Allah's Will, He Himself could certainly have punished them (without you). But (He lets you fight), in order to test you, some with others. But those who are killed in the Way of Allah, He will never let their deeds be lost.

---

* There are many English translations of the Quran. Because Muslims believe the Quran was delivered to Muhammad in Arabic, most Muslims believe that any translation cannot be more than an approximate interpretation. As a result, every translated version of the Quran contains parentheses and brackets to give context and clarify missing pronouns. For the purposes of this book, we are using the translation by Muhammad Taqi al-Hilali and Muhammad Muhsin Khan, titled *The Noble Qur'an in the English Language.* Endorsed by the Saudi government, Dr. al-Hilali and Dr. Khan's translation is the most published Quran in Islamic bookstores throughout the English-speaking world. I have used the exact translation; all parentheses and brackets appearing in Quranic verses (as well as Hadith) can be found in the original text, which is available online at: http://www.noblequran.com /translation/.

And Sura 2, verse 154, clearly outlines that Allah will reward holy warriors who fight on his behalf:

> And say not of those who are killed in the Way of Allah, "They are dead." Nay, they are living, but you perceive (it) not.

What the ambassador of Tripoli was explaining to the future second and third presidents of the United States was the concept of jihad—God's lawful war against nonbelievers. To drive the point home, the ambassador left Jefferson and Adams with a final image of what American sailors would face on the high seas. The two American diplomats recounted what the Barbary ambassador had told them:

> It was a law that the first who boarded an enemy's vessel should have one slave, more than his share with the rest, which operated as an incentive to the most desperate valour and enterprise, that it was the practice of their corsairs to bear down upon a ship, for each sailor to take a dagger in each hand and another in his mouth, and leap on board, which so terrified their enemies that very few ever stood against them, that he verily believed the Devil assisted his countrymen, for they were almost always successful.

Again, the ambassador was hewing closely to Islam's holy text. Prisoners could be killed, sold into slavery, or ransomed. Sura 33, verses 26 and 27:

> And those of the people of the Scripture who backed them (the disbelievers) Allah brought them down from their forts and cast terror into their hearts, (so that) a group (of them) you killed, and a group (of them) you made captives. And He

caused you to inherit their lands, and their houses, and their riches, and a land which you had not trodden (before). And Allah is Able to do all things.

*   *   *

I started with this story because I want you to follow the path of Thomas Jefferson, a path that starts with reading the primary sources and original texts of Islam in an effort to better understand how millions of Muslims interpret their faith.

Every day around the world Islamist fanatics are plotting ways to kill us. They do so under the banner of a supremacist ideology that pits Islam against the rest of the world and commands the murder of those who do not willingly submit.

It is no understatement to say that Islam has the power to change our way of life. It already has. From mindless security protocols, like toiletries stuffed into clear bags and shoes being removed, at airport checkpoints, to entire parts of the globe now being impenetrable to Western travelers, to an emerging nuclear arms race that threatens global stability, to shaming and silencing those of us who defend freedom of speech, Islam is on a crash course with the free world.

The ultimate irony is that, fifteen years after 9/11, we're actually farther away from understanding the threat than we were in the days following the most brutal attack in our history.

That's why this book is necessary.

This work is not meant to be a polemic, but rather an exercise in free inquiry in the tradition of one of our nation's most cherished Founding Fathers. As such, it's going to tell the truth about Islamists and the fundamental things they believe. I'll spare you the political correctness and the pleasant-sounding niceties. The time for worrying about being insensitive or hurting other people's feelings is long past.

Put simply, it *is* about Islam.

People do not want you to know that truth. They don't want to hear it. They certainly don't want to discuss it. The mainstream media has essentially ordered a blackout of anything remotely to do with it.

When you say that the siege against America under way today is about Islam itself, the PC crowd gasps and says you're attacking a religion, or disrespecting people's right to worship how they choose.

That's nonsense. Do Americans have a problem with people worshipping any supreme being they choose? Of course not. Our country was founded on religious freedom. Thomas Jefferson himself ensured that the Constitution protected religious freedom, including for Muslims, Scientologists, Jews, Mormons, Catholics, and everyone else. Our forefathers came here expressly because they wanted every citizen to worship, or not to worship, as they see fit.

Is every Muslim in the world predisposed to violence or thinking that America is the Great Satan? Of course not. Does every Muslim in the world share a belief in spreading a Caliphate or support the mandatory implementation of sharia law? Absolutely not. Here in the United States, many Muslims disagree with the radical beliefs of Islamists around the world.

There's a crucial distinction to be made between Islam and Islamism. When discussing a topic this important, terminology is critical. Islam is the faith of 1.5 billion people around the world. Islamism is the supremacist political ideology that insists on imposing sharia, or Islamic holy law, on the world. Tens of millions of Muslims around the world are Islamists. They include terrorists in groups like al-Qaeda and ISIS—variously known as the "Islamic State in Iraq and Syria" (or Levant, meaning the lands including Syria, Lebanon, Jordan, and Israel, hence ISIL), and Daesh (the Arabic acronym of ISIS, pronounced "desh")—but they also include millions more who may not resort to suicide bombings and beheadings but who would like to see people like you and me convert to Islam or else be treated as second-class citizens. There is no such thing as a "moderate" Islamist.

These Islamists—people who believe in Islam as a political and governing force—are the heart of the problem. They have a clear agenda. They are not trying to hide it. And they are succeeding in executing on it.

There are, however, moderate Muslims—and while I know this comes off as being overly political correct, it's not an exaggeration to say that they are our neighbors, our coworkers, our friends, and our family members. They are the reformers who seek to make Islam compatible with our individual liberties and freedoms and with a twenty-first-century society. They are also the victims. The Islamic State, al-Qaeda, and other Islamist terrorist groups kill their fellow believers for not being Muslim enough. Thousands of Iraqi and Syrian Muslim Kurds have died fighting the Islamic State and its totalitarianism.

But increasingly I fear these Muslims are the exception. But there are troubling signs, including here in America. A June 2015 poll of Muslims living in the United States by the Center for Security Policy showed that a shocking number (51 percent) seek to embrace sharia over the U.S. Constitution. In addition, nearly one in four of Muslims polled believed that "it is legitimate to use violence to punish those who give offense to Islam by, for example, portraying the prophet Mohammed." One in five respondents agreed that "the use of violence is justified in order to make shariah the law of the land in this country" while only 39 percent believed that Muslims in the U.S. should be subjected to American courts.

If, as the Pew Research Center estimates, there are approximately 3 million Muslims in America, that translates to roughly half a million U.S. Muslims who believe acts of terror and murder are legitimate tools in order to replace the U.S. Constitution with sharia law.

One of the consequences of living in a free, open-minded, tolerant nation like ours is that we don't always see what is really going on elsewhere in the world. In the Middle East, for example, there are many countries where the vast majority of Muslims share the fundamentalist view that Islam is the only true religion and that it must be spread through any means necessary. They are growing in power, influence, and size.

Islam—as it is interpreted and practiced by these people—is, quite simply, incompatible with freedom the way we understand it. It is incompatible with open elections, rights for minorities, trial by jury, and all the other institutions familiar to the Western way of life. It is incompatible with basic morals and decency. It is incompatible with man-made laws and the rights of mankind to adapt and progress and modernize.

This book is going to prove that. Not through theory or opinion, but through facts and quotes of primary source material. You can understand the Islamists only if you first understand what they truly believe.

Those who claim Islam is not the problem, or deny that it's incompatible with freedom, are racist, homophobic, and sexist. Why? Because the Islam that millions of Muslims believe in, practice, and promote envisions a world in which we are required to accept a lower standard of life for women, for homosexuals, for Christians, or for anyone else who is different from their standard.

In America we like to believe that all religions are equal. But that's not the truth. A religion that believes in stoning and killing people who don't share their views and values is not equal to the rest. A religion that supports the beheading of human beings in the twenty-first century simply is not equal to Christianity or Judaism or Buddhism or any of the world's great faiths.

The PC police in America will be aghast at this thought—and this book. How, they'll ask, could you say that the radicals and fanatics of Iran or ISIS have anything to do with Islam? *ISIS is a terrorist group that has nothing to do with the Islamic faith.*

That is a lie, and it's time to label it as such.

Islam is at the root of everything that terrorists from ISIS, al-Qaeda, Hezbollah, and Hamas say and do. Islam is the reason they have recruits. To argue that it has nothing to do with terrorism or violence is the equivalent of going back to the sixteenth century and telling Martin Luther that the corrupt actions of the Catholic Church had nothing to do with Christianity.

If you take Islam out of ISIS, you have nothing left. They are called Islamists for a reason: their references to Islam—to what they call a holy war against our Roman Empire—are what help them gain recruits and money and support.

As a nation we bend over backward to accommodate—yes, to *appease*—some of the most vile practitioners of Islam. As I write this, the Obama administration is making a deal with the radical ayatollahs of Iran—a country that roots for the death of the Jews and the end of America; a country that refuses basic rights to women and denies not only the rights, but the very existence, of homosexuals. In Tehran, Bruce Jenner would not have a widely televised special where he talks about his transformation into a woman; he would be in pieces, torn limb from limb, hung from a crane, or stoned to death in public.

Let me repeat that: *stoned to death.* You will find that word repeated again and again throughout this book. Millions of practitioners of Islam believe that God wants us to literally *stone* people to death when we find their lifestyle offensive.

We haven't had stoning in America, well, ever. But in the *Islamic* Republic of Iran, stoning is one of the punishments currently available for a variety of offenses. Here's how a report by Amnesty International put it:

Iran's Penal Code prescribes execution by stoning. It even dictates that the stones are large enough to cause pain, but not so large as to kill the victim immediately. Article 102 of the Penal Code states that men should be buried up to their waists and women up to their breasts for the purpose of execution by stoning. Article 104 states, with reference to the penalty for adultery, that the stones used should "not be large enough to kill the person by one or two strikes; nor should they be so small that they could not be defined as stones."

What the Amnesty International report neglects to mention is the full name of the statutes that allow stoning: the *Islamic* Penal Code of Iran (emphasis added). Here's what Chapter 21 of that code authorizes in cases of *attempted* theft: "up to five years' imprisonment and up to 74 lashes."

Lashes? Also known as flogging, as in taking a strap to human flesh *seventy-four times*. Hitting a human being repeatedly and violently so that pieces of their flesh tear off the body. That's sanctioned under *Islamic* law.

How about forced amputations? This, too, comes from Amnesty International's report on the Islamic Republic of Iran:

> Sentences of flogging and amputations continued to be imposed for a wide range of offences, including alcohol consumption, eating in public during Ramadan, and theft. These sentences were increasingly implemented in public.

Under Islamic law, at least as interpreted by Iran, you can lose a hand for things that teenagers in America do on a typical Friday night. Even crucifixion is not off-limits in Iran as well as in ISIS-controlled areas of Syria.

In this book, we're going to use the Islamists' own words to show what they really believe. To show what they stand for. To show what their laws actually say. To show what they hope to impose on the rest of the world.

Again, we're going to do this *in their own words*.

We're going to quote straight from the Quran, Islam's most holy book, so you can see what it really says. We're going to quote straight from the Hadith, the collected deeds and sayings of Allah's prophet Muhammad, which form one of the primary bases of Islamic law. And we're also going to expose the foolish, naïve, and, as we'll learn in some cases, intentionally deceptive views of Islam apologists in the United States who have worked hard to convince everyone that there is nothing to see here. That there isn't something inherently wrong with the way millions of people are practicing the Islamic religion. That Islam has nothing to do with the fact that so many people want us dead.

The first chapter will take you into the heart of the Islamist agenda—an agenda that seeks to bring about, in the words of many Islamists, Armageddon and the End Times. This is why reasoning or negotiating with terrorists is pointless. They believe they have literally been tasked by Allah with bringing about the end of the world—and that the time for it is rapidly approaching.

Chapter 2 offers some history of the Islamic faith, going back to the time of Muhammad and the spread of Islamic empires.

Chapter 3 chronicles the rise of modern Islamist ideology and the use of terrorism as a response to Islam's stagnation and the rise of Western powers.

Chapter 4 outlines how Islamist terrorists have used everything from 9/11, to the war in Iraq, to the rise of ISIS to bring about a final confrontation with the West, one they hope will result in World War III. We will chronicle, in their own words, their twenty-year plan to build a new empire, or Caliphate, and expand it to the rest of the world.

The book also contains a section about the many lies that are told about Islam and its followers, using other people's words and sentiments as much as possible. The lies include the oft-heard claims that Islam is a religion of peace, that Islam has nothing to do with terrorism, that Islam respects the rights of women and Christians, and that sharia law is a myth made up by Islamophobes.

Finally, we'll talk about the future. What can we do about any of this that will make a real difference? How do we protect ourselves against people who believe they are taking their cues to destroy us directly from Allah?

In doing all this and asking the hard questions we will be following in the path of Thomas Jefferson himself, who read and thought deeply about Islam. He stood as representative of a nation that had hundreds of captives languishing in prisons across North Africa. He was face-to-face with jihad and saw the threat it posed.

Which brings us back to Jefferson's Quran.

Today it resides in the Library of Congress in the great round room that replicates his original collection. Other than the fact the two volumes arrived at the Library of Congress in 1815 from Monticello, how do we know the book is in fact Jefferson's?

On page 113 in volume 1 of George Sale's translation are Thomas Jefferson's own initials beside one of the Quran's most warlike passages: "God hath preferred those who fight for the faith [mujahideen] before those who sit still."

What possessed Jefferson to mark this page, and this page only, in his Quran? We will never know. Perhaps he was struck by Allah's blessings bestowed on the mujahideen—the holy warriors who strive and fight in His name. Perhaps he turned to this passage before his meeting with Abdul Rahman in 1786. Or perhaps he turned to this passage in 1801, when, as commander in chief, he finally gave the order to take America to war against the

Barbary pirates, the mujahideen of the Mediterranean. Regardless, it seems clear that Jefferson undertook a serious effort to understand the motivations of his enemies.

The mujahideen of 2015 are no less devoted than those of 1800. They seek Allah's reward with even greater fervor. So, to truly understand the threat they pose, we must follow Jefferson's example and go straight to the source of their beliefs.

PART ONE
Islam 101

1

ISLAM AND END TIMES

"The Last Hour would not come until the Romans would land at al-A'maq or in Dabiq. An army consisting of the best (soldiers) of the people of the earth at that time will come from Medina (to counteract them). . . . They will then fight and a third of the army would run away, whom Allah will never forgive. A third which would be constituted of excellent martyrs in Allah's eye would be killed and the third who would never be put to trial would win and they would be conquerors of Constantinople."

—Muhammad, according to the Hadith

Dabiq, Syria
November 2014

The man clad in black stood over his victim.

Peter Kassig, an American aid worker, wore an orange jumpsuit. His head was shaved. He was on his knees.

The man in black spoke into a camera with a discernible British accent. "To Obama, the dog of Rome: today we are slaughtering the soldiers of Bashar and tomorrow, we will be slaughtering your soldiers. Soon we will be slaughtering your people on your streets."

As insane videotaped rants go, this one featured production values worthy of a Hollywood studio, complete with sound effects of heavy breathing and an audible heartbeat that seemed to speed up as the sixteen-minute video progressed. The sounds crescendoed right before Kassig and others were decapitated, their heads bloodying the sand.

Though clips of the grisly video were disseminated around the world, virtually no one in the media picked up the most important thing about them: the location of Kassig's slaughter, a town called Dabiq in northwest Syria. The spark of this conflict was lit in Iraq, the video's narrator warned, "and its heat will continue to intensify by Allah's permission until it burns the crusader army in Dabiq. And here we are, burying the first crusader in Dabiq. Eagerly awaiting for the remainder of your armies to arrive."

Kassig's was among the first blood to spill in Dabiq, but millions of Muslims believe (and hope) that it is only the beginning. Dabiq, they contend, will be the site of the most consequential battle in the history of mankind.

The unassuming farmlands surrounding this northern Syrian town may at first seem like an odd place for such a confrontation. But for supporters of the Islamic State of Iraq and Syria, it is the place prophesied by Muhammad where the forces of Christianity and Islam will mass and engage in a final conflagration.

End Times

In Islamic tradition, Dabiq is the site for what the Bible calls "Armageddon." In and around this village the crusaders, or "armies of Rome," as ISIS fanatics like to call them (and as Muhammad is reported to have predicted), will be vanquished once and for all, leaving an open road to Istanbul and Europe beyond. In this telling, Barack Obama and the United States are the leaders of these "forces of Rome" who will send their armies to fight ISIS. What will be left in the wake of the marauding Islamic armies and America's final defeat is the Caliphate, a global governance of Muslims that will impose Islamic law, or *sharia*, on any survivors.

Dabiq is so central to this vision that it is mentioned over and over again in ISIS propaganda. In fact, it is the name of the movement's official digital magazine. The cover of one recent issue featured ISIS's black flag superimposed on a picture of St. Peter's Square at the Vatican.

ISIS followers believe they will make all of this come to pass—that they are actors setting the stage for the final act of history. Their tweets, propaganda videos, and statements are filled with references to the coming Day of Judgment, which will bring about the death of infidels and the resurrection of the righteous. As Graeme Wood, a scholar on the teachings and ideology of ISIS, wrote in the *Atlantic*, "The Islamic State is no mere collection of psychopaths. It is a religious group with carefully considered beliefs, among them that it is a key agent of the coming apocalypse. . . . The reality is that the Islamic State is Islamic. Very Islamic."

To understand the stakes of the battle at hand, it makes sense to start at the end, to understand the cosmic plan in which our enemies believe they are playing a preordained role.

While there are varying interpretations and prophecies of how the end will play out, there is a strong conviction in Islamic circles that we are currently witnessing the disintegration of the world and the beginning of a new era to be ushered in by a mythical figure named the Mahdi and the second coming of Jesus Christ, who together will battle an Antichrist figure known as the Dajjal.

What makes ISIS's (as well as the radical Islamists who share their ideology) interpretation of Islam so unique and dangerous is that they don't just *believe* that the End Times and the Day of Judgment are imminent—there are other religions that share this belief—they believe they are charged with playing an active role in bringing these times about. In their minds, that justifies everything they do. The bloodshed and terror are just means to an end—to *the* end, in fact.

And it's why they will never stop.

The Dajjal versus the Mahdi

On several occasions the Quran mentions the coming Day of Judgment (*yawm al-din*), a horrific time when the Muslim faithful will be separated from the infidels, who will be "led to Hell in crowds," among "boiling water and in the shades of black smoke." In fact, the Quran revels in the torture of nonbelievers after the Day of Judgment, predicting that they will have nothing but "food that chokes" and "boiling water" to drink while wearing "garments of liquid pitch."

On Judgment Day, the Quran states, everyone who has ever lived will be resurrected. They are judged in the presence of Allah, who sends nonbelievers, such as Jews and Christians, to torment and the believers to Paradise:

And the Trumpet will be blown, and all who are in the heavens and all who are on the earth will swoon away, except him whom Allah will. Then it will blown a second time and behold, they will be standing, looking on (waiting). And the earth will shine with the light of its Lord (Allah, when He will come to judge among men) and the Book will be placed (open) and the Prophets and the witnesses will be brought forward, and it will be judged between them with truth, and they will not be wronged. And each person will be paid in full of what he did; and He is Best Aware of what they do.

This will be a great moment for all true Muslims. Not so great for the rest of us.

The Quran is less clear about the major signs that precede the Day of Judgment, but there are ample Hadith—oral traditions of sayings and acts attributed to Muhammad—that offer guidance. The Hadith are second in sacredness only to the Quran. They are the recorded wisdom of Islam's prophet—the model Muslim—and are essential sayings and stories of how Muhammad lived in the seventh century A.D.

But according to the Hadith, first, the birth of the Dajjal, or Antichrist, heralds the beginning of the End Times. It is said that the Dajjal will have one eye, and hair all over his body. Some prophecies attributed to Muhammad say that he will appear on the road between Iraq and Syria.

According to the Hadith of Muhammad, the Dajjal will be born near Iran and Syria at a time when immorality—specifically homosexuality and drug use—reign. Seventy thousand Jews will be seduced by the Dajjal to fight the true Muslims, who will be led by a successor of Muhammad called the Mahdi. Epic battles will ensue.

Many ISIS militants believe that the Dajjal has already been born. They've even distributed photographs on social media of supposedly one-eyed babies. It turns out some of the photographs are of actual real-life children born with one eye (one was born in Bolivia in 2008; the other, born in India in 2006, lived only one day).

The Twelvers and the Shia Mahdi

Islam is divided into two main branches: Sunni and Shia. Sunnis make up 85 to 90 percent of Muslims. The branches share many views, such as their reverence of the Quran as a holy book and their belief that Muhammad was a prophet, but the 120 to 170 million Shia Muslims around the world take a distinctly different view from Sunnis toward the End Times and the role of the Mahdi, who according to their tradition has already visited earth and gone into hiding.

The majority of Shia consider themselves "Twelvers," referring to the number of imams, or leaders, who have been divinely ordained. These successors to Muhammad were infallible and ruled with perfect justice, despite persecution from the Sunni caliphs who attempted to kill most of them.

The first imam was Ali, a son-in-law and cousin of Muhammad. The most recent was Muhammad ibn Hasan ibn Ali, whom Twelver Shia refer to as the Mahdi. In 873, he went into hiding, supposedly at the bottom of a well, to avoid being captured by Sunni authorities. The Mahdi waiting in hiding is called "the occultation," which, in the Shia tradition, continues to this day.

"Henceforth, no one will see me, unless and until Allah makes me appear," one of the Mahdi's representatives told his followers. "My reappearance will take place after a very long time when people will have grown tired of waiting and those who are weak in their faith will say: What! Is he still alive?"

Whereas in the Sunni tradition of Islam, belief in the imminence of the End Times is more confined to radical Salafists, it is very much in the mainstream of Shia belief. The Hidden Imam, or Mahdi, will set into motion a course of events that will end the world, just as it is believed in the Sunni tradition.

While most of the Muslim world is Sunni, the Islamic Republic of Iran is almost exclusively (90–95 percent) Shia. Iran's supreme leader, Ayatollah Khamenei—as the father of the Iranian revolution, Ayatollah Khomeini, before him—is a fervent believer in the End Times and the return of the Mahdi. This informs Iran's geopolitics. Another prominent Iranian ayatollah has promised that when the Mahdi does emerge, "he will behead the Western leaders." Indeed, Iran's headlong pursuit of nuclear weapons is viewed by many as preparation for the confrontation that will ensue when the Mahdi comes out of occultation.

This conflict will be something akin to World War III, with devastation beyond comprehension. Here the Sunni and Shia traditions of apocalyptic thought become united again around the contours of the final cosmic battle, with both sects featuring a surprising ally of the Mahdi fighting the one-eyed Dajjal.

The Return of Jesus Christ

According to both Sunni and Shia traditions, the Mahdi will be joined by Jesus Christ in the bloody battle against the Dajjal. Islam teaches that Jesus, or *Isa* as he is referred to in the Quran, is among the holiest of prophets, second only to Muhammad. He wasn't, as Christians believe, the Son of God, but in fact a messenger sent to herald the coming of the Day of Judgment and impose Islamic law on the world.

The Quran teaches not that Jesus was crucified or killed, but that God brought him to Heaven before he died. And, according to Islamic teaching, Jesus will come again, descending near Damascus. As one Hadith describes it:

> At this very time Allah would send Christ, son of Mary, and he will descend at the white minaret in the eastern side of Damascus wearing two garments lightly dyed with saffron and placing

his hands on the wings of two Angels. When he would lower his head, there would fall beads of perspiration from his head, and when he would raise it up, beads like pearls would scatter from it.

Jesus will be Allah's apostle and, according to some readings, will help him lead by Islamic law. Jesus then will undertake a pilgrimage to Mecca, called *hajj,* and will help the Mahdi oversee and enforce Islamic law around the world.

In essence, according to the Hadith, the original prophet of peace becomes a jihadist warrior of the apocalypse:

> Certainly, the time of prayer shall come and then Jesus (peace be upon him) son of Mary would descend and would lead them in prayer. When the enemy of Allah would see him, it would (disappear) just as the salt dissolves itself in water and if Jesus were not to confront them at all, even then it would dissolve completely, but Allah would kill them by his hand and he would show them their blood on Jesus's lance.

The Caliphate

The establishment of the Caliphate is another sign to Islamists of the impending end of days. The success of ISIS in declaring an Islamic State is proving irresistible to thousands of recruits from around the world, including Europe and the United States, who want to join the battle before the final apocalypse. It gives meaning to the lives of those searching for one. Disaffected youths dealing with the mundane struggles of adolescence can quickly define themselves as ISIS holy warriors fighting in a celestial battle. Every brutal act committed by ISIS, every barbaric murder broadcast on social media, becomes justified in hastening the coming of the final battle at Dabiq and the beginning of the apocalypse.

As a result, ISIS has essentially merged the tenets of Islamic belief with the allure of a messianic cult.

Obama's "JV Team"

The Arab Spring of 2010 was lauded by many in the West as the stirring of democracy and reform across the region. Praise rang out for the uprising and the instability of governments from Tunisia to Egypt to Syria. President Obama applauded it, saying, "The will of the people proved more powerful than the writ of a dictator." Many others in Washington heralded the movement as well, from powerful neoconservatives like Bill Kristol ("One has a right to actually be hopeful about these developments") to the perennially wrong liberals who had been hoodwinked into supporting "moderate" Islamist groups like the Muslim Brotherhood.

The reality was, as usual, quite different. Out of the chaos of the Syrian Civil War emerged the fiercest, most brutal brand of radical Islam the world has ever witnessed: the Islamic State.

What began as a ragtag group of terrorists has emerged as one of the most powerful terrorist armies in the world, eclipsing even al-Qaeda in its allure to recruits and in its barbarity to victims.

President Obama first declared ISIS as "not Islamic" and simply not worth his time discussing or thinking about, telling the *New Yorker*'s David Remnick, "The analogy we use around here sometimes, and I think is accurate, is if a jayvee team puts on Lakers uniforms that doesn't make them Kobe Bryant."

If Obama had done his homework, he'd have known that ISIS members were the most brutal killers on earth, their skills honed fighting against U.S. forces in Iraq and incubated in the chaos of the Syrian Civil War.

Any illusions about ISIS not having to be taken seriously were likely shattered five months later, in June 2014, when the group seized the key Iraqi city of Mosul, stunning the world. ISIS members stormed through berms of sand that had marked the border separating two sovereign nations for nearly a century. A thousand ISIS soldiers took over one of the largest cities in Iraq, which at the time was guarded by approximately thirty thousand U.S.-trained Iraqi soldiers and policemen. The terrorist army took control of tens of millions of dollars' worth of the finest military equipment in the world: M-1 Abrams tanks, Humvees, and automatic weapons. ISIS was no longer just in charge of the eastern deserts of Syria; now it also held one of the cities that had been liberated by U.S. troops from Saddam Hussein only a decade earlier. Soon ISIS controlled all of western Iraq, effectively governing an area larger than Great Britain.

Days after ISIS troops stormed Mosul, ISIS's self-appointed leader, Abu Bakr al-Baghdadi, looked upon thousands of his faithful from the pulpit of the Great Mosque of al-Nuri in Mosul, the city that U.S. forces had pacified and occupied only a few short years earlier. It was June 28, 2014, the first day of Ramadan, a symbolic and holy day in Islamic tradition that would soon prove to be notable for other reasons as well: ISIS had rebranded itself. The group now called themselves the "Islamic State," establishing the first Muslim Caliphate in ninety years.

Al-Baghdadi rebranded himself as well. He would now be known as "Caliph Ibrahim." Secular laws would no longer be enforced—instead, sharia laws determined by the Islamic scholars and jurisprudents appointed by Baghdadi now ruled. Nor would there be petty distinctions like national citizenship. Names like Syria and Iraq had no meaning.

"Rush O Muslims to your state," Caliph Ibrahim said. "Yes, it is your state. Rush, because Syria is not for the Syrians, and Iraq is not for the Iraqis."

Under the new Caliphate, you were either a true Muslim or you were an enemy.

"The Management of Savagery"

For Baghdadi, that day had been nearly fifteen years in the making. Born Ibrahim Awwad Ibrahim al-Badr, Baghdadi was, by most accounts, a quiet, understated man from Samarra, Iraq. Not much else is known about his early years, but it is clear that he received his military and terrorist training alongside Abu Musab al-Zarqawi, the man who had created al-Qaeda in Iraq in 2004 and ramped up a guerrilla campaign against U.S. forces as they were trying to bring peace to the country.

Zarqawi had closely followed an online field manual called *Idarat al-Twahhush,* or *The Management Savagery,* by an al-Qaeda theologian named Abu Bakr Naji. The book, which outlines a strategy to directly draw the United States into a prolonged war in the Middle East, suggested executing a series of terrorist attacks against U.S. forces until the "media halo" of American invincibility was steadily erased. Naji believed that once America was shown to be vulnerable more and more Muslims would realize the power of their faith and join jihad. "The public will see how the troops flee," Naji wrote. "At this point, savagery and chaos begin and these regions will start to suffer from the absence of security. This is in addition to the exhaustion and draining (that results from) attacking the remaining targets and opposing the authorities."

The field manual holds up jihad as the holiest of endeavors. But Naji also isn't shy about admitting what it entails. "One who previously engaged in jihad knows that is naught but violence, crudeness, terrorism, frightening (others) and massacring."

Though American air strikes killed Zarqawi in 2006, al-Qaeda in Iraq, as well as radical Sunnis who allied with the terrorist organization, took Naji's advice to heart. They sought to sow as much chaos as possible and declared open season on Iraq's Shia, whom they call *rafidun*, a derogatory term that means "rejecters" who have perverted the Islamic faith. With deadly car bombs and attacks, Sunnis massacred thousands of Shia in their mosques, during their weddings, at their shrines, and on their holiest days.

The Caliphate and the End Times

Until 2014, the world had been without a Caliphate since the Ottoman Empire was defeated in World War I and a young secularist general named Mustafa Kemal (later Atatürk) came to power in Turkey. In 1924, a democratically elected parliament of Turkey formally abolished the Caliphate.

Reestablishing the Caliphate had long been a goal for Osama bin Laden and al-Qaeda. And like al-Qaeda, ISIS has since ruled through fear and brutality. When they took over parts of northern Iraq that a small religious sect known as Yazidis had called home for centuries, they beheaded captives and abducted children to train as suicide bombers. Hundreds of women were enslaved and raped by ISIS fighters. They broadcast their murders to a global audience for a very specific purpose: to shock and deter. Savagery is central to their method of ruling. It may alienate some potential supporters, but it forces many more into submission.

All of the Islamic State's activities, from its propaganda to its battlefield strategy, are designed to fulfill the prophecies of Muhammad about the coming Day of Judgment. Some within

ISIS believe that Abu Bakr al-Baghdadi is the Mahdi himself. Al-Baghdadi seems to agree with that view, considering he changed his name to include "Muhammad," something that's believed to be a prerequisite for the Mahdi.

Many radicals believe that the Caliphate will be ruled from Jerusalem. That is one reason that ISIS has its sights on Jordan—it is seen as the eastern gate to Israel. The Mahdi will then lead the Muslim world for a period of years, vanquishing the enemies of Islam alongside Jesus Christ.

These may seem like fanciful delusions to many of us. Dreams of grandeur. Twisted interpretations of history. False prophecies. But they are the deep-seated ambitions and fervent desires of our enemies.

We underestimate them at our peril.

2

FROM REVELATION TO EMPIRE

"Then when the Sacred Months (the 1st, 7th, 11th, and 12th months of the Islamic calendar) have passed, then kill the Mushrikun [idolaters] wherever you find them, and capture them and besiege them, and prepare for them each and every ambush."

—Quran 9:5

Mecca
December 22, A.D. 609

The brightness was more disorienting than the total darkness that had enveloped him moments earlier. The mountain cave had been an escape from the chaos of the city below, a place of solitude and prayer for days on end—but now it had been transformed into something else entirely.

Mecca itself was a bustling—some might say sinful—oasis in the middle of a vast, unforgiving desert. The shrine at its center, a cube of black stone containing idols of the many gods of Arabia, was the destination for thousands of travelers who came to pray.

But, to the merchant in the cave, those thoughts seemed far away at the moment.

What had been a quiet, dark place had suddenly been filled with light and a booming voice that called out one word: *iqra,* which means "recite." The command reverberated through the stillness of the cave.

And recite he did. Arabic words filled his head. Words, the merchant had ultimately convinced himself, that were divine in origin. All those who bowed down to false gods would soon know—or be forced to know—the one true God.

And *that* God was currently in the presence of a forty-year-old merchant named Muhammad.

Over the next twenty-two years Muhammad would have visions of the Archangel Gabriel transmitting to him the direct word of God over and over again.

An ordinary merchant had become a prophet.

The life of Muhammad and the divine teachings he received, later compiled in the Quran, form the basis of Islam. Therefore, understanding his life and the contents of the book that 1.6 billion Muslims regard as the perfect, immutable, unchangeable word of God is essential to understanding the religion. The Quran, unlike the Bible, isn't a collection of stories or revelations written in the third person by humans; it is Allah's direct word, in his first-person voice. It cannot and will not ever be changed.

Despite his being one of the most revered and important figures in history, shockingly little is known about Muhammad the man. Western scholars have been largely reluctant to apply the same standards of historical inquiry to Muhammad as they have to other religious leaders, such as Jesus. And their reluctance is easy to understand. Those, such as British scholar Tom Holland, who have dared to look deeply into Muhammad's life have been subjected to death threats.

Here's what we can say with near certainty: Muhammad was a person who lived in the Arabian desert from approximately A.D. 570 to 632. What we cannot say is exactly what went on in the sessions when he reportedly heard and recited the word of God. Complicating matters is the fact that it would be decades before those revelations would be systematically committed to paper as the complete Quran.

After receiving his first revelation in a cave in the mountains, Muhammad returned to his home in Mecca. There he began preaching—first to his astonished family and friends, and then to others in his tribe. With a revelation reminiscent of the passion of Moses and the dedication of Jesus he condemned the polytheists and idolaters of Mecca who had strayed from the ways of God. He railed against the corruption and immorality pervading society.

Much of Muhammad's preaching resembled that of itinerant Christians and monks who occasionally ventured into Arabia, as well as that of the Jews who lived there. In fact, much of the Quran stresses the similarities between Christianity and Judaism and affirms the holiness of the Old and New Testaments and their prophets, from Moses to Jesus. The Quran even suggests that Jesus had predicted Muhammad's coming:

> And (remember) when 'Iesa (Jesus), son of Maryam (Mary), said: "O Children of Israel! I am the Messenger of Allah unto you confirming the Taurat [(Torah) which came] before me, and giving glad tidings of a Messenger to come after me, whose name shall be Ahmed. But when he (Ahmed, i.e., Muhammad) came to them with clear proofs, they said: "This is plain magic."

Muhammad also taught, however, that Christians and Jews had perverted their religions and betrayed true faith in God: Christians worshipped Jesus Christ, which was tantamount to idolatry, and Jews had ignored Jesus as a prophet and the importance of his message.

But, like Christianity and Judaism, Muhammad preached judgment and resurrection after a coming Day of Judgment. There was no god but God, whom he called Allah. While Christians and Jews shared a belief in one god, the tribes in and around Mecca were polytheists, and among those hundreds of gods they worshipped was one known as "Allah."

The Meccan polytheists did not take kindly to Muhammad's message that, by worshipping false idols, they were offending the one true God. As a result, few people, except for Muhammad's closest friends and families, had any interest in listening. The local townspeople of Mecca did not see a prophet but rather a man intent on disrupting the booming tourism industry they had built around their local shrines.

Shrines, of course, that were dedicated to many gods.

The Satanic Verses

Muhammad was nothing if not a pragmatist. Frustrated by his inability to convert Mecca to Islam, Muhammad knew he had to come up with another option. And so the prophet became a politician.

The Meccans offered him a deal. If he would worship the gods of Mecca for a year, then they would worship Allah for a year. Muhammad contemplated the proposition and asked for divine guidance. It was a difficult decision—he had, after all, derided the Meccan gods as false gods. Should he ignore or twist everything God had told him so far? Did the means justify the end? In response, he received a revelation: the three main gods of Mecca could be worshipped, for they had a special relationship with Allah.

The conciliatory measure pleased the Meccans, but according to the Quran, it greatly angered Allah. The revelation, which would later become known as the "Satanic Verses," had been a false one—a result of trickery by the Devil.

"Never did We send a Messenger or a Prophet before you," the Quran says, "but when he did recite the revelation or narrated or spoke, *Shaitan* (Satan) threw (some falsehood) in it. But Allah abolishes that which *Shaitan* (Satan) throws in. Then Allah establishes His Revelations. And Allah is All-Knower, All-Wise."

It was a shocking admission. Satan had apparently infiltrated the prophet's revelation and corrupted the word of God. Who was to say that other parts of the Quran weren't similarly compromised? Was Muhammad an infallible prophet, a flawed messenger, or something else entirely?

The Satanic Verses remain a source of contention for Muslims today, as evidenced by the furious reaction to Salman Rushdie's novel of the same name, which reaction included a fatwa from the ayatollah of Iran sanctioning Rushdie's killing.

At God's behest, Muhammad later rescinded his offer of compromise, enraging the Meccans and further straining their relations with Muhammad and his followers.

When Islam Turned Violent

By 622, thirteen years after Muhammad received his first revelation, the opposition of the Meccans had grown too much for the prophet. He and several hundred followers left Mecca and migrated to the nearby oasis town of Medina—a move that became one of the most significant events in Muslim history: the establishment of a separate community, or *umma,* of believers.

As Muhammad consolidated power in Medina, his ranks

swelled with those convinced of the divinity of his message. Others, however, including Medina's Jewish clans that rejected Muhammad's claim to being a prophet in the tradition of Moses, Isaac, and Isaiah, were still skeptical.

These clans had been generally receptive to Muhammad's message of monotheism at first—Muhammad had even prayed in the direction of Jerusalem to show his respect for the Jewish tradition and to underscore that Allah was the same god of the Torah and Bible—but as his power grew, Muhammad was preaching with increased hostility toward those who did not convert to Islam.

While in Medina, Muhammad continued to receive revelations, but the tone of his message changed dramatically. For the first thirteen years, God's revelations to him had reflected the fact that Muhammad led a beleaguered community in Mecca. The Quran stressed peaceful coexistence with others, if for no other reason than Muhammad didn't have political power.

But that all changed in Medina.

The Medinan verses, as they are called by Islamic scholars, preach open warfare against perceived enemies and are the parts of the Quran most often cited by Islamic terrorists. Jihad is prescribed to defend the faith and vanquish its enemies. As Ibn Ishaq, Muhammad's earliest biographer, recounted, "The apostle had not been given permission to fight or allowed to shed blood. . . . He had simply been ordered to call men to God and to endure insult and forgive the ignorant. . . . When [the Meccans] became insolent towards God and rejected His gracious purpose and accused His prophet of lying . . . He gave permission to his apostle to fight and to protect himself against those who wronged them and treated them badly."

Muhammad now had divine approval to take action against his detractors, including Medina's Jews, toward whom the Quran was not exactly complimentary:

The Jews say: "Allah's Hand is tied up (i.e., He does not give
and spend of His Bounty)." Be their hands tied up and be they
accursed for what they uttered. . . . We have put enmity and hatred amongst them till the Day of Resurrection. Every time they
kindled the fire of war, Allah extinguished it; and they (ever)
strive to make mischief on earth. And Allah does not like the
Mufsidun (mischief-makers).

Jews are repeatedly described throughout the Quran as cun-
ning deceivers and the fiercest enemies of Islam. As his chosen
people, Allah had given them the first revelation through the
prophet Moses (who, in the Quran, is an Islamic prophet whom
the Jews disobey). This earns Allah's wrath. "O you who believe!"
the Quran says, "[t]ake not the Jews and the Christians as *Auliya'*
(friends, protectors, helpers, etc.), they are but *Auliya'* to one another. And if any amongst you takes them as *Auliya'*, then surely
he is one of them."

Jews are further described as killers of prophets. They are
rebellious against Muhammad's rule ("Why do not the rabbis and
the religious learned men forbid them from uttering sinful words
and from eating illegal things? Evil indeed is that which they have
been performing.") and they are called "apes" and "pigs," epithets
still commonly used today by terrorists and anti-Semites.

What to do with the troublesome Jews, some of whom had
made assassination attempts on Muhammad's life? His solution
was to exile two of Medina's Jewish tribes, execute the male members of a third, and confiscate all their property.

With his opponents vanquished, Muhammad set about establishing the foundations of the Islamic community in Medina. He
preached five pillars of faith: *salat* (ritual prayer five times a day),
zakat (almsgiving), *hajj* (pilgrimage), fasting for Ramadan, and
shahadah (bearing witness to the unity of God and Muhammad's

prophethood). Muhammad stood not only as a religious leader, but as a political one, acting as the Muslim community's governor and judge.

There were plenty of positives to come from Muhammad's application of the revelations he continued to receive. Moral and spiritual reform, for example, were very much part of his message; the brutal existence of nomadic desert life, in which women were often viewed as property, gave way to rules that upheld some basic rights (although still not as many as adult males); and the blood feuds that had torn apart and killed members of families for generations were deemed un-Islamic and outlawed.

Birth of an Empire

As Muhammad's political clout grew in Medina he turned his attention back to those in Mecca who had rejected his message. Muhammad and the Muslims began to raid and loot passing caravans of Meccans. As long as the caravans were owned by non-Muslims, they were fair game. The Quran counseled no mercy until the enemies were defeated and ready to negotiate: "When ye meet the Unbelievers (in fight), smite at their necks. At length when ye have thoroughly subdued them, bind a bond firmly: thereafter (is time for) either generosity or ransom, until the way lays down it burdens."

Muhammad himself led his troops into battle, promising Paradise for any Muslim killed fighting on behalf of Allah. Their enemies would be consigned to the fiery pits of Hell.

The first jihad had begun.

Muhammad amassed wealth as his armies raided the goods of merchants, racked up victories against marauding armies, and cut off Mecca from the trade that sustained it. He had no interest in killing all Meccans, merely converting them. To that end, he agreed to a compromise that would make the polytheistic shrine in the middle of Mecca, the *ka'ba*, a holy shrine of Islam and required pilgrimage site for every Muslim. It was a shrewd move that ensured the money would keep flowing into Mecca.

Conquest continued with bloody battles in the Arabian Peninsula. Muhammad united most of the tribes of the Arabian Desert under his political and religious vision. Christians and Jews were allowed to remain in Muslim lands as long as they paid additional taxes. Muhammad provided protection in return for taxes and loyalty to the Islamic faith. Atheists and polytheists were forced to convert to Islam or else face execution.

The violent anarchy of traditional nomadic life would be no more, as clans became a less important test of alliance than loyalty to the Muslim community. Being a Muslim meant—and still means—more than just a set of spiritual beliefs; it means identity with fellow believers. As Muhammad taught, Islam is not just a faith but complete *submission* (a direct translation of the word *islam*) to a holistic political ideology and the inalterable laws established by Allah.

What followed was a ruthless commitment to spread that ideology to the edges of the known world.

An Expanding Caliphate

Muhammad's death in 632 resulted in chaos. He hadn't left directions for who should succeed him as political leader of the growing faith, so a consensus among the powerful Medinan tribes selected a man named Abu Bakr. Bakr, along with the two leaders, or *caliphs*, who succeeded him, amassed the most formidable armies the Middle East had ever seen. They vanquished the Persians in the East and the Byzantine Romans in the West.

The first four caliphs were associates or "Companions" of Muhammad. By virtue of their personal connection to the prophet the Companions were accepted as rulers by the Muslim community. But in a seventh-century desert version of *Game of Thrones*, the power that came with leading a rapidly expanding religion and empire inevitably created epic struggles and wars.

Three of the first four caliphs were assassinated. In 661, the murder of the fourth caliph, Ali, who was a cousin and son-in-law of Muhammad, provoked a civil war and permanent schism between the groups that would eventually become today's Sunni and Shia Muslims. Because of his connection by blood, the Shia believed that Ali's son was the next in line to become caliph and that anyone other than Ali's descendants was a false caliph. The Sunnis, by contrast, accepted the legitimacy of the Umayyad, Abbasid, and subsequent dynasties after Ali's death.

From 661 on, the two sects developed their own traditions and practices. One called themselves "Ahl al-Sunna," the "people of the tradition"—or Sunni. The other, in memory of the man they believed to be the first and last true caliph, took the name "Shiat Ali"—or Shia—the "party of Ali." Rebellions and fighting occasionally broke out, but by and large the borders of the Caliphate expanded. As Europe was beset by a crumbling Roman Empire and warring feudal lords, a civilization grew in the East with Baghdad and Damascus becoming wealthy capital cities. By the beginning of the eighth century A.D., the borders of the Caliphate stretched from Spain to India.

Despite the expansion, the loss of Muhammad's divine revelations and leadership meant that uniting Muslims around a common direction proved to be a challenge. Muslims could not yet rely on the Quran, since it did not exist as a complete written document until years after Muhammad's death, so instead turned to memories and written fragments of God's direct word on leaves and bones; as well as the Hadith, oral traditions attributed to

Muhammad by followers, which were later organized into several collections. Because the Quran was often contradictory and confusing, the Hadith became even more important in determining the rules for daily life.

An entire class of Islamic scholars and lawyers emerged to make sense of what was valid and what was not, with bitter disagreements among them. There are hundreds of thousands of supposedly valid or "strong" Hadith, and most Muslims admit that there are many completely fraudulent or "weak" ones as well. Part of the reason for that is the significant time that elapsed between Muhammad's life and the Hadith. The most authoritative of the Hadith collectors, al-Bukhari, was not even born until nearly 180 years after the prophet's death.

Because politics and religion had been so thoroughly intertwined by Muhammad, there was no separation of church and state in Islam. The caliphs were both religious and political leaders. They established laws based on their understanding of the Quran and sayings of the prophet, the Hadith. These holy laws make up *sharia,* which in Arabic does not mean "law" but "the way" or "the pathway"—implying something much broader than law. Sharia is, in fact, an all-encompassing way of life.

Whenever the law is involved—or, to be more exact, whenever lawyers get involved—things get complicated. Almost immediately after Muhammad's death, Islamic legal scholars wrangled with each other about what various Quranic passages meant, what Muhammad actually did and said, and what to do in cases where their existing sources offered no guidance.

Different schools of legal thought began to emerge, and sharia or Islamic law began to be codified in a formal way. There was unanimity on the basics, and the Caliphate ensured that every Muslim living under its domain abided by them. In family law, for instance, a man could be married to up to four wives at any given time. Slavery was permitted. In criminal law, adultery was punishable by death by stoning. A first offense of theft meant losing a right hand, and a second offense meant losing a left foot. In trials before judges, a woman's testimony counted for half of a man's. Blasphemy, or anything that might be taken as insulting to God or Muhammad, was one of the worst crimes. Depending on the school of law, there were different punishments. They ranged from fines to amputation to hanging or beheading.

The severest crime in sharia is apostasy, or abandoning Islam by converting to another religion or atheism. From the Quran: "Whoever disbelieved in Allah after his belief, except him who is forced thereto and whose heart is at rest with Faith but such as open their breasts to disbelief, on them is wrath from Allah, and theirs will be a great torment." In Muhammad's lifetime, the specific "torment" was clear: death. A Muslim could be punished with death in three cases: murder, "a married person who commits illegal sexual intercourse," and "one who reverts from Islam and leaves the Muslims."

Apostasy was such a severe crime because adherents of Islam considered Islam to be the final, perfect teaching of God. Those who replace it with something else have committed the gravest sin against God.

House of War, House of Peace

Muhammad didn't just bring the world another religion; he brought an empire that was on a collision course with neighboring regional powers and all those across the Middle East who didn't think of themselves as Muslims. Both Muhammad and the Quran taught the supremacy of Islam over other religions and the political duty incumbent on every Muslim to spread the faith by persuasion and example, and if necessary, by the sword as well. Unlike Judaism and Christianity, which began as persecuted minorities of believers, Islam was almost always associated with power and conquest.

Sharia law developed an entire set of rules, laws, and traditions for non-Muslims. If they survived the initial waves of conquest, most non-Muslims lived a second-class existence. Using Muhammad's example or *sunna* (way or tradition), Jews, Christians, and a religious group called Zoroastrians were allowed to retain their faith if they paid a tribute called a *jizya*. Because Christians and Jews bore some resemblance to Muslims in the way they venerated God's prophets and their holy books such as the Bible, they would not be forced to convert to Islam. They would instead be considered *dhimmi*, "protected" or "guilty" people—the word means both in Arabic.

Though it is not mentioned in the Quran or in Muhammad's Hadith, a concept emerged that delineated the world between Muslims and everyone else within the first decades of Islam. *Dar al-Islam,* or the "house of Islam," referred to lands and cultures where Muslims formed a majority, and *Dar al-sulh* referred to non-Muslim nations that had agreed to a peace treaty with Muslims, often including payment of tribute. Everything outside of that was dubbed *dar al-harb,* or the "house of war." Though there could be temporary truces lasting not more than ten years, there was a perpetual state of conflict between Islam and everyone else—a state that exists to this day.

The dividing line between the Muslim and non-Muslim communities, between the Islamic faithful and the unbelievers, became sharper and more humiliating as the Islamic Caliphate grew in power and scope: *dhimmi*s were second-class citizens, without the same rights Muslims had; non-Muslim religious symbols were prohibited from any public display; and the *jizya* tax could be a crushing burden for non-Muslims. In addition, land and property could not be inherited between *dhimmi*s and Muslims, meaning that if someone in a family had converted, there was an incentive for everyone else to convert as well.

The Collapse of "The Islamic Golden Age"

By A.D. 1200, Islam had enjoyed nearly half a millennium of continuous expansion since the time of Muhammad. Muslims had fulfilled their role as the newly chosen people of God who would inherit the earth through conquest and conversion. For five hundred years, it had worked brilliantly. Islamic conquest and conversion had reached well into Europe—as far north as France (halted only by a French duke named Charles Martel, who stopped the northward advance of Muslim armies at the Battle of Tours in 732).

Islam and Christianity clashed throughout the time of the Crusades, but while Europe remained largely disunited under various feudal empires, the Caliphate flourished. The years 700 to 1250 marked the so-called Islamic Golden Age, a period that often gets romanticized by apologists as a time of tolerance and learning. In his 2009 speech in Cairo, Egypt, Barack Obama said that during this period Islam "carried the light of learning through so many centuries, paving the way for Europe's Renaissance and Enlightenment." He went on to praise the "innovation in Muslim communities that developed the order of algebra; our magnetic compass and tools of navigation; our mastery of pens and printing; our understanding of how disease spreads and how it can be healed."

A closer look reveals that the flourishing of Islam during this period was based not only on conquest, but also on cultural reappropriation. Noted scholar of the Islamic world Bernard Lewis has pointed out that Muslim successes around this time were due largely to their military and trading power. "[Muslims,] at the very same time, were invading Europe and Africa, India and China," Lewis wrote, as well as "trading in a wide range of commodities through a far-flung network of commerce and communications." In the process they were inheriting ideas, inventions, and innovations. Muslim scholars translated the Greek philosophers Aristotle and Plato, as well as other great sources of ancient wisdom.

There were sporadic bouts of violence between Muslims and religious minorities during the Islamic "Golden Age." Though it is often portrayed as a time of cooperation and tolerance shown by Muslim rulers to minorities, the rise of the Islamic empire was not always kind to Jews and Christians. The first caliph declared that no Jew or Christian could live in Arabia, the sacred homeland of Islam, and so they were expelled to other parts of the Middle East. In 1066, mobs in Islamic-controlled Spain killed thousands of the area's Jews.

Like all empires, Islam's "Golden Age" eventually came to an end. In 1258, Mongol invaders sacked Baghdad, destroying the seat of the Caliphate. The Caliphate would go on to be inherited by the Ottoman Turks, but it would never again stretch as far across the Middle East or command the same influence.

The decline of the Islamic empire wasn't supposed to happen. Its armies had repulsed Crusades from the west and intruders from the east, but by 1300 the Caliphate was crumbling. In the centuries that followed, Europe underwent a renaissance—reclaiming Spain and Eastern Europe and going on to colonize much of North Africa and the Middle East.

As the Quran and Muhammad both made clear, Muslims were God's newly chosen people. Islam was supposed to expand,

and the *dar al-harb* was supposed to shrink, giving way to a global Caliphate and world of believers. Yet precisely the opposite had happened. It was a world turned upside down.

What went wrong, as Bernard Lewis asked in the title of his 2001 book? What went wrong with the dream of the global Caliphate? How could Islam return to the promise of its founding? There were no shortage of people with answers to those questions.

3

WAHHABISM AND SALAFISM

"The abolition of man-made laws cannot be achieved only through preaching. Those who have usurped the authority of God and are oppressing God's creatures are not going to give up their power merely through preaching."

—Sayyid Qutb, *Milestones*

Ten miles outside Cairo, Egypt
July 21, 1798

Crossing the desert in the July heat had not been pleasant for the thirty-five thousand French soldiers or the imposing man now leading them. The port city of Alexandria had fallen without much resistance, but the rest of Egypt was not likely to succumb so easily. Not if the Mamluks had anything to say about it.

The Ottoman Turkish empire, which had inherited the seat of the Islamic Caliphate, had placed the Mamluks—warriors known as much for their courage as their cruelty—in charge of Egypt. Now Napoleon Bonaparte, walking in the footsteps of Alexander the

Great and Julius Caesar, was intent on changing that by bringing the ideals of the French Revolution to the Middle East. His immediate goal was to expel the British from the Mediterranean, thereby protecting France's southern coast. But his larger designs were far more ambitious: he hoped to cut Britain off from easy access to its colonial territories in India, the jewel of the British Empire.

They were a long way from home, but now they were in sight of Egypt's famed Pyramids—something nearly every Frenchman had seen in books. "Soldiers," Bonaparte said, "from the height of these pyramids, forty centuries look down upon you."

Also looking down upon them was a fearsome line of ten thousand Mamluk warriors bearing sabers on horseback. They charged straight into Napoleon's cannon fire. The battle was over in an hour. Up to six thousand Egyptian men lay dying, alongside a few hundred dead or injured Frenchmen.

The road to Cairo—and the rest of Egypt—was now open.

Napoleon was willing to do and say whatever was necessary to subdue Egypt. He proclaimed that he respected God, Muhammad, and the Quran more than Egypt's own Mamluk feudal lords did. He brought with him historians, scientists, engineers, mathematicians, and Egyptologists and they made historic discoveries, like the Rosetta Stone, which eventually allowed archeologists to unlock the secrets of ancient Egyptian hieroglyphs. Translating "Liberty! Fraternity! Equality!" into Arabic, Napoleon appealed to the people to take power for themselves and to throw out their Mamluk overlords and the Ottoman masters they served.

Napoleon's reign did not last long. The British reacted forcefully by shoring up and expanding their alliances throughout the Middle East, establishing firm control along the Red Sea and Persian Gulf well into the twentieth century. The Russians seized on the opportunity presented by the challenge to Ottoman and British interests by advancing their southern frontier around the shores of the Black Sea, around the Caspian Sea, and into Central

Asia. Together they would eventually combine to expel the French from Egypt.

Napoleon's colonization of Egypt was the first effort among many to bring the lands of the crumbling Ottoman Empire under European control. A century earlier, the Ottoman Turks had occupied most of Eastern Europe and had gotten to the gates of Vienna in 1683. The Great Powers took advantage of the Ottoman Empire's waning influence and started occupying large areas of the Islamic world. The French took Algeria in 1830, and Tunis in 1881, while the British occupied Egypt in 1882 and Sudan in 1889. The age of European empire building continued into the twentieth century with the Italian occupation of Libya in 1912, while Spain and France divided up Morocco between them. Western occupation, which began with Napoleon, unleashed forces that steadily unraveled the entire region over the next two centuries.

In the eyes of millions of Muslims something was deeply wrong with the new order of things. Islamic lands were now occupied by Western powers that had installed puppet governments. Europe had undergone a Renaissance, an Enlightenment, and an Industrial Revolution. Meanwhile the Islamic world was stagnating and falling behind the advances of the West.

Muslims searched for a reason why the march of the Islamic world seemed to be stuck in reverse. The answer many came up with was that their contraction correlated with their straying from the pure tenets of Islam. They had betrayed the legacy of Muhammad and ignored his teachings—and now they were paying the price.

The Desert Winds of Wahhabism

Islam had been born out of the deserts of Saudi Arabia. It would be reborn and returned to its purist form there as well.

Muhammad ibn Abdul Wahhab, born in 1703, was one of Islam's earliest reformers. A Sunni cleric from the central Arabian Desert, he believed that Islam had become corrupted with "superstitions," such as worshipping at shrines and graves of early Muslims. He said that Christians and Jews were "sorcerers" who believed in devil worship.

According to Wahhab, Islam had grown corrupted and soft under Western influences. It ignored the unambiguous teachings of Muhammad, such as the stoning of women who had committed adultery, and the leaders in the Middle East had succumbed to the temptations and comforts of modern times. They were living in a state of ignorance, or *jahiliyya,* much as the Meccans before Muhammad had. Wahhab believed that he had to save Muslims from themselves by cleansing the alien elements from Islam and reviving the faith practiced by Muhammad and his followers.

Wahhab was the father of the modern Salafist movement. *Salaf* means "ancestor" in Arabic, and refers to the first few generations of the prophet's followers, the Islamic equivalent of Christ's early disciples. Wahhab called for a return to the pure Islam of those early generations. He taught that all Muslims should be Salafists—followers of the precedents of those earlier followers of the prophet Muhammad.

Wahhab found a powerful ally in the Saud tribe. Prince Muhammad bin Saud provided the army to build a new state and Wahhab provided the religious faith and fervor to fuel it. "You are the settlement's chief and wise man," Wahhab told bin Saud. "I want you to grant me an oath that you will perform jihad against the unbelievers."

In 1744, Wahhab and bin Saud took an oath to each other and began decades of conquest to unite Arabia and reinstall a righteous Caliphate—much as Muhammad had a millennium earlier. As resistance to the Ottoman Empire grew among the Turks' Arab subjects, the Sauds became an increasingly powerful force. The early Saudi state expanded into Iraq and then Oman. Wahhab and the Saudis denied the legitimacy of the sultan's authority as caliph and his claim as guardian of the holy cities of Mecca and Medina.

What remained of the Caliphate, now in Constantinople, Turkey, was a mere shadow of what it had been in the thirteenth century, when it stretched from Europe to India. In the eyes of pious Muslims, the corrupt caliphs seemed more interested in amassing harems of beautiful women and material wealth than in spreading the word of God preached by Muhammad. Instead of staying faithful to an inalterable set of laws, Muslim leaders had given in to modernity.

The result was a two-hundred-year effort to reclaim the fundamentals of the Islamic faith and re-create the early-seventh-century vision of Islam in Muhammad's image. It was not just a spiritual revolution, but a political one as well. As Muhammad taught, the two were inseparable under Islam. We know this philosophy today as Islamism—the use of Islam as a political system—a revolutionary ideology that aims to restore the glittering Caliphate that ruled at the dawn of the Islamic world.

Sykes-Picot and the Dismemberment of the Ottoman Empire

Over the course of the nineteenth century, the Ottoman Empire was being left behind. Its rulers had fashioned themselves as inheritors of the Caliphate—the rulers of the Muslim community, or *umma,* worldwide. But their lands were being steadily eroded and their power was waning. Europe, which was enriched by the gold and silver of the New World and then by the Industrial Revolution, had economies and militaries far more powerful than those of the Ottoman Turks.

World War I eventually destroyed the Ottoman Empire, but not before the empire first destroyed millions of its own citizens. The first genocide of the twentieth century happened twenty years before Hitler devised the "Final Solution" to exterminate Europe's Jews. In fact, it happened well before *genocide* was even a word.

In 1915, the Ottoman Turks began a systematic campaign against Christians living in their lands who were viewed as disloyal to the empire. The campaign targeted Greeks and Assyrians, but the majority of the barbarism was focused on the Armenians, a people who had founded one of the first Christian nations in the world.

On April 24, the nightmare began. It did not end until as many as one and a half million Armenians were herded like cattle into the mountains and then slaughtered.

During World War I, the Ottoman Turks sided with Germany and Austria. That decision sealed their empire's fate. In the midst of war, the Allies met to carve up the "sick man of Europe"—the Ottoman Empire. In secret negotiations they agreed to divide the Middle East into spheres of British and French control, with some areas ceded to Russia. The treaty, known as the Sykes-Picot Agreement of 1916, created nations and borders where none had previously existed.

To implement this agreement and hasten the end of Ottoman power, Great Britain decided to foment an internal revolt among the Ottoman Empire's restive Arab subjects. They entrusted the task to T. E. Lawrence, the dashing figure remembered today as "Lawrence of Arabia."

Lawrence's great achievement was to convince the two major Arabian powers—the Hashemites and Sauds—to unite against the Ottomans. He made many promises to the Arabs (the majority of which the British had no intention of keeping), but the most important was the promise of creating a unified kingdom of Greater

Syria, which encompassed present-day Syria, Lebanon, Israel, and parts of Iraq and Jordan. Meanwhile, the British government promised the Jewish people a "national home" in Palestine in the form of the 1917 Balfour Declaration.

Unbeknownst to the Arabs (or Lawrence), Sykes-Picot established new states chiefly for the purpose of facilitating control over them by Britain and France. Britain took advantage of Woodrow Wilson's League of Nations to get the international community's seal of approval for their territorial ambitions. The League assigned the administration of territories—or "mandates"—in Palestine and Jordan to Britain, and in Syria and Lebanon to France.

World War I marked the low point in Islam's retreat before Western powers. The Ottoman Empire was dismembered and replaced by a largely secular Turkish republic. In 1924, Kemal Atatürk, the secular founder of modern-day Turkey, abolished the Caliphate. Suddenly, for the first time since the seventh century, there was nobody left to claim the title of caliph, leader of all the world's Muslims. Radical Islamists, such as the followers of ISIS, consider the dissolution of the Caliphate a tragedy of history, committed by Atatürk, whom they refer to as a "Jewish traitor"—an anti-Semitic slur frequently used in the Islamic world to describe deceivers and mischief-makers.

For the Arabs, one of the bitter fruits of Sykes-Picot was the creation of a mandate in Palestine that allowed Jewish immigrants to fulfill the dream of returning to the land promised to them. Two decades before Israel was officially declared a state by the United Nations, Britain and France set up an entire structure governing how Jews and Arabs could coexist in Palestine.

The end of the nineteenth century brought a terrible wave of anti-Jewish persecution in Eastern Europe, chiefly in Russia, where there was a very large Jewish population. Homes were looted and whole villages were driven out of their homes. It was ethnic cleansing on a massive scale. Many of those refugees came to New York City to live in the tenements of the Lower East Side and Brooklyn.

A large number of refugees also went to Palestine, the land of their forefathers, inspired by the vision of Theodor Herzl, an Austrian Jew who launched the modern Zionist movement in the late nineteenth century. They came with the intention of working and living alongside the Arabs in the region, and the fifty other ethnicities and religions of Palestine. But many Arabs had different ideas.

During the 1920s and the 1930s, anti-Jewish sentiment became increasingly violent among the Palestinian Arabs. Attacks became common, and included the massacre of more than 130 defenseless Jewish civilians during the Palestinian riots of 1929.

When the British mandate was set to expire in 1947, the United Nations proposed a partition plan for Palestine, creating a Jewish state and an Arab state, with Jerusalem to be under international administration. Israel readily agreed to the partition plan, but the Arabs of Palestine, and the surrounding Arab states, immediately rejected it. They went to war. Arab armies surrounded the Jewish communities of Palestine, cut off their water, and began to massacre them.

The massively outnumbered and outgunned Jewish people prevailed. Not only did the Jewish armies push Arab forces out of Israel, they miraculously managed to capture land beyond their original boundaries. Israelis today remember it as the War of Independence, and as the beginning of the Jewish state of Israel. The Arabs call it *nakba:* catastrophe.

The creation of Israel and the Arabs' loss proved a useful propaganda tool for those who saw Islam as the answer for an upside-down world. Now it wasn't only European powers that were subjugating the Islamic world: Israel itself was an outpost of

Western secularism in the heart of the Middle East—and an enduring reminder of the humiliation they suffered.

The ruins of the Ottoman Empire also gave rise to another quasi-state that would one day become a powerful nation: Saudi Arabia. The Salafist movement of Ibn Abdul Wahhab, under the protection of the Saud family, was there to claim the title as the new protector of Islam. The Saudis, with the same alliance forged a century and a half earlier between the Wahhabs and the Sauds, again captured the holy cities of Mecca and Medina to the west. To this day the descendants of Wahhab control the religious institutions of the Saudi state, while the Sauds control its political, economic, and military institutions.

The kingdom of Saudi Arabia rose from the ashes of the Ottoman Empire in the Arabian Peninsula having staked everything on positioning itself as the strictest and most Salafist state in the Islamic world. The discovery of oil there in the 1930s by Standard Oil Company of California (later Chevron) also made the Sauds the richest and most powerful family in the Muslim world.

The Nazis, the Muslim Brothers, and the Rise of Militant Islam

The 1920s were a time of disarray for the Muslim world. Even during its centuries-long decline the Ottoman Caliphate had symbolized the unity of the Islamic faithful. After it was suddenly gone in 1924, Muslims had no one to look to as a religion-wide leader, as caliph. Christian powers had occupied and divided up their lands with secret and treacherous treaties like Sykes-Picot. In Bernard Lewis's words: "Like every other civilization known to human history, the Muslim world in its heyday saw itself as the center of truth and enlightenment, surrounded by infidel barbarians whom it would in due course enlighten and civilize." But after the fall of the Ottoman Empire, Muslims watched as their culture was eroded, replaced with Western innovations and traditions like secular constitutions and nation-states that had invaded the Muslim world.

In the eyes of many Muslims, the solution to this upheaval was to revive Islam. The radicals believed that too many Muslims saw their faith as something that was practiced privately, by prayer and personal communication between the individual and God or by attending mosques once a week on Fridays. But some now believed that this was why the Islamic world had fallen so quickly behind the West and, with the end of the Caliphate, was falling even further behind. Islam, they believed, was a complete and total system that prescribed a political vision and social order. Sharia was the only body of law worth recognizing. The nation-states that divided up the world were false boundaries; the only real boundary was between the Muslim community, the *umma* or *dar al-Islam,* and the community of unbelievers, or *dar al-harb.* The only way to properly realize these objectives was to set up an Islamic state to faithfully implement sharia as Muhammad and the first four rightly guided caliphs had done.

This was the message of the Salafist movement, and it began gaining traction across the Arab world—especially in Egypt, where social unrest and discontent with British occupation and their feckless puppet King Farouk simmered. Egypt was struggling. People couldn't put food on their table. In the 1930s, Hassan al-Banna came along preaching a message that resonated. He said misery was caused by two things: Western influence, and the Jews.

"Allah is our goal, the prophet our model, the Koran our Constitution, the Jihad our path and death for the sake of Allah the loftiest of our wishes," al-Banna proclaimed. He would go on to found the Muslim Brotherhood on a platform of violence and hatred that rejected the West and longed to reestablish a Caliphate. In doing so, Hassan al-Banna breathed new life into the fourteen-centuries-old longing for jihad and martyrdom.

As the Muslim Brotherhood grew, they found common cause with the Nazis, who began to fund them and support another founding father of modern jihad: the grand mufti of Jerusalem, Haj Amin al-Husseini.

Al-Husseini personally engaged in violent jihad—armed revolts against Jewish immigrants to Palestine—and enlisted the Nazis to help eliminate the Jews from Palestine. In return for removing the Jews from Palestine and a Nazi guarantee that he would control the Middle East once the Allied powers were defeated, the grand mufti al-Husseini promised Islamic jihad to help exterminate the Jews everywhere in the world. In April 1943, al-Husseini personally organized and recruited a Bosnian Muslim division of SS troops.

"The Muslims inside and outside Palestine welcome the new regime of Germany and hope for the extension of the fascist anti-democratic governmental system to other countries," Husseini proclaimed.

In 1936, al-Husseini inspired an Arab revolt. Then, after fleeing to Lebanon, he used Nazi money to instigate another revolution. He later migrated to Iraq, where he supported the prominent fascist society and focused on radicalizing Islamic youth—a program modeled directly after the Hitler Youth. Soon after, the mufti found himself in Germany, where he stayed during World War II, learning radical anti-Semitism from the people who'd perfected it.

It was the grand mufti al-Husseini, in fact, who gave Hitler the idea of making Jews wear a yellow Star of David. He collaborated with top Hitler henchmen like Adolf Eichmann and Heinrich Himmler. He even took tours of German concentration camps to see the scientific method with which the Nazis destroyed Europe's Jews. He hosted a popular radio broadcast from Germany with thousands tuning in to hear his fiery brand of anti-Semitic Nazi propaganda. "It is the duty of Muhammadans in general and Arabs in particular to . . . drive all Jews from Arab and Muhammadan countries," he declared. "This is the sole means of salvation. It is what the prophet did thirteen centuries ago." He publicly praised Hitler's decision to eradicate the Jews: "Germany is also struggling against the common foe who oppressed Arabs and Muhammadans in their different countries. It has very clearly recognized the Jews for what they are and resolved to find a definitive solution [*endgültige Lösung*] for the Jewish danger that will eliminate the scourge that Jews represent in the world."

The Nazis were eventually defeated in Europe, but their anti-Semitic ideology remained in the heart of the Middle East with al-Husseini. From there, it spread like wildfire in the form of the Muslim Brotherhood.

The Brotherhood, which had about one thousand members in 1936, ballooned to hundreds of thousands strong by the end of World War II and emerged as the originator of a powerful second wave of Salafism. Unlike the Islam of Wahhab, the Muslim Brotherhood's Islam grew out of cities, not the desert, and included many professionals and well-educated Arabs among its ranks. That made the group a particularly flexible and effective force, capable of working within governments as part of the process, and of maintaining unity during periods when they were brutally suppressed.

Precisely because of their flexible and long-term approach, which often espoused temporary nonviolence and willingness to work through the political process in an effort to seem mainstream, the Brotherhood generated many offshoots bent on more direct and immediate forms of jihad, particularly against Israel and the United States. These offshoots, which appeared from one

end of the Sunni Muslim world to the other, included Hamas and
Islamic Jihad among the Palestinians, and the Egyptian Islamic
Jihad, the group that assassinated the great Egyptian leader Anwar
Sadat in 1981 for the "crime" of making peace with Israel. Par-
ticularly devout jihadis among these offshoots eventually united
to form the first globally networked terrorist franchise: al-Qaeda.

The Brotherhood's goal was to unite all Muslims, even the
Shia. And they were incredibly successful. The ideology of the
Muslim Brotherhood gave rise to every major Islamic terrorist organization in the world. For example, Palestine Liberation Organization terrorist Yasser Arafat was a distant relative of the mufti
of Jerusalem, and Hamas was cofounded by Muslim Brotherhood
member Abdullah Azzam. Azzam, who moved to Jordan after the
Six-Day War in 1967 and led paramilitary attacks against Israel,
later became a professor in Saudi Arabia, where he met and men-
tored a young student named Osama bin Laden.

Another leading light of the Muslim Brotherhood was Sayyid
Qutb, who was the group's leader in the 1950s and 1960s. Qutb
called for constant jihad against "enemies of religion," among
whom he included Muslims who didn't adopt a Salafist orienta-
tion and full rejection of modernity and the West. He believed
that true Muslims had the power to excommunicate less faithful Muslims from Islam, thereby condemning them, like other
apostates, to death. This doctrine, called *takfir*, was controversial
among Muslims, but it remains a key component of how radical
Islamists justify the killing of others of their own faith. Violence
was often necessary to spread the word of God. Merely preaching
was not enough.

In addition to being anti-Israel, Qutb was also virulently anti-
American. Qutb hated the materialism of the West, and of the
United States in particular. He had spent time in the small town
of Greeley, Colorado, in 1949 and came away unimpressed. "The
American girl is well acquainted with her body's seductive capac-

ity," he wrote. "She knows it lies in the face, and in expressive eyes, and thirsty lips. She knows seductiveness lies in the round breasts, the full buttocks, and in the shapely thighs, sleek legs—and she shows all this and does not hide it." Qutb saw himself as a latter-day Muhammad, preaching against the sins of a pagan, ignorant, and barbaric culture.

Today, all major jihadi groups can, directly or indirectly, trace their roots right back to the founders of the Muslim Brotherhood.

The Islamic Revolution of Iran

The Shiites of Islam—followers of the caliph Ali—had lived with a legacy of defeat since the civil war that followed the death of Muhammad in the seventh century. Existing at the margins of Islamic society, never recognized by the Sunni caliphs, the Shia developed a contemplative interpretation of Islam. Because they were minorities and lacking in political power, their faith was largely seen as between the individual believer and God.

But in 1979, Shia Islam acquired a virulent new force in Iran, a force that, in some ways, was more absolute and threatening than all the Salafist-inspired movements of the Sunni Arab heartland.

Nearly half of the world's Shia live in Iran, formerly known as Persia. Like the sultans of the Ottoman Empire, the shahs of Iran had ruled over a multiethnic, multireligious empire for centuries. By the late nineteenth century, Persian society was still virtually cut off from the outside world. But the shahs attempted Western reforms and inventions: telegraph lines, railroads, banks, and even constitutional governance. Their willingness to modernize by accommodating imperial European powers roused both nationalist sentiments and religious fervor.

Oil brought the matter to a head in 1951, when Iran nationalized the Anglo-Iranian oil company under the leadership of their new prime minister, Muhammad Mossadeq. Mossadeq's coalition of nationalists and religious conservatives was a volatile stew. When Shah Reza Pahlavi tried to dismiss Mossadeq in 1953 after a successful boycott of Iranian oil by Britain and Western countries, Mossadeq refused to leave and his supporters poured into the streets. Mossadeq won and the shah was forced to flee instead.

With the help of the CIA, the shah was ultimately restored to power—a move that further infuriated Mossadeq's nationalist and religious supporters and alienated and incensed the Shiite clergy, which began to plot an Islamic revolution.

With Ayatollah Ruhollah Khomeini in charge, Iran's Shiite clerics led a popular movement to oust the shah, and then established the Islamic Republic of Iran. They moved quickly to establish their brand of pure Islam, a combination of political and religious authority under the principle of *velayet e faqih*, the "mandate of the wise" or "rule of the jurists."

Khomeini institutionalized the political power of the clerics who followed his revolutionary brand of Islam. The Islamic revolution that it espoused called for open war against Israel and the United States, and included a call for jihad in the constitution for the newly Islamic Iranian republic:

> In the formation and equipping of the country's defense forces, due attention must be paid to faith and ideology as the basic criteria. Accordingly, the Army of the Islamic Republic of Iran and the Islamic Revolutionary Guards Corps are to be organized in conformity with this goal, and they will be responsible not only for guarding and preserving the frontiers of the country, but also for fulfilling the ideological mission of jihad in God's way; that is, extending the sovereignty of God's law throughout the world (this is in accordance with the Koranic verse "Prepare

against them whatever force you are able to muster, and strings
of horses, striking fear into the enemy of God and your enemy,
and others besides them." [8:60])

This allowed the Islamic Revolution to claim a high ground,
above that of the Sunni Muslim Brotherhood, not to mention the
Saudi Wahhabis, who were openly allied with the United States.
Many of the Brotherhood's splinter groups, such as Hamas and
Islamic Jihad, soon held the Islamic Revolution in great esteem—
one reason that Shiite Iran has long been the primary source of
material support for the Sunni terrorists like Hamas and Islamic
Jihad that are fighting Israel in the occupied territories.

Until the rise of al-Qaeda, the Islamic Republic of Iran was
the only Islamist group that directly challenged and made war
with the United States. It started with the seizure of the American
embassy in Tehran and the ensuing 444-day hostage crisis, and
continued with the 1983 attack on the Marine barracks in Lebanon, which killed 241 Americans; the "tanker war" in the Persian
Gulf in the late 1980s; the Khobar Towers bombing, which killed
nineteen Americans in Saudi Arabia in 1996; and its support for
Shiite militias that have killed thousands of Americans in Iraq.
Through Hezbollah ("party of God"), its terrorist proxy army in
Lebanon, Iran has attacked Israel and has continually armed Palestinian terror groups.

The Totalitarian Strain of Islam

The two centuries since Napoleon's conquest of Egypt brought
turmoil and further decline to the Islamic world. Though there
were different theories about what to do, many believed that only
by going back to the seventh century, when the purest version

of Islam ruled, could the Muslim world be made new. Only by uniting politics and religion in the way Muhammad did could Muslims triumph over their powerful Western oppressors.

The utopian vision of the Salafists, from Saudi Arabia's Wahhab to Egypt's Qutb, provided, if nothing else, ruthless consistency. Totalitarian ideologies provide ready answers to everything. They obliterate freethinking and debate, and in their place they prescribe an entire way of life, right down to the minutest of details. They define enemies and friends in black-and-white terms that leave nothing to the imagination.

But totalitarian ideologies also tend to do something else: they obliterate freedom and morality. Anything done to help achieve the goal of bringing about their vision becomes justified, including the murder of children and women.

Americans were about to see that firsthand.

4

REESTABLISHING THE CALIPHATE

Panjshir Valley, Afghanistan
September 9, 2001

He was achingly tired. A lesser man might have thrown in the towel years earlier. After all, he had seen enough war and bloodshed to last many lifetimes. And while the territory he now controlled had been reduced to a small pocket in northeastern Afghanistan, Ahmad Shah Massoud had no intention of yielding to the Taliban's Islamists.

Known as "the Lion of the Panjshir," the name of the valley that he called home, Massoud was leader of the Northern Alliance, a patchwork of tribes and ethnic groups united only in their opposition to the men in dark turbans committed to returning the land to the seventh century. Though Massoud considered himself a faithful Muslim, the brutal Islamist ideology of the Taliban was alien to him.

For the past five years he had fought against the Taliban, who, in his view, were ravaging his homeland with the same kind of barbarism he had seen during the Soviet occupation twelve years earlier. He had long appealed to the United States for help—but none had come.

Now, dressed in his military fatigues and fringed scarf, the bearded Massoud sat on a couch as a Belgian camera crew began to set up for filming. Massoud had done many interviews like this. When he wasn't leading troops into battle, his job was to tell the media about Afghanistan's plight under the Taliban and the peril it posed to countries like the United States.

He had warned them especially about the Taliban's terrorist foot soldiers, the Arabs who called themselves "al-Qaeda," meaning "the Base." These men had pledged *bayat*, or an oath of loyalty, to Sheikh Osama bin Laden. Massoud had met with CIA officers during the Clinton administration to tell them of the evil that had overtaken his land. He'd even offered to undertake a Northern Alliance mission to kill bin Laden. The CIA advised him not to. "You guys are crazy," Massoud told them. "You haven't changed a bit."

The chaos of Afghanistan was Massoud's problem now, but he continued to warn the West that it would soon be their problem, too, unless something changed. He figured that his appeals to Western journalists were the only shot he had at getting Washington and the CIA to change their position and help him take the offensive.

An aide to Massoud asked the two reporters what questions they would be asking on camera. One of the journalists scribbled on his notepad with his blue pen, as if he hadn't heard him. He let several seconds pass before looking up and smiling. "Why are you against Osama bin Laden? Why do you call him a killer?"

The aide began translating the English questions into Massoud's native Tajik, but before he could finish a blinding light enveloped the room. The explosion was heard for miles around.

The two journalists were al-Qaeda operatives, sent on a mission of the highest priority. One of them had strapped explosives around his waist, and the other had packed the video camera with a bomb aimed directly at Massoud's chest.

War Against the Infidels: The Opening Salvo

Al-Qaeda's war against the West began much earlier than September 11, 2001.

There had been a failed attempt to bring down the World Trade Center in 1993, U.S. embassy bombings in 1998, and the attack on the USS *Cole* in a Yemen harbor in 2000, among others. But on September 9, 2001, the twenty-year plan to install a Caliphate and return Islam to global dominance officially got under way.

It was that day that the terrorist group assassinated Massoud, the one man who could have united Afghanistan against the Taliban and al-Qaeda. They knew that, within forty-eight hours, jetliners commandeered by terrorists would be heading to their targets in New York and Washington, D.C., and that this would undoubtedly provoke a fearsome response of American military might. Without a unifying hero like Massoud, the country was all but guaranteed to disintegrate, to be ruled by petty warlords and weak figurehead governments. But it would mostly be chaos—and that's exactly what they wanted.

Those of us who are old enough will never forget the sunny, deep blue skies of that Tuesday morning. The air was perfect for early September—cool, then warming. Then suddenly there was a boom. Crowds began to gather on the sidewalks of Water Street and Wall Street to look up at the burning World Trade Center tower. Then, just as suddenly, another airliner screamed into view and slammed into the other tower.

It was terrorism of a magnitude never before witnessed by mankind. Hundreds of Americans were dying before our eyes live on television. The shock brought home to America just how near and lethal the Islamist danger really was.

The anti-American jihad had scored a historic victory. The first steps of their twenty-year plan had gone off smoothly, and within days, America would be successfully goaded into sending troops into Afghanistan, a country known for centuries as "the graveyard of empires."

It was, after all, the place where the mujahedeen like bin Laden had brought another superpower to its knees in the 1980s. With the support of U.S. money and arms, the mujahideen had expelled their Soviet invaders. It was a dedicated, decade-long effort that proved the resourcefulness, combat capability, and will of the Islamist movement.

The Twenty-Year Plan (2000–2020)

If we want to understand our enemies, it helps to know what they think and they say. The U.S. government spends hundreds of billions of dollars every year gathering intelligence information about al-Qaeda and its affiliated terror organizations. For a tiny fraction of the cost, and with far less danger to our civil liberties, they could read the newspapers and accounts from people who have spent time with the terrorists and understand their goals and grand strategy.

One prominent example is a Jordanian journalist named Fouad Hussein, who spent years working his way into al-Qaeda's inner circle. He has interviewed some of the most sought-after terrorists in the world, earning their trust and getting them to open up about their plans. "I interviewed a whole range of al-Qaida members with different ideologies to get an idea of how the war between the terrorists and Washington would develop in the future," he wrote. In a little-noticed 2005 book, *Al-Zarqawi: The Second Generation of Al Qaeda*, which was published in Arabic, Hussein revealed the terrorist group's twenty-year plan, which, in their own words, has seven different phases.

- ### Phase I: The Muslim Awakening (2000–2003)

  Beginning with 9/11 and ending with the U.S. invasion of Iraq, this phase was aimed at provoking the West. "The first phase was judged by the strategists and masterminds behind al-Qaida as very successful," Hussein reported. "The battlefield was opened up and the Americans and their allies became a closer and easier target."

- ### Phase II: Opening Eyes (2003–2006)

  This second phase was the "mainstreaming" of al-Qaeda's cause within the Muslim world. The terrorist organization becomes a broader ideological movement, the vanguard for a political effort to reawaken millions of followers of Islam and return them to the foundations of their faith. This phase is primarily accomplished through propaganda broadcasts around the world and with tactical battlefield victories in Afghanistan and Iraq. Iraq in particular, which the United States invades in March 2003, is to become "the center for all global operations, with an army set up there and bases established in other Arabic states."

  More and more Muslims are recruited to join the cause, and other like-minded terrorist organizations pledge *bayat,* or allegiance, to bin Laden.

- ### Phase III: Arising and Standing Up (2007–2010)

  The fight expands from Iraq and the assault begins on neighboring Syria, Jordan, Turkey, and Israel, where secular and anti-Islamic governments reign. Special priority would be placed on Syria, Hussein reported.

- ### Phase IV: Collapse (2010–2013)

  Revolution begins to sweep the Middle East, and the infidel governments, such as Egypt's, begin to fall. These hated regimes are to be swept away by popular revolts.

  "The creeping loss of the regimes' power will lead to a steady growth in strength within al-Qaida," wrote Hussein. Attacks continue against the United States, with a special emphasis on cyberattacks to target America's economic might.

- ### Phase V: Caliphate (2013–2016)

  An Islamic state will be formally declared. The West will begin to lose much of its will to fight, allowing al-Qaeda and its allies to re-create the Caliphate for the first time in nine decades. Because Western resistance is so limited, the Caliphate will grow over time in strength and territory. It is the first step in replacing the world order of sovereign nation-states with a new world order divided between the Caliphate and Muslim community of believers (*dar al-Islam*) and the unbelievers (*dar al-harb*), or house of war.

- ### Phase VI: Total Confrontation (2016–2019)

  The shocking rise of the Caliphate will "instigate the fight between the believers and non-believers." This, in the terrorists' view, will be the West's final, dying breath to confront the growing Islamic armies. The West will muster all of its technological capabilities and advantages to destroy the Caliphate and the many thousands of Muslims who have volunteered to fight on its behalf.

- **Phase VII: Definitive Victory (2020)**
  The Caliphate will triumph over the West. The stunning victory will convince the many millions of Muslims who had remained on the fence to join the Islamic state. One and a half billion Muslims strong, the Caliphate will be the world's lone superpower.

Does this all sound absurd? Well, consider that, as of 2015, a decade after the plan was first published by Hussein, the first five phases have been right on schedule.

Phases I and II: The Invasion of Iraq and the Management of Savagery

Al-Qaeda believes that they successfully induced America to invade Iraq in 2003, an event they used to their full advantage to sap the morale, resources, and lives of the most powerful nation of the world. The Iraq War also conveniently removed the major counterweight to the Islamic Republic of Iran, Saddam Hussein. Toppling Saddam set off a wave of events and instability that gave rise to the Caliphate, which currently calls the western half of Iraq home.

Al-Qaeda's leadership has long believed that the road to a Caliphate runs through Baghdad. In 2003, Iraq became a training ground for al-Qaeda and ground zero for the newly forming alliances between the leadership of the terrorist group in Pakistan (Osama bin Laden and his deputy, Ayman al-Zawahiri) and a particularly psychopathic recruit, Abu Musab al-Zarqawi, who had traveled to Baghdad after fleeing U.S. bombing in Afghanistan in 2001. Zarqawi founded al-Qaeda in Iraq and began a merciless campaign against U.S. forces and America's Iraqi Shia allies.

In 2005, Zawahiri wrote a letter to Zarqawi with his marching orders: "The establishment of a caliphate in the manner of the prophet will not be achieved except through jihad against the apostate rulers and their removal."

To do so, they believed, would require the unleashing of brutality not witnessed since the days of the Third Reich. In 2004, a book titled *The Management of Savagery: The Most Critical Stage Through Which the Ummah Will Pass,* by Abu Bakr Naji, began circulating in jihadist circles. Western counterterrorism experts dubbed it "the *Mein Kampf* of jihad"—and for good reason: Naji served as the terrorists' leading intellectual and moral compass.

The Management of Savagery advised al-Qaeda and its fellow travelers to create as much "savagery" and murder as possible so that the world descends into chaos. To Naji's thinking, chaos would ensure that the colonial borders created by the Sykes-Picot Agreement would disappear as governments prove unable to control their populations and impose their secular, ungodly laws. Rebellions would take place across the Muslim world, and no Western power, least of all the United States, would be able to do a thing about it. With continuous attacks bruising and bloodying the world's superpower, America would lose its "aura of invincibility."

In the chaos, Naji argued, a new Caliphate could emerge. "If we succeed in the management of this savagery, that stage—by the permission of God—will be a bridge to the Islamic state which has been awaited since the fall of the caliphate," Naji wrote, a decade before the Islamic State officially was declared. "If we fail—we seek refuge with God from that—it does not mean an end of the matter. Rather, this failure will lead to an increase in savagery."

Naji drew on the example of the first two caliphs after the death of Muhammad to justify his brutal tactics. They "burned (people) with fire, even though it is odious, because they knew the effect of rough violence in times of need." The massacre of other Muslims was commonplace in the years after Muhammad's death. "Dragging the masses into the battle requires more actions which will inflame opposition and which will make people enter into the battle, willing or unwilling. . . . We must make this battle very violent, such that death is a heartbeat away."

In fact, according to Naji, there is mercy in all of this barbarism:

> Some may be surprised when we say that the religious practice of jihad despite the blood, corpses, and limbs which encompass it and the killing and fighting which its practice entails is among the most blessed acts of worship for the servants. . . . Jihad is the most merciful of the methods for all created things and the most sparing of the spilling of blood.

The shocking violence of beheadings, crucifixions, and murder of women and children is anything but senseless. It is purposeful: necessary to strike fear and create a lasting psychological effect that the Caliphate is inevitable and its followers are willing to stop at nothing to impose it.

Zarqawi implemented Naji's barbaric vision with ruthless efficiency. Before he became the leader of al-Qaeda in Iraq, al-Qaeda as a whole was responsible for the deaths of around 3,200 people worldwide. In just two years, Zarqawi's group was responsible for the deaths of twice that many people in Iraq alone.

Iraq is also where al-Qaeda transitioned from a small terrorist group into a broader social movement. With Zarqawi, and his senior lieutenant, Abu Bakr al-Baghdadi (who would go on to become the first caliph), the beginnings of what would become ISIS had formed.

Phases I and II were successfully completed, right on schedule.

Phases III and IV: Arab Spring, Arab Winter, and the Syrian Civil War

As Zarqawi and his followers forced Iraq into the depths of chaos, al-Qaeda's strategy to stoke a global civil war that could lay the foundations for a new Caliphate began to take shape.

One ripe target was Egypt. Ever since the more extreme off-shoots of the Muslim Brotherhood assassinated Egypt's moderate president, Anwar Sadat, in 1981, they have kept their eye on the prize: the final takeover of the most populous and culturally significant nation in the Arab world. It took nearly a quarter of a century, but in 2011 unrest led to the toppling of Egypt's dictator, Hosni Mubarak. He was thrown into prison and the Muslim Brotherhood swept into power.

This was the culmination of what became known here in the West as "the Arab Spring." In one telling of it, the Arab Spring began when a Tunisian fruit vendor set himself ablaze to protest the lack of individual rights in his country. This allegedly led to a sweeping movement where some, but not all, protesters demanded democracy and political freedom. At the time, Barack Obama and neoconservatives alike heralded the triumph of freedom. What followed, they wanted us to believe, would be a mass democratic movement across the Middle East, the very embodiment of the human aspiration to be free.

That, of course, is not at all what happened. And this rosy view was not in any way representative of what was going on at the time.

What the Arab Spring was really about was the ascendance of Islamic supremacy, with Islamist parties such as the Muslim Brotherhood using the euphoria to take power. Calls for democracy are "just the train we board to reach our destination," according to Turkey's Islamist strongman Recep Tayyip Erdogan.

Democracy, at least where it's been tried in Iraq, the Gaza Strip, and Egypt, has led only to the election of undemocratic strongmen and Islamist parties that see democracy as a temporary step toward sharia. The truth is that freedom has a different meaning for most Muslims in the Middle East than it does for the rest of us. In the Islamic tradition, freedom, or *hurriyah,* is freedom from man-made laws. "We want to free all people from being slaves of men and make them slaves to Allah," explained Abu Abdullah, one of the leaders of Hizb-ut-Tahrir, an Islamist political party with thousands of members worldwide.

"Democracy" in the Islamic world, simply put, isn't really democracy—it's Islamic supremacy led by rulers, not representatives. Leaders of Islamic "democracies" are there to interpret and execute God's law. As Middle Eastern historian Bernard Lewis wrote in 1954:

> [T]he political history of Islam is one of almost unrelieved autocracy. . . . [It] was authoritarian, often arbitrary, sometimes tyrannical. There are no parliaments or representative assemblies of any kind, no councils or communes, no chambers of nobility or estates, no municipalities in the history of Islam; nothing but sovereign power, to which the subject owed complete and unwavering obedience as a religious duty imposed by the Holy Law.

Islamism cannot coexist with freedom in any meaningful way. Votes may be held, and constitutions may be written, but societies that insist on a truly Islamic foundation for their political authority do not allow for straying from what's demanded by the Quran and Hadith. As Egypt's leading Muslim Brotherhood scholar, Sheikh Qaradawi, said, "Legislation belongs to God, and we only fill in the blanks."

Put simply, there is the truth as revealed by Islam—and there is everything else. God's truth necessarily suppresses free expression and free will, and gives way to a totalitarianism in which no democracy deserving of the name can function in a meaningful way. It's little wonder why the "mass democratic uprisings" of the Arab Spring withered on the vine and now lie dormant in the bitter winter that has swept from North Africa to the Persian Gulf.

Al-Qaeda and its Sunni Islamist allies not only toppled the most important secular government in the region in Egypt; they also successfully provoked a civil war in Syria against dictator Bashar al-Assad, who belongs to the Alawite (non-Sunni) majority. Syria, as explained earlier, is home to Dabiq, a place viewed by many Muslims as the location of the final battle between the forces of Islam and the infidels. Just as important, it is the doorstep to toppling Jordan and Israel, one good reason why there was a "special focus" on Syria in Phase III of al-Qaeda's twenty-year plan.

In 2011, Assad's opposition was a hodgepodge that included some secularists and reformers who were quickly outgunned, killed, or sent into exile. Those who remained were the hard-core Salafist Islamist holdouts and al-Qaeda affiliates, many of whom were combat-hardened veterans from the wars in Iraq and Afghanistan. These groups were themselves divided, with various smaller groups, such as Jabhat al-Nusra and the Yarmouk Brigade, all vying for influence.

The Obama administration saw little danger in the growing menace. In September 2013, they came within days of providing al-Qaeda with the world's most advanced air force before public and congressional outcry forced them to reverse course.

The Syrian Civil War had created a vacuum in which ISIS could recruit, train, and kill, almost at will. All they needed next was a government.

Phases III and IV were complete, right on schedule.

Phase V: The Black Flag of the Caliphate and the Merging of al-Qaeda and the Islamic State

Five months after President Obama referred to ISIS as the JV team, they established the Islamic State and a Caliphate, a terrorist state in the heart of the Middle East. Its capital is al-Raqqa in eastern Syria. Week by week, the Islamic State has taken more and more territory with impunity.

We are now in the midst of witnessing the merging of al-Qaeda and the Islamic State. As we've already seen, before there was an Islamic State, there was ISIS, and before there was ISIS there was al-Qaeda's Iraq branch. The Obama administration would prefer to keep al-Qaeda separate from the Islamic State so they can continue to boast about how they have "decimated" the terrorist group that struck us on 9/11. They would have us believe that "core al-Qaeda," a narrow and misleading term meant to limit the group to its current leader, the aging Ayman al-Zawahiri, and his immediate inner circle in Pakistan, has little impact anymore.

But this cheerful appraisal of the situation misses the point that al-Qaeda has evolved from a terrorist organization to an ideological movement to which ISIS and dozens of other jihadi groups pledge allegiance. As left-wing journalist Patrick Cockburn, who has spent more time in Syria studying the rise of ISIS than any other Western journalist, wrote:

Al-Qa'ida's name became primarily a rallying cry, a set of Islamic beliefs, centering on the creation of an Islamic state, the imposition of sharia, a return to Islamic customs, the subjugation of women, and the waging of holy war against other Muslims, notably the Shia, who are considered heretics worthy of death. . . . It has always been in the interest of the US and other governments that al-Qa'ida be viewed as having a command-and-control structure like a mini-Pentagon, or like the mafia in America. This is a comforting image for the public because organized groups, however demonic, can be tracked down and eliminated through imprisonment or death. More alarming is the reality of a movement whose adherents are self-recruited and can spring up anywhere.

In 2014, with the declaration of the Islamic State, al-Qaeda ideology and terrorist tactics went mainstream and were adopted by a quasi-government that controls and governs territory. Not coincidentally, this was exactly the plan al-Qaeda had outlined a decade earlier when it predicted that other terrorist groups would adopt its goals and that, by 2013, a new Islamic government would form a Caliphate under its banner.

Phase V was also successfully completed, right on schedule.

Phase VI: Total Confrontation

The Islamists believe we are currently in the sixth phase of their plan right now—a global conflict with the West that will bring about our last, dying gasps, while also expunging those Muslims who deny fundamentalist Islamic authority.

Al-Qaeda and ISIS have targeted for death thousands of Shia in Iraq, whom the Islamic State calls *rafidah,* a slur from early

Islam that means "rejecters," or people who deny legitimate Islamic authority. ISIS, Saudi Arabia, Pakistan, and other Sunni nations of the Gulf are also aligning against the Shia in Iran.

Iran, meanwhile, is fighting back on behalf of the region's Shia population, escalating the civil war within Islam to bloody proportions not seen in more than a millennium. Iran has created a vassal state with the neighboring government in Iraq, with its Shia soldiers and militias becoming the only effective fighting force against the Islamic State. Iran has funded rebellions of Shia minorities in Bahrain and Yemen to foment instability. Iran, in short, is trying to re-create the Persian Empire, which was defeated by the first armies of Islam in the seventh century and became part of the Ummayad Caliphate.

While this vicious conflict within Islam is already well under way, few people in our government even seem to understand it. Silvestre Reyes, a Texas Democrat who was the incoming *chairman of the House Intelligence Committee* (before Republicans reclaimed Congress), was asked whether al-Qaeda was Sunni or Shia. He didn't really know. "Predominantly—probably Shiite," he responded. And Hezbollah in Lebanon? "Hezbollah, uh, Hezbollah . . . Why do you ask me these questions at 5 o'clock?" He later offered an explanation: "Speaking only for myself, it's hard to keep things in perspective and in the categories."

And yet perspective and categories are exactly what we need if we want to understand the war that is engulfing Islam and threatens to expand into a global war, annihilating Israel, and posing a dire threat to America and the West.

If there is a glimmer of hope in all of this bad news it is that the Sunni and Shia extremists hate each other almost as much as they hate Israel and the West. They are already killing each other in droves across Iraq and in places like Yemen where civil wars are breaking out. But here's the thing: while they kill each other with

AK-47s, RPGs, and suicide bombs for now, each side is seeking to be the first to get its hands on the ultimate prize: nuclear weapons. This is a nightmare scenario—one that could literally bring about the End Times in the form of a nuclear winter that engulfs the region, and possibly the world.

The U.S. government is not helping matters. Under the terms of a negotiated nuclear agreement with Iran, the United States will effectively bless Iran's nuclear program in return for a normalization of relations between the two countries. To counter Iran, Saudi Arabia then made the "strategic decision" to acquire "off-the-shelf" atomic weapons from Pakistan.

Given the splintering sides between Team Shia and Team Sunni, it's not inconceivable that a nuclear Saudi Arabia could ally with the Islamic State. Both are ruled by extreme Salafist Sunni Muslims.

The Islamic State is trying to persuade Sunni Muslims that they are the true protectors of Islam. And there are some signs that it's working. Ibrahim Hamidi, a journalist and leading analyst of the Islamic State, told the *New York Times* that the group is "hijacking legitimate demands"—meaning that they are filling a political and social vacuum in the areas they conquer. "Now," Hamidi explained, "with the sectarian polarization of the region, under the skin of every single Sunni there is a tiny Daesh." (*Daesh* is the Arabic acronym for the Islamic State.)

In other words, even the many Muslims who object to the Islamic State's brutal tactics are beginning to sympathize with their goals. They've become so mainstream that there's even a slang word for the many people who are inclined to support ISIS: *Dawoosh,* an Arabic term that means "cute little Daesh."

The Islamic State and Iran are forcing the Islamic world into two camps, opposed to each other by virtue of a 1,300-year-old split but united in their embrace of radical Islamism and totalitarian, apocalyptic ideology. Increasingly there is no room for moderates in the middle.

Most people in the West are still blind to this—but if Phase VI of the plan is executed as effectively and efficiently as the other five phases, they won't be blind for long.

PART TWO

Thirteen Deadly Lies

"If you look for truth, you may find comfort in the end; if you look for comfort you will not get either comfort or truth; only soft soap and wishful thinking to begin, and in the end, despair."

—C. S. Lewis

INTRODUCTION TO PART TWO

We haven't been honest with ourselves for a long time. We've allowed political correctness, fear, and simple ignorance to mask basic truths about Islam and the Quran. These truths need to be confronted in order to defend ourselves, our families, and our country.

In other words, we need to stop lying to ourselves—and, perhaps more important, we need to stop allowing ourselves to be lied to.

We hear lies about Islam nearly every day, in nearly every place, in nearly every manner. They usually originate with elites in the media, in Washington, D.C., and Hollywood. In 2010, for example, National Public Radio aired a bizarre segment with the headline "Is the Bible more violent than the Quran?" (Spoiler alert: liberal NPR says yes!) A few years later, noted Islam expert Ben Affleck took Bill Maher to task for attacking what Affleck called "the officially codified doctrine of Islam." Questioning the tenets of Islam, Affleck claimed, was "gross" and "racist."

The Architect of Lies

How did we get here?

With their supremacist ideology, whether the form practiced

by Abu Bakr al-Baghdadi and the Islamic State or Ayatollah Ali Khamenei and the clerics of the Islamic Republic of Iran, Islamists know what they stand for.

But do we?

I'm not so sure anymore. America and the West are more timid than ever. Those of us who stand up for our most cherished values—freedom of expression, for example—are denounced as insensitive racists and pronounced guilty of hate speech. Government leaders and media types pile on, telling us that we are in no place to criticize other cultures and religions. It's a mentality that has infected the entire discussion—or lack thereof—surrounding Islam and terrorism.

I want to introduce you to someone whom very few people outside of academic circles have ever heard of, yet who has had the most enduring impact on the way we talk and think about Islam and the Middle East. Perhaps no one is more responsible for imposing a straitjacket of political correctness on any discussion involving Islam than the late Edward Said (pronounced SIGH-eed).

Said grew up in Jerusalem and Cairo in an affluent family. He came to America to study at an elite New England prep school, and then went on to Princeton and Harvard, where he got his Ph.D. He eventually became a professor of literature at Columbia University, where in 1978 he published *Orientalism*, a book that forever changed the way academia, the mainstream media, and the West's elites thought about Islam and the Middle East.

Said argued that the entire field of Middle Eastern history and studies in the West was an exercise in creating the perception of a different and inferior "Oriental culture" so that it could be taken over by Western imperialists. He claimed that all Western scholarship on the Middle East and Islam was a form of racism, an intrinsically hostile pillar of imperialism. Any Westerner or non-Muslim who studied Islam or the Middle East, intentionally or not, developed an "absolute and systematic difference between the West, which is rational, developed, humane, superior, and the Orient, which is aberrant, undeveloped, inferior." In other words, Said believed that if you're a person of European descent then talking about the religion of 1.6 billion Muslims is inherently racist.

Said's book created shock waves in the academic world. It was soon translated into more than three dozen languages, and became deeply influential in most of the world's universities. In 2005, Edward Said's books were assigned as reading in at least 868 courses in American colleges and universities, counting only courses whose syllabi were available online. More than forty books have been published about Said and multiple universities offer whole courses about him.

Said accused Western scholars of Eastern studies, particularly Middle Eastern studies, as conscious enablers of exploitation and subjugation. Linguists, historians, anthropologists, and archeologists had all been willing instruments of colonialism and empire building. Western scholars had accomplished this evil work by defining the West in opposition to the "other." In the case of "Orientals" the "other" was someone "to be feared . . . or to be controlled." He claimed that literally everything a European or American said about the Orient made them "a racist, an imperialist, and almost totally ethnocentric." He framed the Israeli-Palestinian struggle in terms of white European colonial oppression of poor, helpless dark-skinned natives.

Multiculturalism started out as a form of enhanced tolerance for cultural differences. Edward Said turned that into an instrument of intolerance, a system for classifying all kinds of comments about Middle Eastern religions, cultures, and societies as racist and forbidden. He taught a whole generation of students how to hurl accusations of "hostility" and "racism" when they disagree with someone.

Our universities are teaching students how to use victimhood, grievance, and taking offense as tools of control. Students are being taught socially acceptable ways to censor each other, to control each other's speech, and to suppress beliefs they don't agree with.

When a military unit is about to make a move or attack a target, they often start with "suppression fire." They sweep everything in front of their attacking unit with artillery and machine-gun rounds, forcing the enemy to duck for cover so their troops can advance. That's pretty much how Said's theories, his framing of the Israeli-Palestinian dispute, and his cult of censorship all advance the Islamist cause and the terrorists who kill in Islam's name.

As Islamists gain momentum, there are seemingly fewer and fewer people who are willing to stand and call the enemy by their name. Said's disciples and his fear-inducing rules for thinking about the world make those people duck for cover.

When they do, the Islamist troops advance even further.

It *Is* About Islam

Think back on the last decade. How many times has the following scenario played out? There's been a horrific terrorist attack somewhere around the globe. Amid the initial confusion, several key facts become clear: The perpetrators were observant Muslims who recorded a video to alert the world they were engaged in jihad. The perpetrators' families and community proudly declare them *shahid*s, or martyrs. Before the day is out, talking heads in the media are showcasing a parade of Ph.D.s and government officials calmly telling the audience that this, in fact, had nothing to do with Islam.

It's been the refrain since 2001, first from the Bush administration, then from Obama's. It could've been a plausible argument had there been one or two terrorist attacks rather than the 25,000 global incidents (according to a website that tracks terrorist activities around the world) we've endured. It could've fooled a lot more people in a time before TV news, the Internet, and social media. But when we see the most graphic barbarism accompanied by constant calls for sharia, or Islamic law—and justified by passages in the Quran and Hadith—it should become plainly obvious that we're being lied to.

In fact, for the mainstream media, the only criterion for alternate theories about the cause of terrorism seems to be that they must have absolutely nothing to do with Islam. Instead the causes cited usually include things like poverty, American foreign policy, and, of course, Israel. As we'll see, they've even tried to make global warming the explanation for why ISIS terrorists have undertaken a campaign of murder sweeping the Middle East.

These people are clueless. But the rest of us don't have to be.

The American people aren't stupid. Even in the face of unrelenting media assurances, bald-faced propaganda, and smug lies from the most powerful public officials, things are so utterly and obviously wrong that even a hypnotized and often distracted nation has a hard time believing them any longer.

In this section of the book we'll do what very few people seem to be willing to: we will take apart the lies we commonly hear about Islam. We will systematically dismantle the notion that terrorist organizations like al-Qaeda, rogue regimes like Iran, apocalyptic armies of ISIS, and their collective vision of a Caliphate have nothing to do with Islam.

Let me say it again: it *is* about Islam.

This is not a book written for people looking to be easily offended. I won't be carefully parsing every word of every chapter to ensure that I am constantly using all the correct PC terminology. Anyone who has listened or watched me for a while knows my stance: people can choose good or evil, peace or violence. The faith of 1.6 billion people around the world is not inherently bad, but those who insist on a fundamentalist, outdated, supremacist reading of it are. This is the key distinction between Islam and Islamism, which is the totalitarian vision that knows no separation between religion and politics and is utterly incompatible with freedom and individual liberty.

From the heartland of Syria, to the government halls of Tehran, to the meeting places of the Muslim Brotherhood and its affiliated organizations here in America, Islamism is on the march. Under the pernicious influence of radicals who seek to impose Islamic law on the world, barbaric practices that Islam sanctioned in the seventh century—killing apostates, stoning women, and hanging homosexuals—are spreading.

Islam is increasingly becoming intolerant, not just of Westerners and others around the world who seek to stand up for basic freedoms and human rights, but of millions of Muslims as well. These voices for moderation, for a classically liberal approach that recognizes faith as something between God and an individual, not to be imposed by governments—are being silenced, and in some instances, targeted and killed.

That is the problem. A reformation within Islam is urgently needed. And yet it may be as far away as it ever has been.

Had followers of Islam worked to systemically reform it—dissociating themselves from the barbaric ways of the past—we would not find ourselves in a place where the religion itself is at the center of the debate, and unfortunately, of so much terror and death around the world. Instead, we are left with a religion that professes to be good and peaceful, but that counts among its faithful millions of followers who are anything but.

How can those things be reconciled? Are we to believe that

terrorists and Islamists—people who are the strictest followers of their faith—are reading the Quran and the Hadith entirely wrong?

If that sounds as absurd to you as it does to me, then it's time to take a closer look at what these main texts of the faith really say and why so many have found in them justification for hatred and violence.

▮ LIE #1 ▮

"ISLAM IS A RELIGION OF PEACE, AND ISLAMIC TERRORISTS AREN'T REALLY MUSLIMS."

"Islam is a religion that preaches peace."

—President Barack Obama

"I stopped calling these people Muslim terrorists. They're about as Muslim as I am. I mean, they have no respect for anybody else's life, that's not what the Koran says."

—Howard Dean, former Democratic Party
chairman, on MSNBC

For decades Americans have been told that Islam is a religion of peace.

This is an endless refrain, repeated by presidents and prime ministers, media figures and sports stars, the pope, and even terrorists themselves.

In the days after the 9/11 attacks the Bush White House went to great pains to stress that the United States was not at war with all people of the Islamic faith. The administration assumed, incorrectly, that Islam is not much different than the host of other religions that differ from Christianity. They wanted to believe that Islam preaches peace—so they decided that it did.

On September 17, six days after the World Trade Center was toppled and the Pentagon smoldered, President George W. Bush went to an Islamic center in Washington, D.C., and sought to distance Islam from the attacks.

"These acts of violence against innocents violate the fundamental tenets of the Islamic faith," Bush said. "And it's important for my fellow Americans to understand that. . . . That is not what Islam is all about. Islam is peace." Former secretary of state Condoleezza Rice also noted "the benevolence that is at the heart of Islam."

The Obama administration has continued this theme and taken it to tortuous extremes. Under questioning from Congress, then–attorney general Eric Holder spent two straight minutes refusing to say the word *Islam* in conjunction with terrorism. "I don't want to say anything negative about a religion," Holder explained in his testimony. Former secretary of state Hillary Clinton has also been overly politically correct, noting that most Muslims are "peaceful and tolerant people" and attacking those who have "distorted" the Islamic faith.

Sometimes telling a lie often enough gets people to believe it.

A 2009 poll conducted by the *Washington Post* and ABC News indicated that 58 percent of Americans believe that Islam is a "peaceful religion." There's been a shift in those numbers recently, thanks in part to the unraveling of the Middle East and the rise of the Islamic State, but not a huge one. A 2015 Rasmussen poll found that 52 percent of Americans now believe that Islam encourages violence to a greater degree than other religions. That still leaves 48 percent of Americans—nearly half the country—

who have bought into the idea that Islam itself really is the "religion of peace" that its apologists claim.

These apologists justify their claim in several ways. First, they discuss the word *Islam* itself, asserting that *Islam* actually translates to "peace," because in Arabic it is based on the same root word, *salam.* That word, *salam,* can be found in the traditional greeting *assalamualaikum* ("Peace be upon you").

But as Middle East scholar Daniel Pipes explains, the word *Islam* more accurately translates to "submission." "There is no connection in meaning between *salām* and *islām,* peace and submission," he writes. "These are two distinct words with unrelated [meanings]. In brief, 'Islam = submission.'"

The notorious British Islamic preacher Anjem Choudary, a vocal supporter of the Islamic State and a cofounder of the terrorist group Al-Muhajiroun, agrees with this analysis. In an op-ed piece justifying the attack by al-Qaeda-linked terrorists on the magazine *Charlie Hebdo,* which killed twelve journalists and a Paris policeman, Choudary wrote:

> Contrary to popular misconception, Islam does not mean peace
> but rather means submission to the commands of Allah alone.
> Therefore, Muslims do not believe in the concept of freedom
> of expression, as their speech and actions are determined by
> divine revelation and not based on people's desires.

But even this is not enough for apologists of radical Islam. Those who cling to the "religion of peace" dogma argue that "submission" itself is a sign of peaceful intention. Submitting to the will of Allah is a personal choice made by every Muslim to help them find peace and tranquility. After all, they claim, many Christians speak about "surrendering" to God's will. An academic project called "Muslim Voices" at the University of Indiana notes that "in Christianity, surrendering to God is a way of putting your life into more capable hands—in fact, Jesus asked many of his disciples to surrender their livelihoods and follow him."

In addition to debating word origins and meaning, advocates of "Islam is peace" cite the highest authority possible, the Quran. Take, for example, President Obama's 2009 Cairo speech. "The Holy Quran," Obama said, "teaches that whoever kills an innocent, it is as if he has killed all mankind; and whoever saves a person, it is as if he has saved all mankind."

If this were in fact the sum of what the Quran says on this topic, then President Obama would have a strong case—but it's not. Obama, like many others, is misquoting the verse, found in Sura 5:32. Here is the actual translation:

Because of that We ordained for the Children of Israel that if anyone killed a person not in retaliation of murder, or (and) to spread mischief in the land—it would be as if he killed all mankind, and if anyone saved a life, it would be as if he saved the life of all mankind. And indeed, there came to them Our Messengers with clear proofs, evidences, and signs, even then after that many of them continued to exceed the limits (e.g., by doing oppression unjustly and exceeding beyond the limits set by Allah by committing the major sins) in the land!

And then note what comes in the very next verse, Sura 5:33:

The recompense of those who wage war against Allah and His Messenger and do mischief in the land is only that they shall be killed or crucified or their hands and their feet be cut off on the opposite sides, or be exiled from the land. That is their disgrace in this world, and a great torment is theirs in the Hereafter.

This is a significant change in tone. Crucial to unlocking the verse's meaning is an understanding of what it means to "wage war" or "do mischief."

One clue is found in the writings of medieval Islamic scholar Ibn Kathir: "'Wage war' mentioned here means, oppose and contradict, and it includes disbelief, blocking roads and spreading fear in the fairways. 'Mischief in the land' refers to various types of evil."

In other words, the Quran states that those who do not follow the tenets of Islam (that is, express "disbelief") are "waging war" against the religion itself. Under the Quran, disbelief alone is enough to justify crucifixion and murder.

Those who do not submit to Islam are "at war" with God himself. This understanding is further clarified elsewhere in the Quran. Here is a quote from Sura 9:29:

> Fight against those who (1) believe not in Allah, (2) nor in the Last Day, (3) nor forbid that which has been forbidden by Allah and His Messenger (4) and those who acknowledge not the religion of truth (i.e., Islam) among the people of the Scripture (Jews and Christians), until they pay the *Jizyah* with willing submission, and feel themselves subdued.

The implications are clear. Failing to submit to Islam puts you at war with God and true believers, and those believers are instructed to fight you until you submit. In that sense, perhaps Islam could indeed be called a "religion of peace"—with peace coming only through submission.

Other evidence from Islam's foundational texts further supports the use of violence in the name of God. The Quran, for instance, reminds Muslims that they are expected to fight even if they might rather not:

Jihad (holy fighting in Allah's Cause) is ordained for you (Muslims) though you dislike it, and it may be that you dislike a thing which is good for you and that you like a thing which is bad for you. Allah knows but you do not know. (Quran 2:216)

The Quran also explains the goal of this fighting—the spread of Islam:

Say to those who have disbelieved, if they cease (from disbelief) their past will be forgiven. But if they return (thereto), then the examples of those (punished) before them have already preceded (as a warning). (Quran 8:38)

And fight them until there is no more *Fitnah* (disbelief and polytheism: i.e., worshipping others besides Allah) and the religion (worship) will all be for Allah Alone [in the whole of the world]. But if they cease (worshipping others besides Allah), then certainly, Allah is All-Seer of what they do. (Quran 8:39)

Muslims are allowed, even commanded, to fight until they achieve universal Islamic worship. This directive is further backed up by the Hadith:

[T]he Messenger of Allah said: I have been commanded to fight against people so long as they do not declare that there is no god but Allah. . . . (Sahih Muslim 1:30)

A subsequent verse in the Hadith gets even more specific about the commands Muhammad received from Allah:

[T]he Messenger of Allah said: I have been commanded to fight against people till they testify that there is no god but Allah, that Muhammad is the messenger of Allah, and they establish prayer, and pay Zakat. . . . (Sahih Muslim 1:33)

Other Quranic passages have been specifically used to justify violence by those committed to carrying it out. Osama bin Laden himself opened a 2002 "letter to the American people" by quoting these verses:

Permission to fight is given to those (i.e., believers against disbelievers), who are fighting them, (and) because they (believers) have been wronged, and surely, Allah is Able to give them (believers) victory. (Quran 22:39)

Those who believe, fight in the Cause of Allah, and those who disbelieve, fight in the cause of *Taghut* (Satan, etc.). So fight you against the friends of *Shaitan* (Satan); Ever feeble indeed is the plot of *Shaitan* (Satan). (Quran 4:76)

In fact, bin Laden was almost certainly aware that the Quran approves of the specific use of "terror"—and thus terrorism— by commanding that Allah's warriors "strike terror into" their foes:

And make ready against them all you can of power, including steeds of war (tanks, planes, missiles, artillery, etc.) to strike terror into the enemies of Allah and your enemy, and others besides whom, you may not know but whom Allah does know. And whatever you shall spend in the Cause of Allah shall be repaid unto you, and you shall not be treated unjustly. (Quran 8:60)

This, too, is supported by the Hadith:

Allah's Apostle said, "I have been sent with the shortest expressions bearing the widest meanings, and I have been made victorious with terror. . . ." (Sahih al-Bukhari 4:52:220)

In the real world, we are confronted constantly by the work of those who believe Allah will be "made victorious with terror."

Ayaan Hirsi Ali, an acclaimed Somali-born women's rights activist and author, has warned the world about Islam for more than a decade. "For more than thirteen years now, I have been making a simple argument in response to such acts of terrorism," she writes. "My argument is that it is foolish to insist, as our leaders habitually do, that the violent acts of radical Islamists can be divorced from the religious ideals that inspire them. Instead we must acknowledge that they are driven by a political ideology, an ideology embedded in Islam itself, in the holy book of the Qur'an as well as the life and teachings of the Prophet Muhammad contained in the hadith."

In case anyone missed what she was saying, she added for emphasis, "Let me make my point in the simplest possible terms: *Islam is not a religion of peace.*"

But you need not take this just from me, or from courageous speakers like Ayaan Hirsi Ali. The leader of ISIS has said the exact same thing.

A May 2015 recording reported to be from ISIS leader Abu Bakr al-Baghdadi opens with his recitation of several verses straight from the Quran. The very first is another translation of Verse 2:216: "Fighting has been enjoined upon you while it is hateful to you." Al-Baghdadi continues:

And He (the Mighty and Majestic) said, "So let those fight in the cause of Allah who sell the life of this world for the Hereafter. And he who fights in the cause of Allah and is killed or

achieves victory—We will bestow upon him a great reward."
(Quran 4:74)

And He (the Glorified) said, "And those who are killed in the
cause of Allah—never will He waste their deeds. He will guide
them and amend their condition, and admit them to Paradise,
which He has made known to them." (Quran 47:4–6)

Later, he provided his own blunt commentary:

O Muslims, Islam was never for a day the religion of peace.
Islam is the religion of war.

Next time you hear the never-ending platitudes about Islam
being a "religion of peace," don't cite my words as evidence to the
contrary. Go directly to the source. Pick up a Quran and find any
of the dozen Suras quoted in this chapter. Or read the words of
our enemies. As Baghdadi put it plainly to each and every one of
us, "Islam is the religion of war."

▌ LIE #2 ▌

"ISLAM IS NOT MUCH DIFFERENT THAN CHRISTIANITY OR JUDAISM."

"There is nothing in the Islam that is more violent than Christianity. All religions have been violent, including Christianity."
—Karen Armstrong, religion writer and former nun

"Remember that during the Crusades and the Inquisition, people committed terrible deeds in the name of Christ."
—Barack Obama

Time and again, in some bizarre attempt at moral equivalence, we've heard the comparisons of Islam and Christianity. Those who kill today in the name of Islam, we're told, aren't that different from those who killed in the name of Christ. After all, they claim, the Bible contains passages that seem to condone violence or slavery.

Philip Jenkins, a scholar of history and religion at Baylor University and Pennsylvania State University, claims that "the Islamic scriptures in the Quran were actually far less bloody and less violent than those in the Bible." Sajjad Rizvi of the University of Exeter has tried to equate Islam and the Judeo-Christian tradition. "Almost all the prophets of the Quran will be familiar to those who know the Bible," he says. "And the Quran explicitly refers to parables, ideas and stories from the Bible. The common roots—and inheritances—of the three faiths make it useful for us to think seriously in terms of a Judeo-Christian-Islamic civilization and heritage that we all share." Karen Armstrong, a former nun and religion writer, argues that "[t]errorism has nothing to do with Muhammad, any more than the Crusades had anything to do with Jesus."

Proponents of the hand-holding, drum-circle view of world religions often point to the common origin of the three monotheistic faiths: Christianity, Judaism, and Islam. This does have a basis in fact as they can each be traced back to Abraham, who is viewed by all three faiths as a great prophet and—to varying degrees—as a literal or figurative father of the religion. In Judaism, he is the patriarch of the ancient Israelites and, therefore, the Jews of today. Christianity grew out of Judaism, and the book of Matthew in the Bible explains that Abraham was an ancestor of Joseph, whose wife, Mary, gave birth to Jesus Christ. Muslims also revere Abraham as a significant prophet. According to Muslims, Muhammad himself is descended from Abraham as well.

The Bible—particularly the Old Testament—contains stories of wars and battles and brutality that were everyday reality in the ancient world. In one passage in Leviticus, for instance, God commands Moses to take a blasphemer outside the camp, after which "the entire assembly is to stone him."

But that was centuries ago. Hebraic law does not command the murder of blasphemers and adulterers. Jews don't routinely resort to practices that date to the time of Moses and David. For Christians, Jesus Christ brought an entirely different understanding of the relationship between his followers and the state. Christ told his disciples, "My kingdom is not of this world," and that they should "[g]ive back to Caesar what is Caesar's and to God what is God's."

In the first centuries, Christians were an embattled minority that fought against the empires that persecuted them. Only three hundred years after the time of Christ did Christianity become associated with temporal or worldly authority with its adoption as the official religion of the Roman Empire. A millennium later, Christianity underwent a reformation that adopted the modern idea of a permanent separation between the church and state.

Islam, by contrast, hasn't reformed at all. The vast majority of Muslims since the time of Muhammad have seen their faith as a holistic, all-encompassing way of life, inseparable from politics and law. All authority in the Islamic faith flows from God. There is no separation of church and state in the Sunni Islamic tradition. The caliph was a religious and political leader in one.

Robert Spencer, director of the Jihad Watch program at the David Horowitz Freedom Center, explains that "Islam has always had a political and social character, including a full program for government." This "program for government" comes in the form of Islamic law—sharia—a series of rules and prescriptions derived from the Quran and other sources of the teachings of Muhammad, such as the Hadith.

Unlike the Jews fleeing Egypt for the promised land of Israel, and unlike Christians escaping martyrdom and the persecution of the Roman Empire, Islam has been a political force from its start, when Muhammad gathered his followers and moved them to Medina from his original hometown of Mecca. This event was so significant that it marks the beginning of time for the faith. The Islamic calendar does not begin at Muhammad's birth or death, nor when he first received visions of Allah, but at the date of this move to Medina, "where [Muhammad] became a political and military leader and Islam became a state." Spencer points out that, to this day, "Islam assumes that its faith must be the ruling ideology of the state."

The capacity for willful ignorance among members of the political and media elite when it comes to the realities of radical Islam never ceases to amaze. They ignore, for instance, the inherently political goals of Islam, such as the desire to impose Islamic (sharia) law as the law of the land and to resurrect the Caliphate that will ensure its enforcement. Other religions make demands on their community of adherents; Islam, by contrast, demands "submission" before Islamic law for non-Muslims as well.

The view that sharia should be a "ruling ideology" enjoys broad support in the Muslim world today. We get into this a bit more later in the book, but what's relevant for this lie about the Islamic equivalency to other major religions is the fact that a vast number of Muslims around the world still support enforcing some of the harshest punishments found in sharia law. These are known as *hudud,* and a 2013 Pew Research Center survey describes them as follows:

> A class of punishments prescribed by the Quran and the sunna [another source of Muhammad's teachings] for crimes considered to be against God. Although interpretations by Islamic jurists vary, such crimes commonly include theft, adultery, making unproven accusations of adultery, consuming intoxicants, armed robbery and apostasy. The prescribed punishments range from lashes to banishment to death.

Majorities of those Muslims who favored imposing sharia law also supported *hudud* punishments for theft, which can include whippings or the cutting off of hands. Among the supporters of such barbaric practices:

Hudud Punishments for Theft

Percentage supporting by country

—Pakistan   88
—Afghanistan   81
—Palestinian Territories   76
—Egypt   70
—Malaysia   66
—Jordan   57
—Iraq   56

And what about women accused of adultery? A majority of Muslims who support the imposition of sharia law in several countries believe those women should be stoned.

Stoning for Adultery

—Pakistan   89
—Afghanistan   85
—Palestinian Territories   84
—Egypt   81
—Jordan   67
—Iraq   58
—Tajikistan   51

Even in Russia, 26 percent of Muslims supporting sharia law shared this view of adultery. You'll note that many of the countries on this list are those that have received billions of dollars and support from the United States government.

In case anyone forgets, this Pew survey was published thirteen years into the twenty-first century. Man has walked on the moon, cured devastating diseases, and invented ways to make information travel around the world instantly. But, in the Muslim world, significant portions of the population still want to cut off thieves' hands, stone cheating spouses, and kill anyone who converts to another religion.

It's not just the "stereotypical" countries that are home to Muslims with these extreme beliefs—the same sentiments have crept into unexpected places, like Norway.

In November 2013, Fahad Qureshi, an Islamic leader in the Scandinavian nation, proclaimed to a large assembly of Sunni Muslims that Americans are being lied to. The Western media, Qureshi said, falsely claim that only "radicals" and "extremist" Muslims support extreme *hudud* punishments for violators of sharia. "Every Muslim believes in these things," said Qureshi. "Just because they are not telling you about it, or just because they are not out there in the media, doesn't mean that they don't believe in them."

Qureshi asked attendees of the assembly to raise their hands if they agreed that "men and women should sit separate." Then he asked, "How many of you agree that the punishments described in the Koran and the Sunna—whether it is death, whether it is stoning for adultery, whatever it is—if it is from Allah and His Messenger, that is the best punishment ever possible for humankind, and that is what we should apply in the world. Who agrees with that?"

Nearly everyone in the crowd raised a hand.

And what about our closest ally, Great Britain? A Muslim leader there, who seeks to bring sharia law to England, declared that homosexuals should be stoned to death, in accordance with Islamic law.

As if this weren't enough to blow up the false-equivalency argument for good, it is also worth addressing one of the apologists' most-beloved topics: the Crusades. Everyone from Karen Armstrong to President Barack Obama, who famously reminded an audience at the National Prayer Breakfast that "people committed terrible deeds in the name of Christ," have used the Crusades to equate Islam with Christianity.

The Crusades did not happen in a historical vacuum. They were, in fact, part of what *New York Times* columnist Ross Douthat called "the incredibly complicated multicentury story of medieval Christendom's conflict with Islam."

Muslim armies had launched plenty of Crusade-like or, more accurately, jihadist efforts against Europe, both before and after the generally accepted period of Christian Crusading. Part of that period overlapped with the "Reconquista," a centuries-long effort to expel Islamic invaders from modern-day Spain and Portugal, which they had controlled since the eighth century A.D. Some scholars maintain that "without centuries of Crusading effort, it is difficult to see how western Europe could have escaped conquest by Muslim armies."

During the four centuries between Muhammad's death and the First Crusade, Islamic warriors and navies launched offensives around the Mediterranean against European forces, including as far away as France. The Crusades were as much a reaction to the Islamic jihad as anything else.

But even the Crusades didn't stop the fighting for good. The ongoing back-and-forth conflict between Christian and Muslim kingdoms continued for centuries, right up until the Ottoman Empire was held back from seizing Vienna in 1683. In fact, radical Islamists' penchant for referring to Americans as "Crusaders" today suggests that, at least in their mind, the conflict may still be going on.

▌LIE #3 ▌

"JIHAD IS A PEACEFUL, INTERNAL STRUGGLE, NOT A WAR AGAINST INFIDELS."

"Jihad as struggle pertains to the difficulty and complexity of living a good life: struggling against the evil in oneself—to be virtuous and moral, making a serious effort to do good works and help to reform society."

—John Esposito, Georgetown University

"Jihad is a personal commitment to service, patience, determination, and taking the higher road, as such, it tasks us with confronting our own weaknesses, vices, and shortcomings; it is about taking personal responsibility."

—MyJihad campaign, 2012

"Many Muslims and Islamic scholars consider the more correct definition [of jihad], refers to the inner struggle to do good and follow God's teaching; Muslims strive to attain this every day."

—Salon.com, 2013

[J]ihad is a holy struggle, a legitimate tenet of Islam, meaning to purify onself or one's community."
                                   —John Brennan, Deputy NSC Adviser, 2010

Within hours of the September 11 attacks, most Americans had heard the word *jihad*. Major television networks and Internet sites showed video of a confident Osama bin Laden declaring that his terrorist organization was on a mission to destroy the United States.

Jihad had come to America.

Nearly fifteen years later, this exotic Arabic word has become frighteningly familiar. And yet there are still many across the world engaged in a massive effort to disassociate the word *jihad* from what we can see with our own eyes—the aggressive war under way against non-Muslims.

A 2003 article in *National Geographic*, for example, quoted Maher Hathout, the author of *Jihad vs. Terrorism*, in an effort to "set the record straight about jihad." Hathout concluded that *jihad* refers to "a range of activities all based on the Arabic meaning of the word 'exerted effort.' In the Koran it's projected as exerting effort to change oneself, and also in certain situations physically standing against oppressors if that's the only way."

In late 2012, Ahmed Rehab, the director of the Chicago branch of the Hamas-linked Council on American-Islamic Relations (CAIR), began a public relations campaign to rebrand the concept of jihad in the United States. He started by taking advantage of a sympathetic media and, once he had the support of donors behind him, plastered buses in major American cities with smiling Muslims testifying to their personal, nonviolent jihads. Rehab explains on his website, MyJihad.com: "Jihad is a personal commitment to service, patience, determination, and taking the higher road, as such, it tasks us with confronting our own weaknesses, vices, and shortcomings; it is about taking personal responsibility. . . ."

Georgetown University professor John Esposito is one of the more prominent of those who've made a good living as an apologist for jihad. From his perch as the director of the lavishly Saudi-funded Prince Alwaleed bin Talal Center for Muslim-Christian Understanding, Esposito has become a prominent figure in the media as a consultant to government officials. His post-9/11 book, *What Everyone Needs to Know About Islam,* set the tone for much of the confusion about the true meaning of jihad. "Jihad as struggle pertains to the difficulty and complexity of living a good life," he wrote. "Struggling against the evil in oneself—to be virtuous and moral, making a serious effort to do good works and help to reform society."

When Esposito isn't busy telling Americans what he thinks we need to know about Islam, he has served as a character witness and cheerleader for the Muslim Brotherhood, both in the United States and abroad. In a letter to a judge, he referred to now-deported Palestinian Islamic Jihad leader Sami al-Arian as "an extraordinarily bright, articulate scholar and intellectual-activist, a man of conscience with a strong commitment to peace and social justice." Despite Esposito's reviews, al-Arian himself confessed to his extensive involvement with the Brotherhood, a State Department–designated Palestinian terrorist organization.

Just as alarmingly, Esposito has expressed admiration for the chief jurist of the Muslim Brotherhood, Sheikh Yusuf al-Qaradawi. He wrote glowingly of the sheikh's "reformist interpretation of Islam and its relationship to democracy, pluralism and human rights." This is the same Qaradawi who, in January 2009, called on Muslims to put the Jews in "their place" as Hitler had done.

"Throughout history," Qaradawi said, "Allah has imposed upon the [Jews] people who would punish them for their corruption. The last punishment was carried out by Hitler. By means of all the things he did to them—even though they exaggerated this issue—he managed to put them in their place. This was divine punishment for them. Allah willing, the next time will be at the hands of the believers."

Thankfully, we don't have to depend on Georgetown professors of Islamic studies, or bloggers, or even presidents to understand what jihad really is—we can discover the truth ourselves in primary Islamic sources. We can—and must—read what Muslims read about their own religion. When we finally make an effort to look, we find that Islamic law is remarkably clear about jihad.

In order to bolster Americans' impression of jihad as a peaceful, internal struggle, apologists refer to a single statement attributed to Muhammad in a Hadith. It is the distinction between the nonviolent "greater jihad" and "lesser jihad," which means warfare.

The Hadith, while authoritative in Islam, does not carry the same weight as the Quran itself, which is believed to be from Allah alone. One of the most recognized and honored scholars of Islamic law, Ibn Taymiyyah, explained the difference between the two jihads and shattered the idea that jihad is anything but holy war against the infidel:

> There is a Hadith related by a group of people which states that the Prophet said after the battle of Tabuk: "We have returned from Jihad Asghar [Lesser Jihad] to Jihad Akbar [Greater Jihad]." This Hadith has no source, nobody whomsoever in the field of Islamic Knowledge has narrated it. Jihad against the disbelievers is the most noble of actions, and moreover it is the most important action for the sake of mankind.

Still, even if an apologist will concede Taymiyyah's point that Muhammad never made a distinction between the "lesser jihad" and "greater jihad," they will insist that, according to Islamic law, Allah will countenance only a "defensive" jihad. Jihad, they argue, is justifiable only once Muslim lands are attacked or Muslims are being persecuted.

Sufi author Kabir Helminski writes in the *Huffington Post* that, according to Islam, "Fighting is allowed only in self-defense, and it is only against those who actively fight against you." He continues, "Yet, Islam is not a pacifist religion, it does accept the premise that, from time to time and as a last resort, arms must be taken up in a just war." That sounds peaceful and moderate enough, right? Who'd argue with a right of a people to self-defense? Or with having to fight a "just war" reluctantly, as a last resort?

The Reliance of the Traveller: The Classic Manual of Islamic Sacred Law, or "Umdat al-Salik" in Arabic, was composed in the fourteenth century by Shihabuddin Abu al-'Abbas Ahmad ibn an-Naqib al-Misri. It is a one-volume authoritative summation of Islamic law from one of its major schools of jurisprudence called *Shafi'i.* Despite its age, it is the single most popular handbook of Islamic law in the United States and a leading authority throughout the world. It was translated into English because so many Muslims in America and elsewhere don't speak classical Arabic. In fact, *Reliance* is the first Islamic legal work in a European language to receive certification from the most important seat of Sunni Islamic jurisprudence, Cairo's Al-Azhar University. In addition, its opening pages contain a similar endorsement from the Muslim Brotherhood's think tank in the United States, the International Institute of Islamic Thought.

Reliance's section on jihad is located in chapter 9, "Justice." It states:

Jihad means to war against non-Muslims, and is etymologically derived from the word *mujahada,* signifying warfare to establish the religion. And it is the lesser Jihad.

The entry on jihad gets even more explicit when *Reliance* outlines "the scriptural basis for Jihad" in three definitive verses from Mohammed in the Quran:

1. "Fighting is prescribed for you." (Quran 2:216)
2. "Slay them wherever you find them." (Quran 4:89)
3. "Fight the idolaters utterly." (Quran 9:36)

As these commands are in the Quran itself, Muslims believe they originated with Allah and, as such, are obligatory. *Reliance* then goes on to reference justifications for jihad warfare in the two most authoritative Hadith collections, Bukhari and Muslim, which relate what Muhammad himself said:

> I have been commanded to fight people until they testify that there is no god but Allah and that Muhammad is the Messenger of Allah, and perform the prayer, and pay zakat. If they say it, they have saved their blood and possessions from me, except for the rights of Islam over them. And their final reckoning is with Allah.

After looking at Islamic law, jihad turns out to be an exhortation to real, physical violence. It is, as well, a command to plunder the possessions of those who do not "testify that there is no god but Allah and that Muhammad is the Messenger of Allah, and perform the prayer, and pay zakat"—or, in other words, become a Muslim.

This interpretation of jihad is supported by numerous other authoritative sources written by Islamic scholars. Ibn Khaldun, one of classical Islam's most prominent scholars, discussed the meaning and goal of jihad as a "holy war" and contrasted it with the aspirations of other religions or nations in his revered text *Muqaddimah:*

In the Muslim community, the holy war is a religious duty, because of the universalism of the Muslim mission and the obligation to convert everybody to Islam either by persuasion or by force. . . . The other religious groups did not have a universal mission, and the holy war was not a religious duty for them, save only for purposes of defense. . . . Among them, royal authority comes to those who have it, by accident and in some way that has nothing to do with religion. It comes to them as the necessary result of group feeling, which by its very nature seeks to obtain royal authority, as we have mentioned before, and not because they are under obligation to gain power over other nations, as is the case with Islam. They are merely required to establish their religion among their own people.

In the 1930s, Hassan al-Banna, the founder of the Muslim Brotherhood, wrote a pamphlet on the centrality of jihad:

Jihad is an obligation from Allah on every Muslim and cannot be ignored nor evaded. Allah has ascribed great importance to jihad and has made the reward of the martyrs and the fighters in His way a splendid one. Only those who have acted similarly and who have modeled themselves upon the martyrs in their performance of jihad can join them in this reward. Furthermore, Allah has specifically honored the Mujahedeen with certain exceptional qualities, both spiritual and practical, to benefit them in this world and the next. Their pure blood is a symbol of victory in this world and the mark of success and felicity in the world to come.

Islam is concerned with the question of jihad and the drafting and the mobilization of the entire [global Muslim community] into one body to defend the right cause with all its strength than any other ancient or modern system of living, whether religious or civil. The verses of the Qur'an and the Sunnah of

Muhammad (PBUH) are overflowing with all these noble ideals and they summon people in general (with the most eloquent expression and the clearest exposition) to jihad, to warfare, to the armed forces, and all means of land and sea fighting.

Some Muslim scholars, like India's Maulana Waris Mazhari, acknowledge that "it is clear that traditional understandings of jihad are urgently in need of careful scrutiny, study and revision." He writes:

The majority of Islamic jurists and Quranic commentators (mufasirin) consider war to be the real basis of relations between Muslims and non-Muslims. They regard the infidelity of non-Muslims as the cause ('illat) of such war. They believe that Muslims must engage in war with non-Muslims continuously till Islam establishes its supremacy over all other religions. Since, in actual fact, this, as Muslims believe, can only happen just before the Day of Judgment, they argue that Muslims must necessarily continue to wage war against non-Muslims till the Day of Judgment finally arrives. The opinion of Imam Shafi'i and some other [Islamic jurists] is even more extreme in this regard—they argue that only Ahl-e Kitab or "People of the Book" can be permitted to stay alive in exchange for paying the jizya, and that all other non-Muslims must accept either Islam or death.

Osama bin Laden, Hamas, the Islamic State, Boko Haram, Hezbollah, and every other Muslim terrorist group justify what they do by claiming they are fighting a defensive jihad. They believe the goal of Islam is to spread its system of law across the world; therefore any *opposition* to spreading Islamic law could be defined as a "defensive" act.

In 1998, bin Laden and al-Qaeda issued a statement to the

West and to the Muslim world, declaring a *defensive* jihad against the United States. It was called "the Declaration of Jihad against Jews and Crusaders World Islamic Front." Notice as you read how important it is for al-Qaeda to back up everything they say with references to figures that Muslims would consider authoritative or legally binding:

> All these crimes and sins committed by the Americans are a clear declaration of war on Allah, his messenger, and Muslims. And ulema have throughout Islamic history unanimously agreed that the jihad is an individual duty if the enemy destroys the Muslim countries. This was revealed by Imam Bin-Qadamah in "Al-Mughni," Imam al-Kisa'i in "Al-Bada'i," al-Qurtubi in his interpretation, and the shaykh of al-Islam in his books, where he said: "As for the fighting to repulse [an enemy], it is aimed at defending sanctity and religion, and it is a duty as agreed by the [Islamic scholars]. Nothing is more sacred than belief except repulsing an enemy who is attacking religion and life."

Bin Laden, and the Islamic authorities he relies on, are in fact referencing Quran 5:33, which reads:

> The recompense of those who wage war against Allah and His Messenger and do mischief in the land is only that they shall be killed or crucified or their hands and their feet be cut off on the opposite sides, or be exiled from the land. That is their disgrace in this world, and a great torment is theirs in the Hereafter.

After the 1991 Gulf War, the United States, at Saudi Arabia's invitation, stationed armed forces in Saudi Arabia to ensure that Saddam Hussein wouldn't again attempt to annex one of Iraq's neighbors. But that wasn't how bin Laden viewed America's actions. He and al-Qaeda charged America with "attacking religion and life" in these Muslim-controlled lands.

Lebanon's late grand ayatollah, Muhammad Hussein Fadlallah, a Shia, defined the nature of the defensive jihad in terms the al-Qaeda leader would certainly approve of (emphasis added):

> Jihad in Islam (the violent confrontation of the enemy) is the fighting movement that *aims at preventing the enemy from forcing its hegemony over the land and the people* by means of violence that confiscates freedom, kills the people, usurps the wealth and *prevents the people's rights in self-determination.* Therefore, *Jihad is confronting violence by means of violence and force-by-force, which makes it of a defensive nature at times and a preventive one at others. . . . In the light of this, jihad is no different than any human and civilized concept of self-defense. It expresses the innate human nature of self-defense, or preventing the others from building the ability for a sudden aggression. There is also the case of* defending the downtrodden who are prosecuted by the arrogant and who have no means of defending themselves.

As Fadlallah made clear, there are plenty of things that Islamic law considers cause for defensive jihad. If Muslims in non-Islamic societies are not permitted by the authorities to live their lives according to sharia—with all its mandatory antidemocratic and outdated rules—it could be considered "persecution" of the Muslim community.

This is a very broad definition that leaves plenty of room for interpretation and justification of defensive jihad. For example, the killers who massacred the staff of the irreverent, satirical magazine *Charlie Hebdo* in Paris did not believe they were taking an offensive action. They believed they were actually *defending* the reputation of Islam's prophet from those who attacked it. More important, though, they believed they were informing the world of the sharia-prescribed penalty for mocking or questioning Muhammad, and thereby dissuading others from following suit.

Even Islamic authorities that are identified as "moderate" by academics and the media, like Yusuf al-Qaradawi—the Hitler-praising Muslim Brotherhood leader and Al Jazeera talk show superstar—accept this rationale for defensive jihad. Qaradawi is the most influential living Sunni imam. His program, *Sharia and Life,* has an estimated audience of some 60 million throughout the Muslim world.

In 2011, Qaradawi famously issued a fatwa outlining the Islamic standard for jihad, including:

> To ensure the freedom to propagate the call to Islam . . . and to remove the physical obstacles which prevent the call to Islam from reaching the multitudes of people. This was the reason for the conquests of the rightly-guided (caliphs) and the companions (of the Prophet), as well as those who followed them in righteousness. (They fought) to remove the power of the tyrants who controlled the necks and minds of men. . . .

This is a very loose standard, and it could apply in a multitude of scenarios where there is any kind of obstacle to mass conversion to Islam, real or imagined. The same logic applies to blasphemy, ridicule, or anything else our First Amendment permits that influential voices like Qaradawi might believe interferes with the "call to Islam." Mocking Muhammad in a cartoon, speaking out against Islamic law, or even writing this book to expose the truth—all could be considered acts that might prevent Americans from converting to Islam, which is the Islamist's goal, and justify violent acts of jihad.

Individual Muslims may have their own peaceful, internal jihads of spiritual and personal growth—but that shouldn't be used to obscure the real threat of violent jihad. Apologists focus on the former in order to make sure we never learn about the latter. Islamic law defines *jihad* to mean "war against non-Muslims" and "warfare to establish the religion," and it is the traditional, sharia meaning of the term that has been a consistent part of Islamic doctrine from Muhammad until today.

▌LIE #4 ▌

"MUSLIMS DON'T ACTUALLY SEEK TO LIVE UNDER SHARIA, LET ALONE IMPOSE IT ON OTHERS; THERE ARE SO MANY DIFFERENT INTERPRETATIONS OF IT ANYWAY."

"In a broad sense, Sharia law is the code of conduct or religious law of Islam. It is a wide-ranging system that encompasses crime, politics, economic, and personal matters such as sexuality, diet, hygiene, prayer, and fasting. . . . [T]here is no one document that outlines a universally agreed upon use of Sharia. This leads to many different interpretations."

—Council on American-Islamic Relations

"There are so many varying interpretations of what sharia actually means that in some places, it can be incorporated into political systems relatively easily."

—Steven A. Cook, Council on Foreign Relations

In an effort to appear tolerant and understanding of Islam, the George Soros–funded Center for American Progress enlisted former Muslim Student Association activist Wajahat Ali to draft a seven-page paper titled "Understanding Sharia Law." In it, Ali writes, "There is no one thing called Sharia. A variety of Muslim communities exist, and each understands Sharia in its own way. No official document, such as the Ten Commandments, encapsulates Sharia. It is the ideal law of God as interpreted by Muslim scholars over centuries aimed toward justice, fairness, and mercy." He went on to conclude: "In reality, Sharia is personal religious law and moral guidance for the vast majority of Muslims. Muslim scholars historically agree on certain core values of Sharia, which are theological and ethical and not political. Moreover, these core values are in harmony with the core values at the heart of America."

Lawyer and author Qasim Rashid, writing in the *Huffington Post,* repeatedly stresses that sharia seeks a society "based on justice, pluralism and equity for every member of that society" and that sharia would not allow these dictates to be imposed on "any unwilling person."

First, let's understand what sharia is. It is a codification of the rules of the lifestyle (or *deen*) ordained by Allah, the perfect expression of his divine will and justice. Therefore it is the supreme law over everything and everyone, regardless of where that individual may live. There isn't a corner of life that sharia doesn't touch; it governs and dictates everything.

Sharia comes from four principal sources: the Quran, the Sunna or Hadith, Ijma, and Qiyas. By now you're already familiar with the central, sacred text of Islam and the example and practices of Muhammad's life as relayed in the oral traditions of the Hadith. *Ijma* means "consensus" and consists of the prevailing opinion of Muslim scholars. Qiyas is reasoning by analogy, which

establishes new precedents in areas where the Quran and Hadith
are unclear.

"Islam, it is generally acknowledged, is a complete way of life,"
writes Imran Ahsan Kahn Nyazee, a leading professor of Islamic
law at the International Islamic University Islamabad, "and at
the core of the code, is the law of Islam. . . . No other sovereign
or authority is acceptable to the Muslim, unless it guarantees the
application of the laws (shariah) in their entirety. Any other legal
system, howsoever attractive it may appear on the surface, is alien
for Muslims and it is not likely to succeed in the solution of their
problems: it would be doomed from the start."

This is the root of political Islam, or what we are calling Islamism. It is the belief shared by millions of Muslims that sharia is
the answer to the world's ills and represents the holistic worldview
of Muhammad and the Quran. It's not surprising then that a 2013
Pew poll of nearly 40,000 Muslims in 39 countries demonstrated
widespread support for the adoption of sharia law.

Support for Sharia

*Percentage of Muslims who favor making sharia the official law in their
country*

—Afghanistan	99
—Iraq	91
—Palestinian Territories	89
—Malaysia	86
—Pakistan	84
—Morocco	83
—Bangladesh	82
—Thailand	77
—Egypt	74
—Indonesia	72
—Jordan	71
—Russia	42

That overwhelming numbers of Muslims should want to live under Islamic law should come as no surprise, especially as we learn more about Islam's goals and underpinnings. For Muslims, living under the law (*deen*) of Allah—which encompasses everything from family law to business and transactional law to international law and more—is a defined religious imperative. In *Islam: A Sacred Law: What Every Muslim Should Know About the Shariah,* author Feisal Abdul Rauf, the imam at the center of the Ground Zero mosque controversy, describes what Islamic law is:

> Since Shariah is understood as a law with God at its center, it is not possible in principle to limit the Shariah to some aspect of human life and leave out others. . . . The Shariah thus covers every field of law—public and private, national and international—together with enormous amounts of material that Westerners would not regard as law at all, because the basis of Shariah is the worship and obedience to God through good works and moral behavior. Following the Sacred Law thus defines the Muslim's belief in God.

Rauf is what the media describes is a "moderate." He matter-of-factly describes that Islamic law traverses the distance between personal religious observance or theology and laws that affect others in the public sphere. As we'll see, our Constitution comes into conflict with Islamic law in numerous places.

In *Shari'ah: The Islamic Law,* renowned Muslim professor Abdur Rahman Doi explains why Muslims in the Middle East and elsewhere feel pressure to want to live according to sharia:

> The Holy Qur'an has warned those who fail to apply the Shari'ah in the following strong words: "And if any fail to judge by the light of what Allah has revealed, they are not better than those who rebel." (5:50) "And if any fail to judge by the light of

what Allah has revealed, they are no better than wrong-doers."
(5:48)

"And if any fail to judge by the light of what Allah has revealed,
they are no better than unbelievers." (5:47)

There's one thing that unites every single one of the world's
Islamic terror groups—from Boko Haram to al-Qaeda and the
Islamic State; from Hezbollah to the Iranian Revolutionary Guard
Corps; and from the Muslim Brotherhood to freelance jihadists
plotting murder in America: the desire to make sharia the law
of the land everywhere on earth. You'd be hard-pressed to find
a letter, press release, tweet, or Facebook post from any militant
Islamic group that doesn't mention the imperative of imposing
sharia, first in Muslim-controlled lands, and then across the globe.

The pronouncements of other Islamist leaders suggest that the
spread of sharia is indeed the clear goal. When ISIS declared a Caliphate in 2014, it declared its mission as "compelling the people
to do what the Sharia (Allah's law) requires of them concerning
their interests in the hereafter and worldly life, which can only be
achieved by carrying out the command of Allah, establishing His
religion, and referring to His law for judgment."

In 2002, Osama bin Laden declared:

Muslims, and especially the learned among them, should spread
Shari'a law to the world—that and nothing else. Not laws under
the "umbrella of justice, morality, and rights" as understood by
the masses. No, the Shari'a of Islam is the foundation. . . . In
fact, Muslims are obligated to raid the lands of the infidels, oc-
cupy them, and exchange their system of governance for an Islamic system, barring any practice that contradicts Shari'a from
being publicly voiced among the people, as was the case in the

dawn of Islam. . . . They say that our *Shari'a* does not impose our particular beliefs upon others; this is a false assertion. For it is, in fact, part of our religion to impose our particular beliefs upon others. . . . Thus whoever refuses the principle of terror against the enemy also refuses the commandment of Allah the Exalted, the Most High, and His Shari'a. . . . And we also stress to honest Muslims that, in the midst of such momentous events and in this heated atmosphere, they must move, incite, and mobilize the Muslim *umma* to liberate itself from being enthralled to these unjust and apostate ruling regimes, who themselves are enslaved to America, and to establish the *Shari'a* of Allah on earth.

Even as it was being courted by the Obama administration the Muslim Brotherhood was honest about its long-standing goals for installing sharia worldwide, declaring in 2010, "The Muslim Brotherhood is an international Muslim Body, which seeks to establish Allah's law in the land by achieving the spiritual goals of Islam and the true religion. . . ."

Of course, none of this is new. Pakistani Abul A'la Maududi, the founder of Jamaat-e-Islami, the largest Islamic organization in Asia, gave a 1939 speech titled "Jihad in Islam" in which he spoke clearly about the goal of installing Islamic law worldwide:

The objective of the Islamic "Jihad" is to eliminate the rule of an un-Islamic system and establish in its stead an Islamic system of state rule. Islam does not intend to confine this revolution to a single state or a few countries; the aim of Islam is to bring about a universal revolution. . . . No revolutionary ideology which champions the principles of the welfare of humanity as a whole instead of upholding national interests, can restrict its aims and objectives to the limits of a country or a nation. The goal of such an all-embracing doctrine is naturally bound to be world revolution.

Like so many prominent jihadists, Maududi was no outcast. He was not only one of the most influential imams of the twentieth century; he was also an internationally recognized Islamic scholar who wrote scores of books, including *The Meaning of the Qur'an,* a popular single-volume commentary widely available in America. At the same time, he was a fierce self-described revolutionary who, in no uncertain terms, sought the overthrow of all non-Muslim forms of government worldwide.

Nearly every article or news report in the Western media about the Islamic State in Iraq or Syria, Boko Haram in Africa, or the Muslim Brotherhood in Egypt remarks on the application of sharia in these places—most often in the context of horrific and medieval sharia-mandated punishments for criminal offenses. Whenever these atrocities are mentioned, we hear Islamic law described as "severe versions of sharia." The journalists and so-called experts want us to believe there are gradations of Islamic law: the bad guys force the "severe" kind on unwilling populations, while "moderate," or even "liberal," interpretations are just as valid and practiced by the vast majority of the world's Muslims.

But we know that's not the truth. There is only one version of sharia—and a great many Muslims around the world will not stop until we are all living under it.

▌ LIE #5 ▌

"AMERICA IS SAFE FROM SHARIA LAW."

"Sharia is as unthreatening to the US legal system as the ideas in the Old Testament. Yet bigoted hysteria is fueling legislation that actually undermines our courts."

—*The Nation*

"There is no evidence that Islamic law is encroaching on our courts."

—American Civil Liberties Union

On the front of the United States Supreme Court building in Washington, D.C., are emblazoned the words "Equal Justice Under Law." Though our justice system is not always perfect, we strive to make sure our courts hold every individual, regardless of his or her background, equally accountable to the laws enshrined in our Constitution and passed by our elected representatives. So what if an American judge sided with foreign religious law that insisted on inequality between believer and nonbeliever instead of our own legal codes? What if you were subjected to an entirely separate shadow legal system?

It admittedly seems like a fevered delusion that this could ever happen in the United States, but it's closer than you think. Islamic sharia law has been slowly integrating itself into American society—and our justice system.

There is a frantic scramble on the left to respond to those warning of the dangers of American sharia with two tactics: calling people "conspiracy theorists," and calling them "Islamo-phobes." The American Civil Liberties Union (ACLU) manages to do both.

The ACLU issued a report on sharia in America with the less-than-reassuring title "Nothing to Fear." In it they assert that "there is no evidence that Islamic law is encroaching on our courts." Cases involving sharia, they claim, are simply "routine legal matters." Those who have a problem with sharia influencing American justice are automatically "anti-Muslim advocates" whose goal is not to preserve liberty, but "to denigrate an entire faith system and to deny its followers the same access to the judicial system enjoyed by citizens of other creeds."

Attorney, law professor, and self-styled sharia expert Abed Awad also wants everyone to rest easy, writing in the *Nation* that we should get used to sharia as just another benefit of globalization:

> The true story of Sharia in American courts is not one of a plot for imminent takeover but rather another part of the tale of globalization. Marriages, divorces, corporations and commercial transactions are global, meaning that US courts must regularly interpret and apply foreign law. Islamic law has been considered by American courts in everything from the recognition of foreign divorces and custody decrees to the validity of marriages, the enforcement of money judgments, and the awarding of damages in commercial disputes and negligence matters.

Who needs a constitution or sovereignty when we can just "regularly interpret and apply foreign law"?

As we saw earlier, sharia is Allah's law—an eternal, unchangeable, and all-encompassing "way," a moral and legal code that prescribes everything down to the minutiae of daily life. There are varying interpretations, but sharia is something that all Muslims are expected to follow, wherever they live, and it must take precedence over the laws of man.

Abdur Rahman Doi, a Malaysian scholar of Islamic law, explains that the Quran mandates that sharia rule over all Muslims everywhere, for all time:

> The entire Muslim Ummah [community] lives under the Shari'ah to which every member has to submit, with sovereignty belonging to Allah alone. . . . Shari'ah was not revealed for limited application for a specific age. It will suit every age and time.

Imran Ahsan Khan Nyazee, a Pakistani law professor, contends that only sharia can properly govern Muslims:

> Any other legal system, howsoever attractive it may appear on the surface, is alien for Muslims and is not likely to succeed in the solution of their problems. . . .

That presumably includes American constitutional law, at least according to the Assembly of Muslim Jurists of America (AMJA), an organization of scholars and clerics that "[issues] fatawa (the plural of "fatwa"—meaning religious formal opinions or rulings) . . . according to the rulings of Shari'ah" for Muslims living in America and the West. At their Fifth Convention, held in Bahrain in November 2007, AMJA decreed:

Allah sent His Messengers and revealed His Books for people to stand forth with justice. The way to do this is to judge by His Laws, to stand up for pure justice and to renounce all the vain desires and human arrangements that go against it. Therefore, it is not lawful to seek judgment from man-made courts of law, unless there is a complete lack of Islamic alternatives. . . .

Muslims are given permission to use secular courts by necessity, but sharia is still established as supreme. In addition, Muslims in the West must find ways to follow sharia however possible:

It is incumbent upon Muslim communities to try to solve their disputes by compromising within the limits of Shari'ah judgment and by seeking out ways that are legal in their countries of residence which would enable them to judge by Islamic Law. . . .

One of AMJA's senior Permanent Fatwa Committee members, Dr. Waleed al-Maneese of the Islamic University of Minnesota, counseled that a Muslim who becomes a judge in America should "understand the Shari'a in such a manner as to be able to rule by it in every case brought before him, or at least as close as he's able to. . . . He also must in his heart hate the man-made law."

The Quran, Hadith, and a consensus of Islamic scholars suggest that Muslims should respect sharia law over the laws of whatever nation they happen to live in. That shouldn't come as a surprise. What should shock us, however, is that *American courts have helped them accomplish this*. The Center for Security Policy has identified at least 146 cases of sharia law coming into conflict with American law. Here are just a few examples:

- **SD v. MJR, New Jersey, 2010:** A Muslim woman was denied a restraining order against her husband, who had repeatedly raped and beaten her. The husband asserted it was his right under sharia law to have sex with his wife at any time, and the trial court held that since the husband believed he was exercising his "religious right," he was not acting with criminal intent. Fortunately this decision was reversed on appeal.

- **In Re: Marriage of Obaidi, Washington State, 2010:** A Muslim woman who was divorcing her husband demanded that he pay her twenty thousand dollars under a prenuptial agreement made in accordance with sharia law. This agreement, however, had been written in Farsi, which the husband did not understand. Despite this fact, the trial court, specifically citing Islamic law, demanded the husband pay the twenty thousand dollars. This was reversed on appeal, and the trial court was found to have "erred by looking to Islamic law."

- **In Re: Marriage of Malak, California, 1986:** A Muslim couple from Lebanon moved to the United Arab Emirates. A few years later, the wife left for America with their two children and eventually filed for divorce and sole custody in California. A sharia court in Lebanon, however, gave custody to the husband, and he asked the California court to enforce this decision. The lower court refused, but on appeal, custody was granted to the husband in Lebanon when the "California appellate court appeared to defer" to the sharia court. This shows that the appeals process cannot always be relied upon.

Perhaps most troubling, in February 2015, the city of Irving, Texas, which is where my studios are located, found itself in the center of a national controversy. The North Texas Islamic Tribunal had established itself as a sharia court in Irving.

I sat down with two of the tribunal's three judges, and while they claimed their authority was limited, they offered some troubling views. One of the judges even praised harsh sharia punishments like cutting off the hands of thieves, "because if he feels my hands were cut because of that, he will think about this 100 times. He will never do it."

The Irving City Council responded by passing a resolution officially recognizing the U.S. Constitution as the law of the land. And yet it passed by only a 5–4 vote. Why? Seemingly because four of the City Council members were more afraid of appearing politically incorrect than they were committed to preserving the integrity of America's laws.

These council members would be wise to study Great Britain, which, by one estimate, had more than eighty sharia courts in 2009. Most of these deal with marriage and family issues, with many of the cases brought by women. A 2013 BBC investigation found that "Islamic rulings given here are not always in the interests of the women concerned, and can run counter to British law." They cited examples of British sharia courts ordering women to go back to abusive marriages or to give up custody of their children to violent spouses.

Back in the United States, the sharia judges in Texas told local media that they've received calls from all over the country from other Muslim leaders looking to set up their own courts. Irving's mayor, Beth Van Duyne, sees where all of this is likely headed. "Our nation cannot be so overly sensitive in defending other cultures that we stop protecting our own," she said.

Unfortunately, that seems to be exactly what's happening.

Being labeled a conspiracy theorist or an Islamophobe is so scary to most people that they won't even raise their hand to affirm that yes, our Constitution is the supreme law of the land.

Political correctness is beating common sense. Once the floodgates open—once a viable system of sharia courts is allowed to operate and coexist with U.S. law—there will be no going back. At that point they won't say we are "conspiracy theorists" anymore; they'll just say we were right.

▮ LIE #6 ▮

"THE CALIPHATE IS A FANCIFUL DREAM."

"When Glenn Beck rants about the caliphate taking over the Middle East from Morocco to the Philippines, and lists the connections between Caliphate-promoters and the American left, he brings to mind no one so much as Robert Welch and the John Birch Society."

—Bill Kristol, *Weekly Standard*, February 2011

"Our strategy is shaped by a deeper understanding of al-Qaida's goals, strategy and tactics that we have gained over the last decade. I'm not talking about al-Qaida's grandiose vision of global domination through a violent Islamic caliphate. That vision is absurd, and we are not going to organize our counter-terrorism policies against a feckless delusion that is never going to happen."

—John Brennan, director of Central Intelligence, June 2011

"No, I don't believe that at all."
—White House spokesman Josh Earnest, when asked, "Do you believe that ISIS has established something of a caliphate?"

Grandiose." "Absurd." "A feckless delusion." "Never going to happen."

That's what John Brennan, a longtime counterterrorism advisor to the Obama and Bush administrations and current director of the CIA, had to say about the idea that a Caliphate might be pitching its tent in some hellhole on the other side of the planet.

Bill Kristol, neocon scribe and architect of Alan Keyes's feckless campaign for the Senate, attacked me a few years back for daring to suggest that Islamist radicals had ambitions to create a Caliphate.

Now, in 2015, an estimated six million people in Syria and Iraq find themselves living under what *U.S. News & World Report,* as well as other outlets, has termed the militants' "caliphate."

So, what exactly is a caliphate?

As discussed in chapter 3, the term has been used to describe Islamic empires since the seventh century A.D. When the prophet Muhammad died in 632, his father-in-law, Abu Bakr, was appointed the first "caliph," or "successor," to rule over the followers and territory that Muhammad had amassed. Throughout many different rulers and succession disputes, the original Caliphate's borders expanded and contracted over time until 1258, when its last capital, Baghdad, fell to Mongol invaders. Shortly thereafter, the Ottoman Turks established a new caliphate based in Constantinople, before it disintegrated in the wake of the empire's defeat in World War I.

Hope for restoring the Caliphate was rekindled in 1928, when Hassan al-Banna started the Muslim Brotherhood in Egypt. According to terrorism researcher Stephen Coughlin, al-Banna viewed the end of the Caliphate as "a calamity that highlighted how far the Islamic world had strayed from the true message and governing system of Islam." Al-Banna was not shy about announcing his group's goal. "It is the nature of Islam to dominate, not to be dominated," the godfather of modern Islamist terrorist groups said, "to impose its law on all nations and to extend its power to the entire planet."

ISIS realized this vision on June 28, 2014, by formally establishing a Caliphate—almost three years to the day after CIA director Brennan's assurances that it would never happen. In their official statement that day, ISIS announced that they had "gained the essentials necessary for khilīfah [caliphate], which the Muslims are sinful for if they do not try to establish."

Muslims around the world faced damnation if they did not fulfill their religious duty to support the new state, according to ISIS. They elevated their leader, Abu Bakr al-Baghdadi, to the position of "imam and khalīfah [caliph] for the Muslims everywhere." He was now to be called "Caliph Ibrahim."

The captain of the "JV" squad apparently woke up one morning and dubbed himself leader of the Islamic world.

Anyone surprised by this (and there are plenty) has simply not been paying attention. In 2005, members of the Bush administration and military leaders told us about terrorists' dreams for a Caliphate. "They talk about wanting to re-establish what you could refer to as the seventh-century caliphate," Vice President Dick Cheney warned, "governed by Sharia law, the most rigid interpretation of the Koran."

Similarly, Secretary of Defense Donald Rumsfeld warned that "Iraq would serve as the base of a new Islamic caliphate to extend throughout the Middle East, and which would threaten legitimate governments in Europe, Africa and Asia."

And then there was this from General John Abizaid, the commander of U.S. forces in the Middle East: "They will try to re-establish a caliphate throughout the entire Muslim world. Just as we had the opportunity to learn what the Nazis were going to do, from Hitler's world in 'Mein Kampf,' we need to learn what these people intend to do from their own words."

But the mainstream media would have none of it. The *New York Times,* among others on the left, took great umbrage at the idea of a Caliphate. In 2005, the *Times* wrote that "a number of scholars and former government officials take strong issue with the administration's warning about a new caliphate, and compare it to the fear of communism spread during the Cold War. They say that although Al Qaeda's statements do indeed describe a caliphate as a goal, the administration is exaggerating the magnitude of the threat."

The *Times* also quoted Shibley Telhami, Anwar Sadat Professor for Peace and Development at the University of Maryland, who assured readers, "There's no chance in the world that they'll succeed. It's a silly threat."

Yet here we are.

Each week, the Islamic State's Caliphate controls an area larger than Great Britain. With nearly every passing day, it absorbs more cities and villages in Iraq and Syria. To date, this desert heartland of the Caliphate puts the Islamic State in control of more than six million people.

The Caliphate continues to expand into oil-rich areas, which provide millions of dollars in funding for increased terrorist activity and expansion. And unlike most pure terrorist organizations, ISIS governs the territory it captures, providing water, roads, and a justice system operated under sharia law. From Libya to Egypt to Yemen and Nigeria it has far-flung cells operating in more than a dozen countries with outposts where it governs pockets of territory.

The term *caliphate* has deep meaning and cultural resonance for Muslims around the world. While it's true that the vast majority of them do not recognize the legitimacy of the Caliphate established by the Islamic State, it has attracted a steady stream of recruits and other means of support as the fulfillment of a political vision that was erased from the face of the earth for ninety years. The new Caliphate is becoming a self-fulfilling prophecy as Islamist radicals flock to join a weak but Allah-ordained political entity destined to spread to the corners of the earth. Osama bin Laden once said, "when people see a strong horse and a weak horse, by nature, they will like the strong horse." As the Caliphate expands and the West does nothing to stand in its way, it's pretty clear that hundreds of thousands of Muslim youths see the strong horse and want to be part of the winning team.

It's also important to remember why the Caliphate is so important in the first place: it's a necessary step to bring about the return of the Mahdi, the final successor to Muhammad before the Day of Judgment. Islamists do not just want money, power, or land. All of these things are necessary, but they are a means to an end.

That end is nothing less than the End Times themselves.

We know that extremists have had a very specific plan to achieve this goal in place for years. As chapter 4 describes, Zawahiri, al-Qaeda, and its ISIS allies have a detailed seven-stage vision, which was published in 2005. Their strategy anticipated a U.S. response to 9/11 that would draw America into war in Afghanistan and Iraq, and successfully predicted the so-called Arab Spring, when secular governments would topple, and the creation of an Islamic Caliphate sometime between 2013 and 2016—years before they actually occurred.

Phase 7, to be completed by 2020, is when "one-and-a-half billion Muslims" join the Caliphate, ensuring its "definitive victory." Given their track record so far (the predicted Caliphate arrived right on time), we have every reason to take them seriously.

The Islamic State has been ground zero for some of the worst crimes against humanity in modern times. Sexual slavery, mass executions, and beheadings are broadcast around the world. They use the Quran and sharia to justify their actions, and to govern the territory they control under their self-declared "Caliphate." They do not kill and conquer in their own name, but in the name of Allah. The question of whether any of this is "legitimate" in the eyes of other Muslims is irrelevant. The Islamic State does not need or care about recognition as a true Caliphate from anyone else. It will continue to act like one and grow as one until, according to their plan, they have more than a billion Muslims under their control and the rest of the world is powerless to stop them.

▮ LIE #7 ▮

"ISLAM IS TOLERANT TOWARD NON-MUSLIMS."

"Throughout history, Islam has demonstrated, through words and deeds, the possibilities of religious tolerance and racial equality. . . . Islam has a proud tradition of tolerance."
— President Barack Obama in Cairo, 2009

"If Islam's sole interest is the welfare of mankind, then Islam is the strongest advocate of human rights anywhere on Earth."
— Hip-hop artist and actor Mos Def

"Never in its history did Islam compel a single human being to change his faith."
— Muslim Brotherhood theorist Said Qutb

You're probably familiar with that purple "COEXIST" bumper sticker—the one where the *C* is an Islamic crescent, symbolizing the unshakable Muslim commitment to peace and interfaith dialogue. It's a familiar refrain, one heard over and over again from Islamists and their apologists alike: Islam's history is one of cooperation and peaceful coexistence with non-Muslims.

Like so much of the material in the Quran and Islamic law, teachings on how to treat Christians, Jews, and other unbelievers often appear murky and contradictory. But, as discussed earlier, these teachings become painfully clear if you know where to look, and know which later Medinan passages replace the earlier, more peaceful Meccan ones. The abrogative structure—meaning that verses in the Quran from an earlier time period are superseded as doctrine by verses revealed by Muhammad at a later time—makes Allah's true message easy to spot: all non-Muslims must be "subdued."

Like many of the more brutal elements of Islam, the persecution of non-Muslims at the hands of Islamist fanatics has seen a resurgence as the global jihad movement has gained strength. Barbarism toward and murder of nonbelievers became the law of the land in the Islamic State Caliphate after it announced that Christians were legitimate targets for death. *Dabiq*, the Islamic State's official propaganda magazine, has listed "the Jews, the Christians, the Rafida [Shia] and the proponents of democracy" as its main enemies deserving of jihad.

Many Muslims are, of course, tolerant and pluralistic people, proud citizens of the twenty-first century who realize that medieval-style religious persecution has no place in the world today. But the fact remains that the Quran and Islamic law contain ample justification for subjugating non-Muslims to Muslim power. Our enemies acknowledge this justification openly—we ignore it at our own peril.

It should be apparent to anyone reading this book that the Quran itself often works *against* those who present a benevolent, tolerant image of Islam. In this case, however, the Quran seems to have given them evidence to back up their views. It is found in Sura 2:

There is no compulsion in religion. Verily, the Right Path has become distinct from the wrong path. (Quran 2:256)

This seems nice and pluralistic. The very first phrase, "There is no compulsion in religion," is seized upon by some as proof that Islam, by nature, is peaceful and content to leave other religions alone. Juan Cole, a professor at the University of Michigan, even includes the verse in his list of the "Top Ten Ways Islamic Law forbids Terrorism." According to Cole's analysis, "Islam's holy book forbids coercing people into adopting any religion. They have to willingly choose it."

That would seem to tie up the issue nicely, and reduce concerns about Islamic treatment of nonbelievers to mere "alarmism." But digging further into the Quran brings to light some contradictory messages.

Let's go back to Cole, who also claims that verse 2:256 "was never abrogated by any other verse of the Quran," meaning it would be established as the ironclad word of Allah on the topic. But Cole's case is not exactly ironclad itself. In fact, Stephen Coughlin, one of the top Defense Department experts on Islamic law until his politically motivated dismissal, uses verse 2:256 as a classic case study for the concept of abrogation.

Coughlin points out that the pluralistic message of verse 2:256 is actually abrogated in the very next chapter, Sura 3, by the following verse:

And whoever seeks a religion other than Islam, it will never be accepted of him, and in the Hereafter he will be one of the losers. (Quran 3:85)

There may be no "compulsion," but there is no "acceptance," either. Coughlin goes on to argue that the final abrogation of the seemingly benign verse 2:256 is found in Sura 5:

O you who believe! Take not the Jews and the Christians as *Auliya'* (friends, protectors, helpers, etc.), they are but *Auliya'* to one another. And if any amongst you takes them as *Auliya'*, then surely he is one of them. Verily, Allah guides not those people who are the *Zalimun* (polytheists and wrong-doers and unjust). (Quran 5:51)

According to Coughlin's analysis, "Surah 2 is abrogated by Surah 3, and Surah 3 facilitates Surah 5." Because Sura 5 "reflects a divine command from Allah," it becomes "the end-state understanding of how an informed Muslim is to regard Christians and Jews."

Other Quranic verses seem to contribute to the idea that Sura 2 is not the final word on the matter. In one particularly biting verse, those who suffer Allah's wrath—as unbelievers do—are referred to as "apes and swine":

> Shall I inform you of something worse than that, regarding the recompense from Allah: those (Jews) who incurred the Curse of Allah and His Wrath, those of whom (some) He transformed into monkeys and swines, those who worshipped *Taghut* (false deities); such are worse in rank (on the Day of Resurrection in the Hell-fire), and far more astray from the Right Path (in the life of this world). (Quran 5:60)

The verse that precedes this one makes it clear that this warning is being addressed to the "People of the Scripture" or "People of the Book," a common Quranic expression for Jews and Christians ("O people of the Scripture (Jews and Christians)! Do you criticize us for no other reason than that we believe in Allah, and in (the revelation) which has been sent down to us and in that which has been sent down before (us), and that most of you are *Fasiqun* [rebellious and disobedient (to Allah)]?")

In fact, this phrase surfaces in another passage that goes far beyond mere name-calling:

Fight against those who (1) believe not in Allah, (2) nor in the Last Day, (3) nor forbid that which has been forbidden by Allah and His Messenger (4) and those who acknowledge not the religion of truth (i.e., Islam) among the people of the Scripture (Jews and Christians), until they pay the *Jizyah* with willing submission, and feel themselves subdued. (Quran 9:29)

Subdued. That is the proper state, according to the Quran, for anyone who does not believe in Allah. Over the course of history, the process of "subduing" unbelievers has taken a number of forms.

Muslim armies of previous eras were not above slaughtering those they conquered who refused to "submit" to Islam. For example, Muhammad led his armies to slaughter hundreds of the males of the Jewish Banu Qurayzah tribe in Medina. The men were beheaded and the women and children were taken into slavery. When twenty thousand soldiers of the Ottoman Empire—the last caliphate—captured the city of Otranto, Italy, after a two-week siege in 1480, they killed 813 of its citizens who remained true to their Christian faith. The Martyrs of Otranto were among the first group of people to be canonized by Pope Francis in 2013.

There was also the massacre and enslavement of millions of Hindus on the Indian subcontinent in the eleventh and twelfth centuries, the 1.5 million Christian Armenians killed in 1915, and the more recent beheadings of Christians by ISIS.

Death was not always the only option, however. Once conquered by a Muslim force, non-Muslims could also become a *dhimmi*—a "protected person"—who would still be allowed to live in the Muslim-run community. But *dhimmi* can also mean "guilty." And for the guilty, there was a price for protection—often literally. Recall the Quran: "Fight . . . until they pay the *Jizya* with willing submission, and feel themselves subdued." According to Hugh Kennedy of the University of London, this passage explains "that the People of the Book (that is Christian and Jews who have revealed scriptures) should be spared as long as they pay tribute and acknowledge their position as second class citizens."

This "tribute" is the *jizya,* a tax paid by *dhimmi*s that amounts essentially to blood money. Kennedy notes that *dhimmi*s were also often required to pay poll taxes and other levies. In addition, *dhimmi*s are known to have been subjected to other regulations such as restricted religious practices, required shows of deference to Muslims, and wearing distinctive clothing items.

Some Muslim rulers actually preferred to maintain control over a large number of *dhimmi*s from whom they could extract *jizya* tribute, as opposed to forcing them to convert to Islam (which would eliminate their extra tax). "The produce of the jizya," Kennedy notes, "was very useful because it was paid in cash. This became specially valuable in the years when structure of caliphal finance collapsed."

This should all sound somewhat familiar. The soldiers of the Islamic State, today's Caliphate, have systematically executed Christians, along with other Muslims, both inside and outside their conquered territory. In lawless Libya, for example, they have executed Christians and threatened the entire "nation of the cross." In videos that went viral around the world, the narrator at one point says to Christians: "You pay (tax) with willing submission, feeling yourselves subdued." He quotes almost directly from verse 9:29.

In Mosul, Iraq, the Christian community, which numbered in the tens of thousands, was given an ultimatum that would have made just as much sense to Christians facing Muslim conquest centuries ago. "We offer them three choices," ISIS said of Mosul's Christians. "Islam; the dhimma contract—involving payment of jizya; if they refuse this they will have nothing but the sword." Christians abandoned Mosul in droves.

ISIS delivered an even worse fate to Iraq's Yazidi minority, a community with an ancient faith tradition that combines elements of Christianity, Shiism, and ancient religions. Tens of thousands were forced to flee their homes in the Sinjar area of northern Iraq as ISIS forces advanced. Many sought refuge in the mountains and endured a brutal state of siege. When the soldiers of the Caliphate arrived, thousands of Yazidis were slaughtered and several thousand women and girls were captured for ISIS to hold as modern-day sex slaves. A "menu" was circulated listing the prices of Yazidi and Christian girls. A female prisoner between one and nine years old could be bought for $172. ISIS took pains to attempt to justify this practice by citing sharia law.

History is repeating itself. Once again, a Caliphate is demanding blood money from nonbelievers. Those who don't pay up get "the sword." But the justification for exacting payment of *jizya* has not changed; it's right there in the Quran.

If that's your idea of tolerance for other faiths then I'm afraid we have very different definitions of that word.

▮ LIE #8 ▮

"ADDRESSING FRUSTRATION, POVERTY, JOBLESSNESS IN THE MUSLIM WORLD—MAYBE EVEN CLIMATE CHANGE— WILL END TERRORISM."

"Efforts to counter violent extremism will only succeed if citizens can address legitimate grievances through the democratic process and express themselves through strong civil societies."

—President Barack Obama

"We fight poverty because hope is an answer to terror."

—President George W. Bush

"We need in the medium and longer term to go after the root causes that lead people to join these groups, [such as] lack of opportunity for jobs."

—Marie Harf, State Department spokeswoman

"Severe drought helped to create the instability in Nigeria that was exploited by the terrorist group Boko Haram. . . . It's now believed that drought, crop failures, and high food prices helped fuel the early unrest in Syria, which descended into civil war in the heart of the Middle East."

—President Barack Obama

They are angry—and perhaps justifiably so." This is a near-constant refrain we hear about the violent Islamist radicals who murder and brutalize innocent people, cut off journalists' heads, and dismember children: these poor, sensitive souls are frustrated by their lot in life. They are mired in poverty, suffering at the hands of powerful rulers. They are suffering from droughts and crop failures caused by the CO_2 emissions from your SUV. They are suffering because of colonialism. They are suffering because of racism. They are suffering because of Islamophobia.

The subtext is almost always that these terrorists are angry because of something America has done.

Maybe their brother was killed in a drone attack. Maybe they heard about a Quran being burned or flushed down the toilet at Guantánamo. Maybe they saw images on Al Jazeera of Palestinian refugees suffering at the hands of Israel's bloodthirsty leaders—images that were probably not even taken in Gaza but are actually of violence in Syria at the hands of Bashar al-Assad. Or maybe they suffer because of the cruel, cynical bargains Western nations have made with Middle East dictators in a quest for oil.

Whatever the reason, the thinking goes, these angry young men need our help and our understanding. Author Bill Siegel has written masterfully about this tendency to blame ourselves for terrorist actions. In his book *The Control Factor,* Siegel suggests that when faced with a threat from radical Islam whose singular goal is our destruction, we tend to frame our perceptions in order to give us the impression we are in control of something we are not. Making ourselves the cause of the terrorists' violence (because of oppressive colonial actions of the past, support for tyrannical powers in Muslim nations, occupation of Muslim lands, insulting of the Prophet, Israeli treatment of Palestinians, or occupation of disputed territories, failing to address Arab or Muslim poverty and lack of education, etc.), as uncomfortable as that may make us feel, is still less threatening than the realization that we are absolutely not in control. It lets us believe that since we are to blame, we can fix it by changing ourselves. The truth is that we are not and cannot.

Siegel explains that this compulsion to blame ourselves resembles the relationship between addicts and enablers. An addict typically blames his behavior on the enabler, who accepts responsibility and endlessly searches for ways to fix it. Unfortunately, this spawns a deadly cycle that grows more intense: while the enabler believes in good faith that they are helping to right a wrong, the transfer and acceptance of responsibility only invites more of the same behavior. Only when we are fully able to see the threat for what it truly is, Siegel suggests, will we be able to muster the appropriate will and clarity to transform our relationship and fight it. Put simply, they come after us because we are not them; not because of anything we do.

As a result, terrorists continue to posture as victims. And we continue to fall for it.

There is an endemic need within many free people, particularly on the left, to try to empathize with those who hate us. To *understand* our enemies so that we can bring them around. To use the Marxist lenses of class struggle and income inequality to examine problems that have nothing to do with economics whatsoever. They revel in psychobabble so that they might be able to do something to lessen the anger these poor and unfortunate terrorists must be feeling and to assuage their own guilt for living a well-heeled life in a prosperous country.

That, at any rate, is the approach that President Obama has repeatedly taken since he first held public office. As a state senator in Illinois, Obama proclaimed, "Most often, though, [terrorism] grows out of a climate of poverty and ignorance, helplessness and despair."

Referencing terrorist Umar Farouk Abdulmutallab, Obama cited the plight of Abdulmutallab's native country of Yemen: "We know . . . Yemen [is] a country grappling with crushing poverty and deadly insurgencies."

"We cannot kill our way out of this war," said State Department spokeswoman Marie Harf. "We need in the medium and longer term to go after the root causes that lead people to join these groups, whether it is lack of opportunity for jobs . . . We can help them build their economies so they can have job opportunities for these people."

Many others on the left have followed this same line of thinking. Touré Neblett, one of the cohosts of MSNBC's *The Cycle,* once said that "Muslim poverty is what threatens our security. Giving these men the chance to work here could diminish their poverty, their anger, and their misunderstanding of the U.S. before they are radicalized. . . ."

It's easy to understand why some would prefer terrorists to be motivated by base emotions like anger. If someone is angry with you, you can talk to them. Reason with them. Address their grievances. It's the equivalent of the foolish U.S. legislator who once said during World War II, "Lord, if only I could have talked to Hitler, all of this might have been avoided."

The problem with the idea that terrorists are attacking us because they are frustrated and angry about their status in life is that it just isn't true. Terrorists aren't attacking us because of our policies or past behavior or because we said something to offend them. They are attacking us because they are motivated by an ideology that urges them to kill in the name of God, that upholds martyrdom over life, that insists martyrdom will be rewarded with heavenly pleasures.

Let's think for a moment about what the president is saying. Yes, the fact that you can't vote in a meaningful election in Syria is terrible. If you have a grievance about that, it's legitimate. But does that really have any impact on the thinking of lunatics who believe that murdering innocent people will get them a reward in heaven?

Would Osama bin Laden have called off 9/11 if he'd been given a voter registration card?

If poverty and anger at the establishment were the predominant motivation for terrorism, then there should be bombs and suicide attacks going on every day in parts of Washington, D.C., or Detroit or South Central Los Angeles.

Osama bin Laden, the author of one of the most effective acts of terrorism against the West in history, was a Saudi millionaire who, by some estimates, was worth $300 million. The Taliban, as rulers of Afghanistan, had it better than most of the people unfortunate enough to have been subjected to their brutal rule. That didn't stop them from supporting terrorism.

Study after study has been done about those who join Islamic terrorist groups. In fact, one study by British researchers found that wealth and education were *positive* indicators for possible terrorist activities. Another survey of four hundred al-Qaeda terrorist biographies found that more than 60 percent of members had college degrees, and that many came from middle- or upper-class backgrounds. A study of Palestinian suicide bombers found that "[n]one of [the bombers] were uneducated, desperately poor, simple-minded, or depressed. Many were middle class and, unless they were fugitives, held paying jobs. . . . Two were the sons of millionaires."

A 2004 Harvard study began with the "reasonable assumption that terrorism has its roots in poverty." By the end, the study determined there was "no significant relationship" between economic conditions and terrorism. "In the past, we heard people refer to the strong link between terrorism and poverty," said Alberto Abadie, associate professor of public policy at Harvard's John F. Kennedy School of Government, "but in fact when you look at the data, it's not there. This is true not only for events of international terrorism, as previous studies have shown, but perhaps more surprisingly also for the overall level of terrorism, both of domestic and of foreign origin."

Islam expressly forbids anger as a justification for jihad. Consider the words of James Cromitie, a New Jersey native who converted to Islam in prison and gave himself the name Abdul Rahman. In 2009, Cromitie was arrested by the FBI after attempting to organize a terror plot to blow up two New York synagogues and launch Stinger antiaircraft missiles at a National Guard base.

During his long conversations with an FBI confidential informant (CI), Cromitie discussed a confrontation he'd had with a Jewish man at his hotel.

CROMITIE: But sometime I just want to grab him and ahhh, just kill him. But, I'm Muslim, insha 'Allah, Allah will take care of it.

CI: Insha 'Allah, if you, brother, if you really have to do something, you have to do something in jihad, and try and do something . . .

CROMITIE: No, because, because you angry.

CI: Angry.

CROMITIE: No, you have to do it where it's fisabilillah.

Fisabilillah. The phrase means, literally, "in the cause of Allah." And, according to the Quran, it's the only legitimate reason for a Muslim to engage in jihad.

Cromitie is not alone when he rejects a worldly motivation, such as anger, as a reason for killing. One of al-Qaeda's earliest members, Sayyid Imam al-Sharif, also known as Dr. Fadl, wrote "Jihad and the Effects of Intention Upon It," in which he cited Quranic verses and authentic hadiths in order to affirm that the desire for wealth, fame, glory, or petty emotions was not sufficient for a jihadist to obtain a heavenly reward.

Among the reported quotes of Muhammad and Hadith that Fadl cites is this one: "Whoever is killed beneath a blind banner, becoming angry for the group and fighting for the group, then he is not from my Ummah." Despite the claims to the contrary by a sympathetic media, anger over colonialism or wounds from "foreign domination" isn't the reason for jihadist violence. It's just an excuse.

Instead, firmly based in Islamic theology, Fadl urged would-be terrorists:

> So strive for righteous intentions so that you will benefit from your actions and your jihad. As the Shari'ah has made the rewards of Jihad contingent upon the correct intentions of the one performing . . .

In other words, terrorists lining up to don suicide vests because they're angry or because they just got a pink slip at work are actually giving up their ticket to paradise.

Given this clear line, why are our Western leaders indulging in the dangerous fantasy that alleviating the anger and hopelessness that exist in the Muslim world would make everything fine? Because believing *we* are responsible for terrorism assuages the modern West's profound sense of guilt and self-doubt. They want to believe that there is a way to end terrorism without violence; that if we just throw enough money at the problem, it will eventually go away.

Of course that will not work. Terrorists' grievances have less to do with personal anger and disaffection and more to do with the religious ideology they've sworn their lives to. This necessitates a fundamentally different approach. They cannot be appeased. They cannot be reasoned with. They cannot be bribed with better jobs or cars or democratic rights.

They can only be defeated.

▌ LIE #9 ▌

"CRITICS OF ISLAM ARE BIGOTS."

"I consider it part of my responsibility as president of the United States to fight against negative stereotypes of Islam wherever they appear."

—President Barack Obama

"Islamophobia is a growing phenomenon in our society that needs to be challenged through proactive efforts. Everyone needs to do their part."

—CAIR national executive director Nihad Awad

On the afternoon of April 26, 2014, Paul Weston, a British candidate for election to the European Parliament, was arrested as he gave a speech in the city of Winchester. In the course of his remarks, Weston mentioned the "curses" of Islam, which he called "dreadful" for its devotees. He had deplored the idea that "every woman must belong to some man as his absolute property," and argued that Islam "paralyses the social development of those who follow it." He concluded by calling Islam "a militant and proselytizing faith."

Weston was placed under arrest for "suspicion of religious/

racial harassment" and was jailed for several hours before being released.

Many people quickly condemned Weston as an "Islamophobe" for his speech. It's a trendy new phrase unleashed by apologists to scare people away from criticizing Islam.

But here's the most interesting part of the story: The words Paul Weston spoke that day—and for which he was arrested—were not his own. They were originally written by a man to whom modern Britain owes nothing less than its very existence: Sir Winston Churchill.

Churchill had penned the lines decades earlier in a book titled *The River War: An Account of the Reconquest of Sudan*:

> Improvident habits, slovenly systems of agriculture, sluggish methods of commerce, and insecurity of property exist wherever the followers of the Prophet rule or live. Thousands become the brave and loyal soldiers of the faith: all know how to die but the influence of the religion paralyses the social development of those who follow it. No stronger retrograde force exists in the world. Far from being moribund, Mohammedanism is a militant and proselytizing faith.

In present-day Great Britain, Winston Churchill, savior of Europe, defender of the West, champion of democratic values, and close ally of Franklin Roosevelt, would likely be behind bars, branded as a notorious Islamophobe who dared to offer criticism about Islam and its teaching.

Islam apologists go to great lengths to prove that people are perfectly free to question Islam—so long as they stay within carefully prescribed limits. For example, the Council on American-Islamic Relations (CAIR) claims, "We do not label all, or even the majority of those, who question Islam and Muslims as Islamophobes. Equally, we believe it is not Islamophobic to denounce crimes committed by individual Muslims or those claiming Islam as a motivation for their actions."

Yet that is exactly what they do.

CAIR and its secular leftist allies, like the ironically named group Fairness & Accuracy in Reporting (FAIR), delight in levying the charge of "Islamophobia" at people who do simply "question Islam and Muslims."

In fact, FAIR has a Nixonian "hit list" of their supposed enemies, which they label as "some of the media's leading teachers of anti-Muslim bigotry, serving various roles in the Islamophobic movement." These nefarious ne'er-do-wells, the group goes on to claim in paranoid fashion, "form a network that teaches Americans to see Islam in fearful terms and their Muslim neighbors as suspects." Among those targeted: Bill O'Reilly, the writer Mark Steyn, Daniel Pipes, and Sean Hannity.

And, of course, me.

The George Soros–funded group Media Matters has its own version of a hate list, which (curiously) includes only conservatives as anti-Islam bigots: Brian Kilmeade, Roger Ailes, Newt Gingrich, Rev. Franklin Graham, and Greg Gutfeld.

And, of course, me again.

The origins of the term *Islamophobia* have unsurprisingly been traced back to the United Kingdom. In a 1997 report from the Runnymede Trust, which bills itself as "the UK's leading independent race equality think tank," the group described "Islamophobia" as "unfounded hostility towards Islam, and therefore fear or dislike of all or most Muslims."

That's actually not a bad definition. "Unfounded" hostility toward Islam and dislike of all or most Muslims may very well be "Islamophobic"—but that definition certainly doesn't apply to me, and I'll bet that it doesn't apply to any of the other people on the FAIR and Media Matters hit lists, either.

Besides, that is not how "Islamophobia" has been defined by

groups like CAIR, which, it should be noted, has a checkered history of radical connections—including links to Hamas and the Muslim Brotherhood—and was an unindicted co-conspirator in the U.S. government's case against the Holy Land Foundation, which gave money to Hamas. This is how CAIR defines the concept: "Islamophobia is closed-minded prejudice against or hatred of Islam and Muslims. An Islamophobe is an individual who holds a closed-minded view of Islam and promotes prejudice against or hatred of Muslims."

The convenient part for them is that the definition of "closed-minded" and "prejudice" is whatever they want it to be. It's pretty clear that CAIR's definition of "Islamophobia" includes anyone who's ever said anything even slightly negative about Islam or who's challenged others to think critically about the connection between Islam and Islamic terrorism. As it happens, that's a long list of people, including some of the most distinguished minds in the Western world, from Tocqueville to Patton to former American presidents.

In 1843, for example, the acclaimed author Alexis de Tocqueville wrote that he had studied the Quran "a great deal." His conclusion was that "there have been few religions in the world as deadly to men as that of Muhammad."

John Quincy Adams, the former president of the United States and a champion for the rights of freed slaves, also reportedly blasted Islam in remarks that would lead him to be condemned and jailed today.

"He [Muhammad] declared undistinguishing and exterminating war, as a part of his religion, against all the rest of mankind," Adams noted. "The precept of the Koran is perpetual war against all who deny that Mahomet is the prophet of God."

General George Patton, one of the liberators of Europe, also had unflattering things to say about Islam. "To me," Patton said, "it seems certain that the fatalistic teachings of Muhammad and the utter degradation of women is the outstanding cause for the arrested development of the Arab. He is exactly as he was around the year 700, while we have kept on developing."

Liberal Bill Maher has noted that "there's only one faith" that "kills you or wants to kill you if you draw a bad cartoon of the prophet" and that "there's only one faith that kills you or wants to kill you if you renounce the faith." He added this is not just a small group of zealots. "It's more than just a fringe element." He went on to say that comparison of Muslim violence to Christianity was "liberal bullshit."

There are plenty of serious people who've made smart observations about Islam over the years—throwing around the charge of "Islamophobia" has become a knee-jerk reaction, a cudgel for clobbering anyone who dares to seek (or speak) the truth. Its purpose, and the agenda of groups that use the term, is the distinctly illiberal goal of stifling different points of view.

"Islam makes very large claims for itself," the late Christopher Hitchens, an acclaimed writer who was the toast of leftist elites, once wrote. "In its art, there is a prejudice against representing the human form at all. The prohibition on picturing the prophet—who was only another male mammal—is apparently absolute. So is the prohibition on pork or alcohol or, in some Muslim societies, music or dancing. Very well then, let a good Muslim abstain rigorously from all these. But if he claims the right to make me abstain as well, he offers the clearest possible warning and proof of an aggressive intent."

That's not bigotry or intolerance or irrational fear of someone different. That is just someone speaking the truth. Those who tend to hurl allegations of hate, intolerance, and bigotry at those of us who have the temerity to question and challenge some of the teachings and traditions of Islam are in fact projecting the reality of their own hate, intolerance, and bigotry on the rest of us.

We cannot let accusations from others distract us. You know what's in your heart, and I know what's in mine. Question with boldness, speak the truth, and the rest will take care of itself.

▌ LIE #10 ▌

"ISLAM RESPECTS THE RIGHTS OF WOMEN."

"While it needs to be acknowledged that atrocities have been committed against women overseas in the name of Islam, it also needs to be acknowledged that such practices have no basis in the religion itself. More than 1400 years ago Islam afforded women rights comparable to those in our contemporary international human rights documents."

—Ghena Krayem and Haisam Farache,
op-ed, *Sydney Morning Herald*

"Contrary to how popular culture portrays Muslim women's rights and privileges, Islam gives women many rights, including the right to inherit, to work outside the home, and to be educated. As in all cultures and communities, these rights are often violated. This is the result of the intersection of Islam with existing cultural norms, which may reflect male-dominated societies. In Muslim communities, women often have a strong influence in the family, the workplace, the religion and society in general."

—"Beliefs and Daily Lives of Muslims," PBS *Frontline*

Violent acts of terrorism in the name of Islam are all too common. Less visible, but no less shocking, are the individual acts of cruelty perpetrated against women in the name of radical Islam. While some would undoubtedly prefer to ignore this fact, those who commit these attacks can easily find justification for them under Islamic law.

Islam has apologists both inside and outside the faith who argue that there is nothing in the teachings of the religion that could lead to repression or violence against women. To them, it's always something else, some sinister outside force that creates a situation for which Islam is unjustly blamed.

Two Australian Muslims, an imam and a scholar in Islamic family law, cowrote a disturbing op-ed defending sharia that was published in the *Sydney Morning Herald* in 2008. In it they claimed that Islam pioneered the field of women's rights centuries ago and that "atrocities . . . committed against women overseas in the name of Islam"—which they at least acknowledge have occurred—"have no basis in the religion itself." Instead, they blame "other factors, notably cultural practices alien to the religion itself."

The television program *Frontline,* which airs on the U.S. government–subsidized Public Broadcasting Service, takes the blame game a level further. According to its "Teachers Guide" on the "Beliefs and Daily Lives of Muslims," the violation of the rights of women in Muslim communities "is the result of the intersection of Islam with existing cultural norms, which may reflect male-dominated societies." Islam itself, they seem to suggest, is a feminist paradise, upset only by a violent patriarchy that is separate and apart from the religion itself.

In fact, the Quran does seem to back up the idea that women—at least Muslim women—are on equal footing with men, at least when it comes to rewarding their faith:

So their Lord accepted of them (their supplication and answered them), "Never will I allow to be lost the work of any of you, be he male or female. You are (members) one of another. . . ." (Quran 3:195)

Whoever works righteousness, whether male or female, while he (or she) is a true believer (of Islamic Monotheism) verily, to him We will give a good life (in this world with respect, contentment and lawful provision), and We shall pay them certainly a reward in proportion to the best of what they used to do (i.e., Paradise in the Hereafter). (Quran 16:97)

These verses pertain to the rewards women will receive in the afterlife, which may well be equal to those of men. But on earth, the reality for women under Islamic rule is very different. A look at the Quran and other Islamic teachings shows that denigration of women, and even violence against them, are hardly "alien to the religion." A number of Quranic verses establish a clear-cut difference in the rights of men and women in various aspects of daily life—and the men always seem to get the advantage:

A man can marry multiple women (as long as he feels he can manage it):

And if you fear that you shall not be able to deal justly with the orphan-girls, then marry (other) women of your choice, two or three, or four but if you fear that you shall not be able to deal justly (with them), then only one or (the captives and the slaves) that your right hands possess. That is nearer to prevent you from doing injustice. (Quran 4:3)

Women automatically receive less in inheritance:

Allah commands you as regards your children's (inheritance); to the male, a portion equal to that of two females; if (there are) only daughters, two or more, their share is two thirds of the inheritance; if only one, her share is half. (Quran 4:11)

In a trial, one male witness is worth two females:

. . . [G]et two witnesses out of your own men. And if there are not two men (available), then a man and two women, such as you agree for witnesses, so that if one of them (two women) errs, the other can remind her . . . (Quran 2:282)

In divorce cases, men automatically have a higher degree of rights:

. . . divorced women shall wait (as regards their marriage) for three menstrual periods, and it is not lawful for them to conceal what Allah has created in their wombs, if they believe in Allah and the Last Day. And their husbands have the better right to take them back in that period, if they wish for reconciliation. And they (women) have rights (over their husbands as regards living expenses, etc.) similar (to those of their husbands) over them (as regards obedience and respect, etc.) to what is reasonable, but men have a degree (of responsibility) over them. (Quran 2:228)

Appearing on NBC's *Today* show in 2007, Massoumeh Ebtekar, the first woman to serve as a cabinet secretary in Iran, claimed that things were looking up for women in her country. "It takes time to change the laws in favor of women," she said, "but we have had lots of improvements."

I suppose it's not hard to improve when you're starting from such a barbaric place. Here are just a few things a woman in Iran was still banned from doing under Islamic law back when Ebtekar appeared in 2007:

- Expose her head

- Apply for a passport without her husband's permission

- Sing any way she chooses

- Divorce her husband without cause (husbands can divorce for any reason)

- Commit adultery—and live

- Inherit an equal share as her brother

- Watch men play sports (with a few exceptions)

- Marry a non-Islamic man

- Be in a relationship with another woman

- Publicly socialize with men

- Sit in the front of a bus

- Run for president

- Travel, work, or go to school without her husband's permission

- Attend her father's funeral without her husband's permission

- Express opposition to the government (countless numbers have been tortured for doing so)

- Have unsanctioned interviews with foreign media

- Maintain custody of her children—should her husband decide to have another wife

- Object to having acid thrown in her face

- Choose not to have children (law pending)

- Have sex outside of marriage

- Get a degree in engineering, physics, computer science, English literature, or business

But at least she can drive, unlike women in other Islamic countries, like, say, Saudi Arabia.

Yet none of this has stopped the empty-headed fools at *Vogue* magazine from dubbing Tehran—yes, *Tehran*—the "next Aspen." They apparently didn't realize that, under Iran's Islamic law, women are not even allowed to ski unaccompanied on slopes.

Perhaps the one verse in the Quran that gives men the greatest blanket dominion over women also serves as a detailed guide on how to inflict punishment:

Men are the protectors and maintainers of women, because Allah has made one of them to excel the other, and because they spend (to support them) from their means. Therefore the righteous women are devoutly obedient (to Allah and to their husbands), and guard in the husband's absence what Allah orders them to guard (e.g., their chastity, their husband's property, etc.). As to those women on whose part you see ill-conduct, admonish them (first), (next), refuse to share their beds, (and last) beat them (lightly, if it is useful), but if they return to obedience, seek not against them means (of annoyance). Surely, Allah is Ever Most High, Most Great. (Quran 4:34)

Muslim women who may be perceived by their husbands as behaving with "ill-conduct" should be admonished, then denied marital relations, and then beaten. Thankfully, they can be forgiven—as long as they obey, of course.

Another verse from the Quran gives Allah's permission to

keep women as captive slaves for sexual relationships outside marriage:

> Also (forbidden are) women already married, except those (captives and slaves) whom your right hands possess. Thus has Allah ordained for you . . . (Quran 4:24)

In the Islamic tradition, those "whom your right hands possess" is a euphemism for slaves, who were allowed to be kept as spoils of war.

While the Quranic justification for treating women in unfair and violent ways is clear, one would hope those views would have evolved in the intervening centuries. In 1997, Yousef al-Qaradawi, an influential cleric, told his television audience:

> Beating is permitted [to the man] in the most limited of cases, and only in a case when the wife rebels against her husband. . . . The beating, of course, will not be with a whip, a stick, or a board.

This is especially disturbing considering the widespread view in the Muslim world that wives must be subservient to their husbands. This was confirmed by a 2013 Pew Research Center survey, which asked Muslims (both men and women): "Must a wife always obey her husband?" In 20 of 23 countries surveyed, at least half responded "yes."

Islam's retrograde views toward women aren't just confined to the realm of the theoretical. In Pakistan, a woman can prove rape only if four adult males of "impeccable" character witness the actual penetration. An Islamic "marriage guide" called A Gift for Muslim Couples advises husbands on the best ways to beat their wives. (It turns out that it's most effectively done with a "hand or stick or pull her by the ears.") And female genital mutilation, one of the most barbaric practices conceived by the human mind, is practiced in some parts of the Islamic world as a way of supposedly controlling the sexual urges of women.

We see in the Islamic State how radical Islamists use the Quran to justify unspeakable horrors that, in a sane world, would earn blanket condemnation from self-proclaimed feminists like Lena Dunham, Susan Sarandon, Jane Fonda, Sandra Fluke, and the pretentious pant-suited phonies of the National Organization of Women (NOW).

As the Islamic State's Caliphate expands across Iraq and Syria, stories of women living under sharia law are becoming even more harrowing. One ISIS savage by the name of Abu Anas al-Libi has reportedly killed more than 150 women and girls for refusing to become "jihad brides," temporary sex slaves for ISIS fighters. They include girls 14, 15, and younger. Women captured by the Islamic State are so traumatized by the rape and torture that they are strangling each other to commit assisted suicide. ISIS has ordered all girls and women in Mosul, Iraq, between the ages of 11 and 46 to undergo female genital mutilation.

Worse is the fate that awaits non-Muslim women, such as the Yazidi minorities of northern Iraq. The surviving victims have given lurid, medieval descriptions of the Caliphate's slave markets:

> They put us up for sale. Many groups of fighters came to buy. . . . Sometimes they brought girls back who had been beaten, injured. When they recovered, they were sold again. Eventually, they took all the girls.

ISIS's "Research and Fatwa Department" did, of course, make sure to issue a pamphlet carefully outlining rules for the treatment of slaves, including sexual relations with those who have not yet reached puberty. It was blandly titled "Questions and Answers on Taking Captives and Slaves," and came complete with Quranic citations.

Given what we have seen, this shouldn't surprise anybody. If people are only willing to open their eyes and look to the sources of Islamic thought they will see that subjugation of women falls right in line with the vision for a "modern" Caliphate.

"IRAN CAN BE TRUSTED WITH A NUCLEAR WEAPON."

"Nuclear weapons and other weapons of mass destruction have no place in Iran's security and defense doctrine, and contradict our fundamental religious and ethical convictions."

—Iranian president Hassan Rouhani

"We are, in fact, closer than ever to the good, comprehensive deal that we have been seeking, and if we can get there, the entire world will be safer."

—Secretary of State John Kerry

Barack Obama seemingly has an obsession with making a nuclear deal with the leaders of Iran. Back in 2007, he talked eagerly about engaging in "aggressive personal diplomacy" with the clerics in Tehran. Even Hillary Clinton mocked Obama at the time as "naïve" on foreign policy.

If only we'd talk to our enemies. It's a refrain we've heard many times in history; often from people who wrongly assume that every leader is rational and receptive to diplomacy. In fact, that was the stance of many on the left for most of the Cold War as they railed against Ronald Reagan, the "warmonger" who led a military buildup to confront the Soviet Union. Time and again, we heard them argue for "peaceful coexistence" with the Soviets. Negotiation, discussion.

When Reagan and Margaret Thatcher and Pope John Paul II and Lech Walesa and others stood up to the threat, and then toppled Soviet governments, the lies those leftists had told were exposed. In fact, we learned, it was true that many Soviets wanted to invade or destroy the United States. They had plans for conquering Western Europe and then America and believed that communism was the future for mankind.

The Left was wrong during the Cold War. And they are even more wrong today about Iran.

After his reelection in 2012, Obama doubled down on his pursuit of Iran, calling for "a more serious, substantive" discussions about their nuclear ambitions.

Three years later, after negotiating a deal that would allow Iran to develop nuclear capability for "peaceful" purposes, Secretary of State John Kerry gloated, "This is an agreement that is based on transparency, accountability, verification."

Echoing Kerry, President Obama has repeatedly claimed that Iran has no aspirations for a nuclear weapon—citing an alleged fatwa from Iranian supreme ruler Ayatollah Ali Khamenei that possessing such a weapon was anti-Islamic.

Obama has celebrated, in his words, "a deal that allows them to have peaceful nuclear power but gives us the absolute assurance that is verifiable that they are not pursuing a nuclear weapon." The president added that "if in fact what they claim is true, which is they have no aspiration to get a nuclear weapon, that in fact, according to their Supreme Leader, it would be contrary to their faith to obtain a nuclear weapon, if that is true, there should be the possibility of getting a deal."

Okay, fair enough. But that is not true.

As a recent article in *U.S. News & World Report* concluded, there is no evidence of any fatwa of this sort from Khamenei—and even if there were, why on earth would we believe him? James S. Robbins, a senior fellow in national security affairs at the American Foreign Policy Council, did some additional research on this supposed fatwa, writing:

> The nearest thing to an official text can be found on the web page of Iran's Permanent Mission to the United Nations. This version, dated Feb. 19, 2012, declares that "The Iranian nation has never pursued and will never pursue nuclear weapons. There is no doubt that the decision makers in the countries opposing us know well that Iran is not after nuclear weapons, because the Islamic Republic, logically, religiously and theoretically, considers the possession of nuclear weapons a grave sin and believes the proliferation of such weapons is senseless, destructive and dangerous." That's all well and good, but it is not exactly a fatwa. It makes no reference to the Quran or any other Islamic text or tradition, as other religious edicts traditionally do. It reads more like a statement of government policy, and as such, can be changed with the circumstances. In fact, even genuine fatwas can be amended and changed by circumstances.

In 2012, Alireza Forghani, a former Iranian governor and advisor to Ayatollah Khamenei, wrote an article, widely publicized in Iran, arguing that, in fact, Muslims must have access to nuclear weapons. "The Islamic world should rise up and shout that a nuclear bomb is our right," Forghani wrote, "and disrupt the dreams of America and Israel."

Here's the truth, and it's pretty simple: The radicals in charge of Iran seek our destruction. They want to kill us. But don't just take my word for it—they say it themselves. There's a mural on display in the Iranian capital of Tehran—a mural that would not be permitted unless it reflected the views of the Iranian government—that has the phrase "Down with the U.S.A." printed on it in English. That's bad enough, but far worse is the actual translation in Persian, written at the bottom of the mural: "Death to the U.S.A."

"Death to America" is a chant that Iranians utter all the time—during political rallies and even during Friday prayers. It's often accompanied by a burning of the American flag.

In March 2015 Ali Khamenei, Iran's supreme leader and a leading Muslim cleric, shouted "Death to America" during a speech to a frenzied crowd in Iran. He said this while President Obama was citing Khamenei himself as a source for why we should trust Iran on a nuclear deal.

We are negotiating with these people?

We are making it possible for them to obtain nuclear capabilities?

Are we insane?

Iran does not want to be our friend. They do not want peaceful coexistence.

They want us, the Great Satan, gone.

To say otherwise is a very dangerous lie.

Benjamin Netanyahu, the prime minister of Israel, understands this. Netanyahu has told Americans that a nuclear Iran is a far greater threat than ISIS. He has pleaded with Americans to listen to his warnings and has been virtually ignored by the Obama administration. The president even refused to meet with Netanyahu on a recent visit to Washington, D.C. The frosty relationship with the White House notwithstanding, Netanyahu found a welcome reception for his message in the halls of the U.S. Congress, where he was given the hero's welcome he deserved.

"Once Iran, the preeminent terrorist state of our time, acquires nuclear weapons," Netanyahu warned, "it will be a hundred times more dangerous, a thousand times more dangerous and more destructive."

Netanyahu sees right through the bald-faced lies Iranian diplomats tell the West—and there are plenty of them. For example, referring to the Old Testament, Mohammad Javad Zarif, Iran's foreign minister, said, "If you read the Book of Esther, you will see that it was the Iranian king who saved the Jews." Iran, you see, is an historic *friend* to the Jewish people, and has absolutely no designs on destroying Israel. These are the kind of statements that get sent around in press releases and fact sheets by the Iranian Information Ministry, the U.S. State Department, and other regime lackeys.

But dig a little deeper and you'll see that Iran openly admits its intention to pursue nuclear weapons and destroy Israel. They tend to say these things in Farsi so that they don't get played on a loop in Western media, but consider the following quotes:

- **IRANIAN PRESIDENT MOHAMMAD KHATAMI (2000):** "If we abide by real legal laws, we should mobilize the whole Islamic world for a sharp confrontation with the Zionist regime . . . if we abide by the Koran, all of us should mobilize to kill."

- **AYATOLLAH ALI KHAMENEI (2001):** "It is the mission of the Islamic Republic of Iran to erase Israel from the map of the region."

- **FORMER COMMANDER OF IRAN'S REVOLUTIONARY GUARD CORPS, YAHYA RAHIM SAFAVI (2008):** "With God's help the time has come for the Zionist regime's death sentence."

- **KHAMENEI'S REPRESENTATIVE TO THE MOUSTAZAFAN FOUNDATION, MOHAMMAD HASSAN RAHIMIAN (2010):** "We have manufactured missiles that allow us, when necessary to replace [*sic*] Israel in its entirety with a big holocaust."

- **COMMANDER OF THE BASIJ PARAMILITARY FORCE MOHAMMAD REZA NAQDI (2011):** "We recommend them [the Zionists] to pack their furniture and return to their countries. And if they insist on staying, they should know that a time will arrive when they will not even have time to pack their suitcases."

- **AYATOLLAH KHAMENEI (2012):** "The Zionist regime is a cancerous tumor and it will be removed."

- **MEMBER OF THE ASSEMBLY OF EXPERTS AHMAD ALAMOLHODA (2013):** "The destruction of Israel is the idea of the Islamic Revolution in Iran and is one of the pillars of the Iranian Islamic regime. We cannot claim that we have no intention of going to war with Israel."

- **KHAMENEI'S REPRESENTATIVE IN THE REVOLUTIONARY GUARD, HOJATOLESLAM ALI SHIRAZI (2013):** "The Zionist regime will soon be destroyed, and this generation will be witness to its destruction."

- **AYATOLLAH KHAMENEI (2014):** "This barbaric, wolf-like & infanticidal regime of Israel which spares no crime has no cure but to be annihilated."

- **DEPUTY HEAD OF THE REVOLUTIONARY GUARD HOSSEIN SALAMI (2014):** "We will chase you [Israelis] house to house and will take revenge for every drop of blood of our martyrs in Palestine, and this is the beginning point of Islamic nations awakening for your defeat."

- **HOSSEIN SALAMI (2014):** "Today we are aware of how the Zionist regime is slowly being erased from the world, and indeed, soon, there will be no such thing as the Zionist regime on Planet Earth."

- **SECRETARY-GENERAL OF THE COMMITTEE FOR SUPPORT FOR THE PALESTINIAN INTIFADA, HOSSEIN SHEIKHOLESLAM (2014):** "The issue of Israel's destruction is important, no matter the method. We will obviously implement the strategy of the Imam Khomeini and the Leader [Khamenei] on the issue of destroying the Zionists. The region will not be quiet so long as Israel exists in it. . . ."

- **COMMANDER IN CHIEF OF THE REVOLUTIONARY GUARD MOHAMMAD ALI JAFARI (2015):** "The Revolutionary Guards will fight to the end of the Zionist regime. . . . We will not rest easy until this epitome of vice is totally deleted from the region's geopolitics."

Threatening the annihilation of a nuclear-armed country is not something that a government that acts rationally or sees things through the lens of self-interest does. As discussed in chapter 1, Iran's leadership is guided by a belief in the impending return of the Twelfth Imam, a return that coincides with the destruction of the world and the Day of Judgment. According to various Hadith, the return of the Mahdi is preceded by total conflict that envelops the Middle East. Iranian regime officials have stated that the Mahdi cannot come under the current circumstances; only war with and the eventual destruction of Israel can bring about the End Times. As Muhammad said according to one Hadith:

> The last hour would not come unless the Muslims will fight against the Jews and the Muslims would kill them until the Jews would hide themselves behind a stone or a tree and a stone or a tree would say: Muslim, or the servant of Allah, there is a Jew behind me; come and kill him. . . ."

In other words, annihilating Israel is the next step to ensuring the return of the Mahdi.

Former Iranian president Mahmoud Ahmadinejad's last speech at the United Nations in 2012 was filled with rhetoric about the Shia prophecy of the return of the Twelfth Imam. "God Almighty has promised us a man of kindness, a man who loves people and loves absolute justice, a man who is a perfect human being and is named Imam al-Mahdi, a man who will come in the company of Jesus Christ, peace be upon him, and the righteous," he said. "The arrival of the Ultimate Savior will mark a new beginning, a rebirth and a resurrection." Remember, Ahmadinejad's insistence that the Mahdi is coming was not a closed-door speech at a mosque in Tehran; it was an address to the most prestigious international forum in the world.

Other members of Iran's political-religious establishment see their nation's destiny as linked to the Mahdi's emergence, and see events in Iran's past and future as signs of his return. Reuters reported that Ruhollah Hosseinian, a politician and Islamic scholar, called the country's 1979 revolution "the prelude to the appearance of the Mahdi." He also sees the alliance of Iranian forces with Hezbollah in Syria as the fulfillment of an eighth-century prophecy and another "sign of the coming of his holiness"—because one

Islamic prophecy speaks of armies "with yellow flags" like those that Hezbollah flies.

Iran analyst Saeed Ghasseminejad, writing in the *Times of Israel,* reported a conversation between one of Iran's nuclear scientists—later killed by a car bomb—and Ayatollah Azizollah Khoshvaght, a member of Supreme Leader Khamenei's inner circle. The scientist asked Ayatollah Khoshvaght when the Mahdi would appear, and Khoshvaght replied: "It depends on what you are doing in Natanz." Natanz, of course, is one of Iran's main nuclear facilities.

According to Ghasseminejad, another cleric, Ayatollah Ali Saeedi—the supreme leader's personal representative to the Iranian Revolutionary Guard Corps (IRGC)—reportedly claimed: "Ayatollah Khamenei is preparing Mahdi's reappearance and IRGC is the instrument to do it." Iran's top leaders see themselves as personal instruments for bringing about the Mahdi's return.

These are the fervent beliefs of the men and women who sat across from U.S. diplomats in Geneva, negotiating over the legitimacy of the Iranian nuclear program.

If Iran obtains a nuclear weapon, there is the distinct possibility, if not likelihood, it will use it to destroy Israel and threaten the United States.

We know this because its leaders have said so over and over again.

"THE MUSLIM BROTHERHOOD IS A MODERATE, MAINSTREAM ISLAMIC GROUP."

"The term 'Muslim Brotherhood' . . . is an umbrella term for a variety of movements, in the case of Egypt, a very heterogeneous group, largely secular, which has eschewed violence and has decried Al Qaeda as a perversion of Islam. . . . They have pursued social ends, a betterment of the political order. . . ."
—Director of National Intelligence James Clapper, 2011

"Allah is our objective. The Prophet is our leader. The Koran is our law. Jihad is our way. Dying in the way of Allah is our highest hope. Allahu-Akbar! Allahu-Akbar!"
—Muslim Brotherhood chant

Hassan al-Banna created the Muslim Brotherhood, or Ikhwan (pronounced "ik-wahn") as it's called in Arabic, in 1928 as a way of reestablishing the Caliphate. Since that time it has counted among its members jihadist luminaries such as

Sayyid Qutb and Ayman al-Zawahiri. The sprawling group now has chapters in countries around the world, including a well-connected and increasingly powerful American one.

In 2011, the Brotherhood's large Egyptian arm seized power after the ouster of Hosni Mubarak during the Arab Spring. They did this with the active, even vocal backing of the Obama administration. Secretary of State Hillary Clinton met with then–Muslim Brotherhood ruler Mohammed Morsi in Cairo. (Three years later, Morsi was convicted by an Egyptian court and sentenced to death for his part in the uprising.) That might be surprising, except that, two years earlier, Obama had invited Brotherhood members to his Cairo speech.

President Obama and his intelligence chief, James Clapper, apparently believe that the Muslim Brotherhood is the "good guy" Islamist alternative to "bad guys" like al-Qaeda and ISIS. The Brotherhood, in their view, is moderate and mainstream and worthy of our support.

Nothing could be further from the truth.

It was almost by accident that the FBI discovered the archives of the Muslim Brotherhood in North America. Had Ismail Elbarasse not been detained on the Chesapeake Bay Bridge with his wife in August 2004, we might still be under the illusion that the Brotherhood and its affiliated groups in America were the simple secular advocacy groups they claimed to be—just another identity group lobbying organization, like an NAACP or Catholic League for Muslims.

But after Elbarasse's wife was caught videotaping the support structures of the Chesapeake Bay Bridge from their car, suspicions were raised. When authorities pulled over the car, they discovered an outstanding warrant for Elbarasse. It turns out he was wanted as a material witness in a case concerning fund-raising for Hamas. The FBI subsequently executed a search warrant on the Elbarasses' house. Hidden in a subbasement in their Annandale, Virginia, home were eighty banker boxes' worth of documents.

These papers confirmed what most counterterrorism experts had long suspected: many of the Muslim-American groups in the United States were controlled by the Muslim Brotherhood, and their goals, as clearly outlined in the documents, were anything but benign.

Among the documents was one called "An Explanatory Memorandum on the General Strategic Group for the Group in North America." Dated May 22, 1991, the memo was written by Mohamed Akram, a member of the board of directors for the Muslim Brotherhood and a leader of Hamas, and had been approved by the Brotherhood's Shura Council. It is sixteen pages of chilling reading, but here's the key passage:

> The process of settlement is a "Civilization-Jihadist Process" with all the word means. The Ikhwan [Arabic for Muslim Brotherhood] must understand that their work in America is a kind of grand jihad in eliminating and destroying the Western civilization from within and "sabotaging" its miserable house by their hands and the hands of the believers so that it is eliminated and God's religion is made victorious over all other religions.

Akram had no intention of any non-Brotherhood member ever seeing the memo, but the FBI presented it as evidence in a 2007 terrorism-financing trial. As a result, the Muslim Brotherhood's plan to transform America into an Islamist society became public for the first time.

Contrary to the opinions of pacifists and apologists, the Muslim Brotherhood didn't just spawn the world's most lethal terrorist groups; it is just as committed to the destruction of Western secular democracy as its more violent cousins. As Mohammed Badie, the Brotherhood's supreme guide, put it, "Resistance is the only solution against the Zio-American arrogance and tyranny." He also explained how that "resistance" would need to work: "The improvement and change that the [Muslim] nation seeks can only be attained . . . by raising a jihadi generation that pursues death just as the enemies pursue life."

The Muslim Brotherhood is committed to a long-term "civilization jihad," a term the Brotherhood uses and mentioned in its Explanatory Memorandum to distinguish itself from the more violent forms of jihad. In some ways, this type of jihad actually poses a more insidious long-term threat to the West. While it may not involve detonating suicide vests and beheading infidels, it is a plan to influence and infiltrate Western societies through *dawa*, which literally means the calling of non-Muslims to join Islam or proselytism. "We will conquer Europe, we will conquer America not through the sword but through *dawa*," says Yusef al-Qaradawi, Egypt's leading Muslim Brotherhood scholar. *Dawa*, in case you were wondering, is the principal means of the Muslim Brotherhood's stealthy civilization jihad.

The Brotherhood's goal is nothing less than to Islamicize our free societies. They are working toward that goal through political and psychological warfare that includes cultural subversion, the co-opting of senior leaders, influence operations, propaganda, and other means of pushing sharia into Western societies bit by bit.

This is a highly coordinated effort that shames and intimidates opponents while persuading allies and fence-sitters that sharia and submission to Islam are the correct path. "We should all be very careful not to be colonized by something which is coming from this consumerist society," said Tariq Ramadan, grandson of the Muslim Brotherhood's founder, Hasan al-Banna. "It should be us with our understanding of Islam, our principles, colonizing positively the United States of America." (This from a man that *Time* magazine listed among the world's top "thinkers" and whom *Slate* called "one of the most important intellectuals in the world" and the "Muslim Martin Luther.")

The Brotherhood's plan starts with the creation of small Muslim enclaves, communities that are entirely separate from the secular laws of our nations and in which Muslims are free to live under sharia. "Were we to convince Western leaders and decision-makers of our right to live according to our faith—ideologically, legislatively, and ethically—without imposing our views or inflicting harm upon them, we would have traversed an immense barrier in our quest for an Islamic state," the Brotherhood's Qaradawi has said. That exact thing is already happening in Europe, where vigilante sharia squads are popping up, enforcing rules prohibiting alcohol and haranguing people who don't dress modestly enough.

Key to the Brotherhood's plans is a rejection of assimilation, and maintaining the Islamic supremacist view of the *dar al-Islam* (house of Islam) opposing the *dar al-harb* (house of war, or the rest of us). This is where the Brotherhood's commitment to *dawa* is problematic for those of us here in America who believe that our Constitution should be the law of the land for all of our citizens, no matter their religion.

This is the civilization jihad in action—a parallel, but more subtle agenda compared to the violent jihad pursued by ISIS and al-Qaeda. Both are necessary for them to achieve their goals. Both are working.

One of the most troubling things about the Muslim Brotherhood is the slippery way in which the group denies any association with the Islamic supremacist tenets it espouses. They are seemingly okay with these lies because of the concept that lying in defense of Islam is not only permissible, it is encouraged. The *Reli-*

ance of the Traveler, a legal text cited by many Islamic scholars and a go-to for the Muslim Brotherhood, counsels:

> This is an explicit statement that lying is sometimes permissible for a given interest. . . . When it is possible to achieve such an aim by lying but not by telling the truth, it is permissible to lie if attaining the goal is permissible and obligatory to lie if the goal is obligatory.

This is known as the Islamic doctrine of *taqqiya*—lying for the sake of Islam. Quran 3:28 says, "Let not the believers take the disbelievers as *Auliya* (supporters, helpers, etc.) instead of the believers, and whoever does that will never be helped by Allah in any way, *except if you indeed fear a danger from them*" (emphasis added).

Taqqiya is used to conceal, obfuscate, or disguise one's beliefs or convictions to confuse the enemy. It's a classic technique used by the Muslim Brotherhood when they say one thing to Westerners and the opposite to their followers. It's why Essam el-Errian, member of the Egyptian Brotherhood's guidance council, took to the pages of the *New York Times* at the height of the Arab Spring to proclaim, "We aim to achieve reform and rights for all: not just for the Muslim Brotherhood, not just for Muslims, but for all Egyptians." They sought nothing of the sort. Soon after the Brotherhood consolidated power, Coptic Christians were massacred and persecuted.

The Muslim Brotherhood has integrated itself into American culture by using various front groups (which don't come with the violence and terror-connected baggage) to promote its cause. For example, the Brotherhood created the Muslim Students Association (MSA) to organize on campuses, as well as numerous other groups: the Association of Muslim Social Scientists (AMSS), the Association of Muslim Scientists and Engineers (AMSE), the Islamic Medical Association (IMA), the Muslim Community Association (MCA), and others. The Brothers also formed other student groups in the 1970s, including the Muslim Arab Youth Assembly (MAYA) and Muslim Youth of North America (MYNA), and the Islamic Society of North America (ISNA).

Some governments already recognize the threat posed by the Muslim Brotherhood. In November 2014, the cabinet of the United Arab Emirates published a list of terrorist organizations that makes no distinction between groups like ISIS, al-Qaeda, Boko Haram, and the Muslim Brotherhood.

But not the United States government. Our leaders seem to think these guys are our friends.

As counterterrorism intelligence officer Stephen Coughlin recounts, in October 2011, individuals associated with the U.S. Muslim Brotherhood wrote to the White House demanding an "embargo or discontinuation" of the dissemination of "information or materials relating to Islamic-based terrorism." It seems that the words *terrorism* and *Islam* apparently couldn't be used in the same sentences. The Brotherhood demanded retraining or "purges" of those at the White House involved with any of those materials. Shortly thereafter, Coughlin reports, John Brennan, a senior White House aide who is now director of the CIA, responded, "We share your sense of concern over these recent unfortunate incidents, and are moving forward to ensure problems are addressed with a keen sense of urgency."

Brennan directed that the "White House immediately create an interagency task force to address the problem" and said that the people or the documents that the Muslim Brotherhood deemed "biased, false, and highly offensive" would be removed. This was part of a pattern and practice of the White House going out of its way to placate the Brotherhood, even sending senior officials, such as the FBI director, to meet with the Brotherhood, over the objections of Congress.

The Brotherhood's campaign to intimidate and silence officials in Washington who link Islam and terrorism is working brilliantly. The 9/11 Commission Report used the word *jihad* 126 times, *Muslim* 145 times, and *Islam* 322 times. A decade later, they have been virtually banished from official U.S. government documents. The FBI's Counterterrorism Analytical Lexicon and the 2009 National Intelligence Strategy have zero mentions of *jihad*, *Muslim*, or *Islam*. Instead, they refer to "violent extremism" in general.

This is madness. We need to see people and groups for what they really are—not what we want them to be. The Brotherhood is at the center of a civilization jihad. It is not bloody or violent (yet) but it is just as threatening to the long-term survival of our Constitution as anything the Islamists in the Islamic State or Iran are planning.

▌ LIE #13 ▌

"ISLAM RESPECTS FREEDOM OF SPEECH."

"The Quranic standard of speech promotes independent thought while encouraging respectful disagreement. . . . In a sentence, Islam champions free speech while promoting a moral speech that obliges Muslims to attain a higher standard of wisdom."
— Author and attorney Qasim Rashid, *USA Today*

"Our basic position is that the First Amendment means that everyone is free to be a bigot or even an idiot[.]"
—Ibrahim Hooper, Council of American-Islamic Relations (CAIR)

"As Americans we understand the importance of the right to free speech and freedom of expression. American Muslims value this right on behalf of every American citizen and would never shy away from ever defending this right."
—Islamic Circle of North America

On May 3, 2015, roommates Nadir Soofi and Elton Simpson drove a thousand miles from Phoenix, Arizona, to the Curtis Culwell Center in Garland, Texas, where the American Freedom Defense Initiative (AFDI) had gathered for its inaugural Muhammad art exhibit and contest. These two "lone wolves," armed with AK-47 assault rifles and wearing body armor, rolled up to the convention center's entrance and opened fire on police and security guards posted outside.

One security guard was shot in the ankle, but the nearly two hundred people in attendance were fortunate that a police officer shot and killed both men before they could carry out a jihad-inspired act of mass murder.

The FBI quickly established that Soofi and Simpson were radical Muslims who frequented ISIS chat boards, downloaded jihadist videos, and pledged allegiance to *Amirul Mu'mineen*—meaning "the leader of the faithful" in the Islamic State. ISIS, in fact, took credit for the attacks and promised that more would be coming.

The "Draw Muhammad" contest and ADFI are the work of Pamela Geller, who may be the most tireless voice against homegrown jihadism and creeping sharia in America today. She isn't afraid of making people uncomfortable by telling hard truths, and she's made plenty of enemies on both sides of the aisle as a result.

Geller chose the Garland location because it was the same site where a "Stand with the Prophet" conference was held in January. She and about two thousand supporters protested that event, which came just a few weeks after the *Charlie Hebdo* massacre in Paris.

When Geller announced the ten-thousand-dollar cartoon contest, she said: "This event will stand for free speech and show that Americans will not be cowed by violent Islamic intimidation. That is a crucial stand to take as Islamic assaults on the freedom of speech, our most fundamental freedom, are growing more insistent." Geller assured would-be attendees that the event would have heavy security, but added, "If we don't show the jihadis that they will not frighten us into silence, the jihad against freedom will only grow more virulent."

It turns out that she was half right. Geller and her group showed they were not afraid to stand up for their rights in the face of real threats. But the jihad against freedom has become more virulent in spite of it.

It wasn't surprising that ISIS claimed credit for inspiring the Garland attack. Or that someone like Anjem Choudary, the media's go-to extremist imam, would tell Geller on Fox News that she "knew the consequences" of holding a contest that depicted Muhammad—an act that many Muslims, not just jihadists, believe is a grave insult.

No, the real insult was the media's rush to condemn Geller and blame her free speech event for inspiring an act of jihadi violence.

The Garland incident could not have been more clear-cut. Here was a group of Americans assembled peacefully to exercise their First Amendment rights, only to come under armed assault by men who *wished to kill them for looking at cartoons*. For their bravery in the face of terror, the *New York Times* presumed to tell Geller and her supporters that their freedom of speech was inferior to . . . well, to the sort of freedom of speech the *Times* deems more acceptable.

"There is no question that images ridiculing religion, however offensive they may be to believers, qualify as protected free speech in the United States and most Western democracies," the *Times*' editors began in an editorial published a few days after the attack. "There is also no question that however offensive the images, they do not justify murder, and that it is incumbent on leaders of all religious faiths to make this clear to their followers."

The editorial should have ended there—short, sweet, and unobjectionable. Instead, the editors decided to ladle on heavy dollops of contempt for their fellow Americans. "But"—*But!*—"it is equally clear that the Muhammad Art Exhibit and Contest in Garland, Tex., was not really about free speech. It was an exercise in bigotry and hatred posing as a blow for freedom . . . to pretend that it was motivated by anything other than hate is simply hogwash."

So the *New York Times* editorial board is populated with mind readers all of a sudden? They know with absolute certainty that Geller's event was all about "bigotry" and "hatred"—and nothing else? Talk about hogwash.

The *Times'* editors weren't alone in missing the point.

Journalists lined up to denounce the cartoon contest and basically accuse Geller of walking alone in Mosul at night wearing a short skirt. Surely she knew what would happen next! Chris Matthews mused on MSNBC that Geller somehow set up Soofi and Simpson—as if they couldn't help but drive fifteen hours to commit unspeakable acts of violence. Rukmini Callimachi, a *New York Times* reporter who covers Islam and terrorism, took to Twitter to ask: "Free speech aside, why would anyone do something as provocative as hosting a 'Muhammad drawing contest'?" Free speech *aside*? You can't put it "aside"—it's the whole point!

If Callimachi had asked the same question of a rape victim, she would have been hounded off the Internet and probably fired. But the media has different standards for outspoken conservative women who are unwilling to surrender their rights to religious zealots.

CNN's Chris Cuomo berated Geller on his program, accusing her of planning the contest to spark a violent confrontation with "crazy extremists" who "bought into an ideology that is sick." He then absurdly compared drawing pictures of Muhammad to an overused racial slur. "The N-word gets treated the same way that depictions of Muhammad does," Cuomo said. "We don't say it because it's offensive, not because legally I can't." We have reached the point where TV talking heads can no longer tell the difference between bona fide political speech and simple racist invective.

On Fox News, Greta Van Susteren said that Geller's free speech rights should not trump police officers' safety. "My message is simple—protect our police. Do not recklessly lure them into danger, and that is what happened in Garland, Texas, at the Mohammed cartoon contest," she said at the top of her May 5 program. "Yes, of course, there's a First Amendment right and it's very important, but the exercise of that right includes using good judgment."

There is actually no "but" in the First Amendment. And Greta seemed to forget that government exists to protect *us* and *our* rights, not the other way around.

Despite the intensity of coverage, many news media outlets opted to blur out the images, seemingly relying on the theory of "better safe than sorry."

The truth is that our media and our politicians have been wobbling on freedom of speech for quite a while.

When cartoons of Muhammad were originally published in the Danish newspaper *Jyllands-Posten* in 2005, they sparked protests and riots throughout Europe and the Middle East. At the time, to their lasting disgrace, the vast majority of major American newspapers, including the *Wall Street Journal, New York Times, Washington Post, Chicago Tribune,* and *Los Angeles Times*, refused to show readers the cartoons that had caused so much havoc. Only a small number of publications—including the *New York Sun,* the *Philadelphia Inquirer,* and the left-wing *Harper's* magazine—printed even one of the controversial illustrations. Most chose to hide behind the fig leaf of religious sensitivity.

As a spokesman for the *Wall Street Journal* explained, "Readers were well served by a short story without publishing the cartoon. We didn't want to publish anything that can be perceived as inflammatory to our readers' culture when it didn't add anything to the story." Apparently, *Journal* readers couldn't be trusted to decide for themselves whether the cartoons were offensive or newsworthy.

You might have at least expected the Association of American Editorial Cartoonists (AAEC) to join in solidarity with their colleagues in the Netherlands. If so, you'd have been disappointed. "Just because you have the right to publish these, that does not mean you have the obligation," said Nick Anderson, who was the AAEC's vice president when the cartoon controversy reached its peak. He asserted, without a shred of evidence, that *Jyllands-Posten*'s editors "wanted to put a stick in the eye of their local clerics and did this intentionally, belittled and mocked the founder of a religion." He told the *New York Times* that the few U.S. newspapers that published the cartoons had fallen into a trap. "If you're doing it in solidarity, look at with whom you're expressing solidarity."

Anderson should have taken his own advice and looked into the cartoonists and editors he claimed had no motivation other than to aggravate Muslims. He might have found some insight in the editorial by Flemming Rose, *Jyllands-Posten*'s culture editor, who explained the newspaper's reasons for publishing the cartoons. "Modern, secular society is rejected by some Muslims," Rose argued. "They demand a special position, insisting on special consideration of their own religious feelings. It is incompatible with contemporary democracy and freedom of speech, where one must be ready to put up with insults, mockery and ridicule.

"It is certainly not always attractive and nice to look at," he continued, "and it does not mean that religious feelings should be made fun of at any price, but that is of minor importance in the present context. . . . We are on our way to a slippery slope where no-one can tell how the self-censorship will end. That is why *Morgenavisen Jyllands-Posten* has invited members of the Danish editorial cartoonists union to draw Muhammad as they see him."

By the time the twelve cartoons had circulated widely—along with two fabricated, deliberately incendiary images depicting Muhammad with a pig's snout and a dog mounting a Muslim bowed in prayer—the newspaper's editors and cartoonists were overwhelmed with death threats. Many were forced into hiding, and a few cartoonists still require twenty-four-hour police protection to this day.

Rose later explained that he didn't believe at first that publishing the illustrations had anything to do with traditional freedom of speech. "I said that this act was about self-censorship, not free speech," he told Daniel Pipes of the *Middle East Quarterly*. "Free speech is on the books; we have the law, and nobody as yet has thought of rewriting it. This changed when the death threats were issued; it became an issue of the sharia trumping the fundamental right of free speech."

That fundamental right has been trampled even further in the years since. The *Charlie Hebdo* massacre helped cement the media's new ethos of self-censorship and cowardice. *Jyllands-Posten* provided a sadly ironic coda to that horrific day with another editorial—this time explaining why the newspaper would *not* republish any cartoons or illustrations.

"We have lived with the fear of a terrorist attack for nine years, and yes, that is the explanation why we do not reprint the cartoons, whether it be our own or *Charlie Hebdo*'s," *Jyllands-Posten*'s editors admitted. "We are also aware that we therefore bow to violence and intimidation . . . it shows that violence works."

Islam apologists go to great lengths to attempt to disconnect these acts of violence from Islamic doctrine; to present them as something unrelated to the religion's core tenets. University of Michigan professor Christiane Gruber wrote in the aftermath of the *Charlie Hebdo* attacks that there was actually no ban on using Muhammad's image in Islam. She cited a number of examples of Muhammad's image being used in the past and claimed there was no justification in the Quran or elsewhere in Islamic law to support such a ban.

Widening the lens, others argue that Islam actually welcomes and protects free speech, making the act of killing someone who offends the religion distinctly un-Islamic. Qasim Rashid, a lawyer and author, condemned the Paris attacks and noted in a *USA Today* op-ed that the Quran "promotes independent thought" and that "Islam champions free speech." He even provided verses from the Quran in support, claiming that instead of violence, Muslims are encouraged to exercise "respectful disagreement." For instance, he cited Sura 5:9, which reminds believers to "let not a people's enmity incite you to act otherwise than with justice."

Ibrahim Hooper, the national spokesman for CAIR, wrote that "Islamic traditions include a number of instances of the prophet having the opportunity to strike back at those who attacked him, but refraining from doing so."

Russell Brand, the alleged comedian who likes to generate publicity by ignorantly charging into political debates, offered an even less informed argument, asking in disbelief, "How can any spiritual scripture be used as justification for mass murder?" He maintained that the *Charlie Hebdo* killers "do not represent Islam any more than George Bush, Tony Blair and Halliburton"— invoking the war in Iraq—"represented Christianity."

Muslims and others understandably want to separate these attacks from mainstream Islam. You can either take their word for it, or you can do the research and look into Islamic law and teachings for yourself. Among the things you will find: an established tradition that prohibits use of the prophet's image and constrictions on free speech, especially when the prophet is involved.

An Islamic text known as the Ash-Shifa, by Qadi Iyad—described by its current publisher as "perhaps the most frequently used and commented upon handbook in which the Prophet's life, his qualities and his miracles are described in every detail"—is very specific about what must be done with those who disrespect Muhammad:

> Know that all who curse Muhammad, may Allah bless him and grant him peace, or blame him or attribute imperfection to him in his person, his lineage, his *deen* [religion] or any of his qualities, or alludes to that or its like by any means whatsoever, whether in the form of a curse or contempt or belittling him or detracting from him or finding fault with him or maligning him, the judgment regarding such a person is the same as the judgment against anyone who curses him. He is killed as we shall make clear. This judgment extends to anything which amounts to a curse or disparagement. We have no hesitation concerning this matter, be it a clear statement or allusion.

In the next section, the Ash-Shifa provides succinct instruction from al-Husayn Ibn Ali, son of the fourth caliph and grandson of the prophet through Muhammad's daughter Fatima. According to al-Husayn Ibn Ali, Muhammad said: "Whoever curses a Prophet, kill him. Whoever curses my Companions, beat him." Qadi Iyad's writings clearly justify, and go on to establish scholarly consensus for, violence against anyone who exercises their free speech in a way derogatory toward Muhammad.

There is no room for compromise whatsoever when it comes to the honor or dignity of the prophet Muhammad. This also applies to depicting his image, according to modern Islamic scholar

Azzam Tamimi: "The Koran itself doesn't say anything, but it is accepted by all Islamic authorities that the Prophet Muhammad and all the other prophets cannot be drawn and cannot be produced in pictures because they are, according to Islamic faith, infallible individuals, role models and therefore should not be presented in any manner that might cause disrespect for them."

Another modern cleric, Sheikh Ibrahim Mogra, presented the issue in even simpler terms: "Islam in general specifically forbids the usage of imagery, and when it comes to depicting the messenger Muhammad, peace be upon him, that prohibition becomes even more relevant: we are not allowed to depict him in any shape, any way or form."

When the creators of the animated TV comedy series *South Park* sought to depict an image of Muhammad in an episode in 2006, the mere suggestion sparked an outcry among Muslim groups. A radical Muslim organization issued a death threat, saying that the show's creators, Trey Parker and Matt Stone, would be murdered like Theo van Gogh, who was killed in 2004 after producing a documentary on the mistreatment of women in Islamic societies.

The threats against the *South Park* creators included lines from a sermon by al-Qaeda imam Anwar al-Awlaki, who said that anyone defaming Muhammad should be murdered: "Harming Allah and his messenger is a reason to encourage Muslims to kill whoever does that."

Executives at the Comedy Central network, which produced the show, panicked. Muslims all over the world had rioted after what they considered an insulting depiction of the prophet appeared in a Danish newspaper. The executives feared similar reprisals.

The controversy baffled South Park's creators. This, after all, was a program that regularly offended Catholics, Jews, Mormons, and many others. "We can do whatever we want to Jesus, and we have," said creator Matt Stone. "We've had him say bad words. We've had him shoot a gun. We've had him kill people. We can do whatever we want. But Mohammed, we couldn't just show a simple image."

The executives at Comedy Central folded. Instead of depicting Muhammad in the episode, *South Park* ran a black screen that read "Comedy Central has refused to broadcast an image of Mohammed on their network."

The *South Park* guys rejected claims that the network was simply being tolerant to Muslims. "No, you're not," Stone responded in an interview with ABC News. "You're afraid of getting blown up. That's what you're afraid of. Comedy Central copped to that, you know: 'We're afraid of getting blown up.'"

Under the Islamic idea of free speech, some things simply cannot be discussed, well, freely. This is explained by renowned sharia scholar Yusuf al-Qaradawi, who maintains that "Islam stresses the principle of freedom"—but with a catch. "[T]his freedom is guaranteed on the condition that religion should not be toyed with, and people's honor and dignity should not be transgressed upon."

A 2012 Pew Research Center analysis found that nearly a quarter of the world's countries and territories—many in the Muslim world—have antiblasphemy laws or policies on the books. As the report noted, "The legal punishments for such transgressions vary from fines to death." A list of those countries includes Islamic nations such as Algeria, Egypt, Sudan, Saudi Arabia, Kuwait, Jordan, Oman, Qatar, Afghanistan, Pakistan, and Iran. And as we detail in other sections of this book, many Islamic societies certainly don't allow free expression for women, non-Muslims, or gays.

Some of these blasphemy cases make headlines internation-

ally. In 2013, a blogger in Tunisia was jailed for "insulting Islam."
The following year in Pakistan a popular TV station was attacked
by the government for "blasphemy" for playing a song that was
considered offensive to the Muslim faith. As Reuters reported,
"Blasphemy carries the death penalty in Pakistan but is not defined by law; anyone who says their religious feelings have been
hurt for any reason can file a case."

Even more disturbing is that many countries, including the
United States, are trying to make Islam's narrow version of free
speech part of international law. In an example of the power of
the Islamic agenda, and of the eagerness of the American political
establishment to go along in the spirit of "cooperation," Muslim
countries have succeeded in persuading the United Nations to
pass a resolution that seeks to "criminalize" certain types of speech
that might offend Islam. This is part of a long-standing effort by
Muslim leaders to "have the United Nations adopt an international resolution to counter Islamophobia and to call upon all
states to enact laws to counter it, *including deterrent punishment*"
(emphasis added).

In March 2011, these apologists began to get their wish. The
United Nations Human Rights Council passed Resolution 16/18,
which encourages countries "to foster a domestic environment of
religious tolerance, peace and respect" by, among other things,
"[a]dopting measures to criminalize incitement to imminent violence based on religion or belief."

The seemingly innocuous resolution was pushed by the Organization of Islamic Cooperation (OIC), a group consisting of
fifty-seven Muslim nations, and enthusiastically supported by the
United States. Hillary Clinton, who was secretary of state at the
time, called it "an important statement that must be followed by
sustained commitment."

Of course, the entire purpose of this resolution was not to

protect Christians or Jews being persecuted in the Muslim world, but to censor anyone from daring to offend Islam.

Clinton admitted as much on July 15, 2011, when she traveled to Turkey to meet with the secretary-general of the Organization of Islamic Cooperation, Ekmeleddin Ihsanoğlu. There, standing with Islamic leaders, she pledged to help the OIC pass the resolution in the UN and "to use some old-fashioned techniques of peer pressure and shaming" to silence Americans who don't toe the line.

The OIC secretary-general himself told a French television station that he was in favor of stopping the publication of Muhammad cartoons, and that those who continue to do so will face the consequences. "If you don't respect the feelings of one-and-[a-] half billion people, and if you don't feel yourself responsible not to insult them," he said, "then we have a problem." Failure to avoid criticism of the prophet, he went on to add, would lead to demonstrations and violence.

The OIC's demands have real international implications. "Not shadowy extremists but representatives of actual governments—nearly 60, in fact—have demanded that Western nations suppress speech that casts Islam in a bad light," notes Jeremy Rabkin, a professor at the George Mason University School of Law.

But the United States, under the Obama administration, seems to be firmly on board with this idea. After all, our country's top diplomat, acting in an official capacity, went to a foreign land and vowed to foreign leaders that the United States government would use extralegal practices to shame and intimidate American citizens to stop them from exercising what should be their constitutional First Amendment right to free speech. The repercussions from this are only just beginning to be felt.

According to at least one survey, American Muslims have similarly restrictive views, placing religious restrictions above their adopted country's constitutional protections. When asked, "Do you believe that criticism of Islam or Muhammad should be permitted under the Constitution's First Amendment?" 58 percent of U.S. Muslims surveyed replied, "No."

Of course, it's easy to be a fan of free speech and the First Amendment when people say things you agree with. It's much harder when you try to imagine upholding the right of someone to say the most offensive thing imaginable to you. And that is the entire point. The depictions of Muhammad may well be offensive to some, just as putting Christ in urine and calling it "art" may be offensive to others.

I may not like protests at soldiers' funerals or the fact that some in the media openly mock my Mormon religion—but I will stand up for their right to do it.

When we kowtow to anyone or anything and hold it up as being so sacred that it is above reproach, we've not only lost our spines; we've lost our freedom.

PART THREE

What Can Be Done

"Truth advances, & error recedes step by step only; and to do to our fellow-men the most good in our power, we must lead where we can, follow where we cannot, and still go with them, watching always the favorable moment for helping them to another step."

—Thomas Jefferson, 1814

On June 26, 2015, the Supreme Court of the United States ruled in favor of gay marriage. In the United States, this led to an outcry among those disagreeing with the decision. In the Middle East, it led to butchery.

Members of ISIS threw homosexuals off the roof of a building. On social media, they even used the hash tag "#Love Wins" to mock the Court's decision.

That same month, ISIS put other victims in a steel cage and lowered them into a pool of water. Cameras were attached to the cage so that a global audience could watch these "infidels" suffer a horrific death as the water rose to the roof the cage, drowning those inside.

Still another set of victims had wires put around their necks, so a video camera could record their heads being blown off.

None of these shocking forms of murder is going to make most of the world care, and here's why: We've been deceived. We've been rendered blind. We've been trained by phony politicians in Washington to focus on bogus "injustices" on the home front—the so-called wars on women or against gays.

There *is* a war against women going on, to be sure. There is a war against gays under way. But these wars are not here in

America. They are over there. They are in the Muslim world. But we don't hear Lena Dunham or George Takei talking about that.

Try to lecture a gay man in Iran—if one dared to surface—about American "intolerance" to homosexuals and he'd laugh at you. Tell a Yazidi refugee about the "plight" of American women being denied birth control and she'd scoff at you. The petty nonsense we preoccupy ourselves with in America is laughable. Even worse, it's dangerous.

There simply is no comparison.

Real injustices are happening right now—in plain view—but we can't see them, since so many contrived, phony injustices are constantly placed in our way.

We have to start over. We have to get back to basics. We have to relearn how to become strong men and women. Strong in faith. Strong in values and principles.

We have to reset our own priorities. And then lead others to the light.

Jihad's cost to civilization is incalculable. Over the centuries Muslim armies have burned libraries, razed cities, and conquered large swaths of the Middle East, Asia, Africa, and Europe. They have enslaved, starved, and massacred millions of men, women, and children—all in the name of Islam.

As we've seen, the jihadists are *not* distorting their religion. They believe they're acting in accordance with their faith and they can cite chapter and verse to justify every beheading, crucifixion, act of vandalism, and degradation of the "infidels" who happen to get in their way.

Our elected leaders often refuse to acknowledge these facts. President Obama says our enemies are "people who have perverted Islam." President George W. Bush said that al-Qaeda terrorists were "traitors to their own faith, trying, in effect, to hijack Islam itself."

Their reticence is understandable in some ways. The Bush administration wanted to head off accusations that the United States was at war with Islam, and by extension more than 1.5 billion Muslims worldwide. President Bush, in fact, often described the War on Terror as "a war against individuals who absolutely hate what America stands for" and as "a war against evil, not against Islam."

The problem with those descriptions is that they obscure who we're fighting and what victory might look like. There's no question that evil does exist. But it has a name: *Islamism*. Saying that Islamism has nothing to do with Islam is like saying that a particular cut of beef has nothing to do with a cow. They are inexorably linked; one grows inside the other. There are plenty of ways to practice Islam—and plenty of choices in cuts of steak—but they all come from the same place.

President Obama himself said in a CNN interview in February 2015 that there is "an element growing out of Muslim communities in certain parts of the world that have . . . embraced a nihilistic, violent, almost Medieval interpretation of Islam." But, he then added, "It is absolutely true that I reject a notion that somehow that creates a religious war because the overwhelming majority of Muslims reject that interpretation of Islam. They don't even recognize it as being Islam."

In reality, tens of millions of Muslims *do* recognize it as being Islam. It does no good to sugarcoat the truth. Our leaders may say we're not fighting a religious war, but the jihadists most certainly are.

This book is a start at arming you with the truth. But it's just a start. We have to do more. An educated citizenry needs to fight back. And here's how to do it.

1. WE MUST UNDERSTAND THE ENEMY

We cannot be afraid to understand our opponents—domestically or internationally—on their own terms, defined by the rules and teachings that motivate them and organize their philosophy.

Yet our inability, or perhaps our unwillingness, to come to terms with an enemy that openly declares its philosophy, the laws under which it operates, and its goals is a reflection of what our society has become.

Our willful blindness—whether due to political correctness or outright fear—is *killing us*.

Too many Americans still take at face value the lies of our nation's leaders that Islam is fundamentally "a religion of peace" and that the likes of ISIS, Boko Haram, and al-Qaeda have distorted it and are therefore "not Islamic." We also take for granted the separation of church and state in America. But there is no separation of mosque and state in orthodox Islam. The only true law is the law of Allah.

As we've seen throughout this book, Islamic rules of war and for the proper subjugation of pagans, Christians, and Jews have been spelled out clearly for Muslims from the very beginning, more than 1,400 years ago. Their teachings about war, conquest, and submission remain central to orthodox Islam today. Those messages are heard every Friday in mosques from Ann Arbor and Boston to London and Cairo, and all the way to Islamabad and Jakarta.

ISIS is literally razing the birthplace of human civilization in Iraq and Syria to build a new Caliphate. In early 2015, the Islamic State pillaged and smashed priceless artifacts in Iraq's Mosul Museum. A masked ISIS spokesman explained in a video that the ancient Assyrians and Akkadians were "polytheists," so it was right to destroy what remained of their civilization: "These statues and idols, these artifacts, if God has ordered its removal, they became worthless to us even if they are worth billions of dollars."

Soon afterward, ISIS vandals demolished the ruins of Hatra, a key stronghold and trade center of the Parthian Empire, which had been a major power in ancient Persia some two thousand years ago. They also pillaged and demolished hundreds of artifacts in the ancient Assyrian city of Nimrud, where the Tower of Babel once stood, before leveling the entire place with explosives. In some cases, ISIS's religious objections to supposed "idols" are secondary to making a profit off them. The group has smuggled and sold millions of dollars' worth of ancient artifacts. "They steal everything that they can sell, and what they can't sell, they destroy," said Iraq's deputy minister for antiquities and heritage.

Boko Haram—a group whose name translates roughly to "Western education is forbidden"—has slaughtered thousands of Christians in Nigeria. The group, which formally pledged allegiance to the Islamic State in March 2015, takes Christian girls as young as nine or ten years old as sexual slaves. Boko Haram's leader, Abubakar Shekau, is completely unapologetic about the practice. "There are slaves in Islam," he said in 2014, "you should know this. Prophet Muhammad took slaves himself during [the] Badr war."

The Badr "war" was the decisive battle in A.D. 624 that led to Muhammad's conquest of his home city of Mecca and, eventually, the entire Arabian Peninsula. Twenty-first-century jihadists would like nothing more than to repeat that history.

Jihad's depredations aren't limited to the Middle East, Africa, or South Asia. Al-Qaeda made its intentions—and its total rejection of Western norms—known to the United States and the world long before Osama bin Laden became a household name. A document discovered in Manchester, England, called "The Al Qaeda Manual," in fact, transparently lays out the organization's mission:

> The confrontation that we are calling for with the apostate regimes does not know Socratic debates . . . Platonic ideals . . . nor Aristotelian diplomacy. But it knows the dialogue of bullets, the ideals of assassination, bombing and destruction, and the diplomacy of the cannon and the machine gun.
>
> . . . Islamic governments have never and will never be established through peaceful solutions and cooperative councils. They are established as they have [always] been:

"by pen and gun;

"by word and bullet; and

"by tongue and teeth."

Never before in our history has the United States had to account for the personal and private beliefs of its enemies. When the United States fought Nazism and fascism, Franklin D. Roosevelt and the *New York Times* didn't say, "Not all Germans . . ." or "Not all Italians . . ." Most Americans understood that "not all Russians" wanted to eradicate the United States during the Cold War. Nevertheless, the regimes of Nazi Germany, fascist Italy, and Soviet Russia were implacable foes and existential threats to our way of life. They needed to be defeated militarily *and* ideologically.

The same must be said of Muslims who rally under the black flag of jihad. In February 2015, the left-leaning *Atlantic* magazine published a blockbuster story by Graeme Wood titled "What ISIS Really Wants." I talked about it at length on my radio program. The article is a must-read for anyone who seeks genuine understanding about the Islamic State's goals.

Wood begins by assuring his readers that "nearly all" Muslims reject ISIS. "But," he writes, "pretending that [the Islamic State] isn't actually a religious, millenarian group, with theology that must be understood to be combatted, has already led the United States to underestimate it and back foolish schemes to counter it."

Wood points out that many Americans "tend to see jihadism as monolithic, and to apply the logic of al-Qaeda to an organization that has decisively eclipsed it." That's a mistake, he argues. I agree with him that while there are different shades of jihad, all of those factions rely on the same holy book, traditions, and religious laws.

More important, Wood argues, the Islamic State's jihadists

are "not modern secular people, with modern political concerns, wearing medieval religious disguise. . . . In fact, much of what the group does looks nonsensical except in light of a sincere, carefully considered commitment to returning civilization to a seventh-century legal environment, and ultimately to bringing about the apocalypse."

As we've seen, the voices of jihad have made their purpose plain again and again. They are bent on a new Holocaust, one that engulfs Christians and Jews in the Middle East and around the world. So how many more innocent Christians need to be crucified or beheaded until we start taking ISIS at its word? How many Jews have to die before we understand that Hezbollah and Hamas, along with their patrons in Iran, really mean what they say about wiping Israel off the map?

It's true that many Muslims in the United States and abroad reject and condemn violent jihad. But it doesn't follow that the violent jihadists of ISIS, al-Qaeda, and their confederates are not truly Islamic. And it certainly doesn't mean that Muslims reject everything that ISIS, al-Qaeda, and the others espouse.

A 2013 Pew poll found sizable minorities of Muslims in eleven countries—including nominal U.S. allies—held favorable views of al-Qaeda, Hamas, and Hezbollah. One in five Egyptians approve of al-Qaeda's work, while 23 percent of Indonesians—a nation with a "moderate" Muslim population of more than 202 million, the largest on earth—say they support the terrorist group's goals. Overall, about one-third of Muslims approve of Hamas, and one in four think highly of Hezbollah.

If that isn't worrisome enough, 15 percent of Muslims in Turkey support suicide bombing and a little over half of all Turks whom Pew surveyed say they aren't the least bit worried about Islamic extremism. Don't forget, Turkey is a NATO ally that has long aspired to join the European Union. Islamism's resurgence in the former seat of the Ottoman Empire appeared to suffer a setback in June 2015, when President Recep Tayyip Erdogan's "Justice and Development Party" lost its parliamentary majority for the first time since 2002. It's a hopeful sign, but whether extremism begins to lose its appeal in Turkey remains to be seen.

Apologists for jihad, whether it's the Council on American-Islamic Relations, the Islamic Society of North America, agenda-driven pseudo-academics such as Karen Armstrong and Juan Cole, or their stenographers in the mainstream press, insist against all evidence to the contrary that the ideology of ISIS and Boko Haram and al-Qaeda "comes from nowhere."

Even our military's top brass seemingly cannot grasp the enemy's religious aims or theological appeal. The *New York Times* in 2014 highlighted the work of a special civilian task force assembled by Major General Michael K. Nagata, commander of U.S. Special Operations forces in the Middle East, to make sense of ISIS and its goals. "We do not understand the movement, and until we do, we are not going to defeat it," Nagata said, according to confidential minutes of a conference call with several experts that the *Times* obtained. "We have not defeated the idea. We do not even understand the idea."

The report relates how Nagata's team consists of more than three dozen outside experts, including business professors and neuroscientists, to figure out the "intangible means" the Islamic State uses to control large populations, and the "magnetic, inspirational" way ISIS attracts so many young men and women from around the globe to fight. "I do not understand the intangible power of ISIL," Nagata said. "This may sound like a bizarre excursion into the surreal, but for me it is about avoiding failure."

General Nagata is right to worry about failure. We *are* failing. But with all due respect to the general, who has served his country with distinction for more than three decades in some of the worst places on earth, he won't find the answer he's looking for in cutting-edge neuroscience or marketing research. Our cultural and political elite may be steeped in secularism and liberalism, but our enemies are deadly serious about their faith and traditions.

When ISIS leader Caliph Abu Bakr al-Baghdadi says, "O Muslims, Islam was never for a day the religion of peace. Islam is the religion of war," he means it. When al-Baghdadi says, "Your Prophet . . . was dispatched with the sword as a mercy to the creation. He was ordered with war until Allah is worshipped alone," he isn't being obtuse. When the self-proclaimed "Caliph" quotes Muhammad addressing the "polytheists" of Arabia and says, "'I came to you with slaughter.' . . . He never for a day grew tired of war," that isn't a mixed message in need of expert parsing.

Why is that so difficult to understand?

Stop and think about the madness of our nation's cultural and political elite. They lack the moral and intellectual clarity to win this *religious* war. They cannot tell friend from foe. They're ignorant of the lessons of history. They have no courage of their convictions, because their convictions are hollow.

If we rely on them to understand our enemy it will be too late. It's up to us.

2. WE MUST BE UNAFRAID TO SPEAK

Do not be deceived. Our enemies understand better than our leaders do that jihad is expansive. And so is our enemies' desire to change America. They would have us cower in fear and shame, censoring our thoughts and words in accordance with their standards.

Gradually, they expect, the United States through guilt and well-intended tolerance will submit to sharia law—and eventually to the Caliphate.

Given all that we've seen and learned in the years following the 9/11 attacks, it still comes as a shock to see how the highest levels of the United States government have pandered to Muslim radicals. As noted, the Obama administration has welcomed members of the Muslim Brotherhood to the White House and to meetings with representatives of the State Department.

This pattern is not unique to President Obama, however. The Bush administration made similar overtures to Morsi and the Muslim Brotherhood. According to the Clarion Project, President Bush was due to meet personally with Muslim leaders—many with Brotherhood connections—in 2001. One of the invitees, Abdurahman Alamoudi, had also met with officials in the Clinton administration. Alamoudi would later be sentenced to twenty-three years in prison for plotting with Libyans to assassinate the crown prince of Saudi Arabia.

That meeting, which was to happen on September 11, was, of course, canceled. But President Bush—along with every other American—nonetheless became well acquainted with radical Islam that day.

These are the people our government apparently listens to. It has gone on for years. If we want those in power to instead listen to the American people, we have to make sure they cannot ignore our message. We must understand the truth, and once armed with that knowledge, we cannot be afraid to speak up.

The most deadly thing the jihadists can do—short of detonating a nuclear weapon or electromagnetic pulse—is to get us to subvert our own precariously dangling Constitution to accommodate them.

That plan of attack is already well under way. We've already seen how criticism of Islam or Muslims is routinely denounced as "Islamophobia." We've seen how intimidation, fear, and violence are directed against people who dare speak out. We witnessed the disgraceful media response to the thwarted terrorist attack on the "Draw Muhammad" contest in Garland, Texas, which laid the blame for a shoot-out that left two ISIS-inspired gunmen dead on the free speech event's organizers. And we've seen how the Brotherhood's "civilization jihad" is working in parallel to the more violent jihadist efforts in the Middle East.

You would think our press would recognize the threat. After all, aren't they in the First Amendment business? Haven't the *New York Times* and other newspapers insisted on publishing U.S. secrets in the fight against al-Qaeda in the name of the public's right to know? Yet, at the same time, they've gone out of their way to deny, deflect, and deceive the public when it comes to the truth about jihad and radical Islam. They seem to be in total denial that Islamic extremists pose a bona fide threat, or that a Caliphate is something that *anybody*—let alone tens of millions of Muslims— actually wants.

Fourteen years after 9/11, the press, with few exceptions, still refuses to consider the *possibility* that a terrorist plot or attack may be the work of jihadists with global designs rather than a simple "lone wolf" or disgruntled individual who happens to be Muslim. They won't call radical Islamists by their proper name. Either the media elite are afraid to tell the truth, or they're afraid of what the American people will demand upon learning the truth.

For example, the media readily accepted the Defense Department's line that Major Nidal Hasan's November 5, 2009, shooting rampage at Fort Hood in Texas—which left thirteen people dead—amounted to a tragic case of "workplace violence." At best, Hasan was a "lone wolf" who acted on his own initiative. Any relationship between his shouts of "Allahu Akbar" as he gunned down his victims with the same battle cry used by countless jihadists in Iraq and Afghanistan must have been purely coincidental.

Never mind the lengthy email correspondence Hasan carried on with Anwar al-Awlaki, the American-born radical Yemeni cleric who was a major influence among English-speaking jihadists before he was killed in 2011 by a U.S. drone strike. And never mind Hasan's lengthy monologues to practically anyone who would listen about how he was "on the wrong side" in the U.S. Army, and how he considered himself a "Soldier of Allah."

As Hasan awaited his court-martial in 2012, he wrote: "I, Nidal Malik Hasan, am compelled to renounce any oaths of allegiances that require me to support/defend [*sic*] man made constitution (like the constitution of the United States) *over the commandments mandated in Islam.* . . . I therefore formally renounce my oath of office . . . this includes my oath of U.S. citizenship" (emphasis added). That doesn't sound like a man who simply had a problem with the army's human resources department.

After seeing the government and media cognitive dissonance play out over and over again in their coverage of the latest jihadist atrocity, I probably shouldn't be surprised about anything anymore. But even I was shocked at the media's response to the Boston Marathon bombing in 2013. ABC News wasted no time asking, "Could this be homegrown terror?" and was likely disappointed when the answer came back "no." The bombing, it turns out, was carried out by brothers Dzhokhar and Tamerlan Tsarnaev, who just happened to be Muslim émigrés from Chechnya who were radicalized in Boston.

Tamerlan died from injuries he sustained in a gun battle with the Boston police, during which his brother Dzhokhar ran him over with a stolen SUV. Dzhokhar was eventually captured after a standoff with police when a homeowner found him hiding in a boat behind his house in the Boston suburb of Watertown. Expecting he wouldn't survive his confrontation with the authorities, Dzhokhar scrawled a note inside his hiding place. It read, in part: "[W]e Muslims are one body, you hurt one you hurt us all, well at least that's how Muhammad (pbuh) wanted it to be . . . the ummah is beginning to rise . . . know you are fighting men who look into the barrel of your gun and see heaven, now how can you compete with that. We are promised victory and we will surely get it."

Predictably, within days of Tamerlan's death and Dzhokhar's arrest, U.S. officials were telling the media that the brothers were "lone wolves" motivated by radical Islam but not connected with any terrorist group. In the first six months of 2015, the FBI had announced arrests of at least thirty U.S. citizens involved in a "lone wolf" terrorist plot of some kind. That's on top of the recent "lone wolf" attacks in Canada where, in separate incidents, terrorists murdered a soldier in Quebec and then, just two days later, another soldier in Ottawa. Reports say that both killers had recently converted to Islam.

A "lone wolf" here, a "lone wolf" there—at some point, you'd think the media would press law enforcement officials and our leaders to admit we have a growing pack of jihadi wolves stalking us in our own backyard.

Instead, they tiptoe around the truth. Homeland security secretary Jeh Johnson says the government is concerned "about the independent actor, and the independent actor who is here in the homeland who may strike with little or no warning." Yet Johnson is maddeningly vague about who those independent actors might be or what cause they might espouse. It could be a right-wing militia member for all he knows, or maybe the Weather Underground is making a comeback. The people responsible for defending the nation simply won't publicly admit the connection between jihad abroad and the threat of jihad at home.

The government is not just wishy-washy about connections to Islam; it also often provides halfhearted defenses of free expression in the face of repeated attacks. In response to the Danish cartoon flap, Bush State Department spokesman Sean McCormack called the illustrations offensive and said, "Anti-Muslim images are as unacceptable as anti-Semitic images, as anti-Christian images, or any other religious belief."

First of all—no—none of these things are unacceptable; they are the very definition of protected speech. But even if we go along and play that game, the obvious difference is that Christians and Jews don't try to murder people who publish anti-Christian or anti-Jewish cartoons.

The Obama administration actually took the side of the jihadists over free speech. The president, along with Secretary of State Hillary Clinton and U.S. United Nations ambassador Susan Rice, tried to blame an anti-Islam YouTube video for the September 11, 2012, attacks on the U.S. embassy in Cairo and the horrific murders in Benghazi, Libya, of U.S. ambassador J. Christopher Stevens and three other consulate personnel. The administration went so far as to arrest the video's producer and director, Nakoula Nakoula, for allegedly violating conditions of his parole in a completely unrelated case. Nakoula wound up spending a year in a federal prison cell because the Obama White House apparently needed a scapegoat for its inept handling of a foreign policy disaster.

Two weeks after the Benghazi debacle, the president addressed the United Nations and made an outrageous comparison between Americans who insult Muslims and Muslims who want to kill Americans, Christians, and Jews. "The future must not belong to those who slander the prophet of Islam," the president told the assembled dignitaries, most of whom routinely persecute and jail political and religious dissenters in their home countries.

"Yet to be credible," he added, "those who condemn that slander must also condemn the hate we see when the image of Jesus Christ is desecrated, churches are destroyed, or the Holocaust is denied."

The president could have set an example to the nation and the world by standing before the General Assembly and saying the future must not belong to those who would kill for the prophet of Islam. He could have made a clear and unequivocal statement that the United States stands for unfettered freedom of speech and true freedom of religion. Instead he descended into moral equivalence and political pandering.

In the face of this crisis, the United States not only needs leaders to stand in the face of violence and intimidation; it needs citizens who are unafraid to speak the truth about the origins of the threat we face and hold our leaders accountable when they resort to political correctness or refuse to call a spade a spade.

3. WE MUST UNDERSTAND OUR TRADITIONS—AND OURSELVES

At this moment, all around the United States, mosques and community organizations affiliated with the Muslim Brotherhood are quietly pushing to introduce sharia law into the fabric of our society and our judicial system. And they're succeeding.

As we covered earlier, Muslims in the Dallas suburb of Irving, Texas, established what the Christian Broadcasting Network described as "the first official shariah law system in the United States." Tribunal judge Imam Moujahed Bakhach denied that the sharia court he runs with three other local imams is anything like what orthodox Islamic teachings say. "The misconception about what they see through the media is that sharia means cut the head, chop the heads, cut the hands and we are not in that," he said. "We are not here to invade the White House or invade Austin."

It's true that sharia isn't *only* about cutting off heads and hands as punishment. Islamic law also has rules about what Muslims may eat and drink, how Muslims should dress, how a woman's court testimony is worth only half of a man's, and how religious minorities must be treated as inferiors. But groups like the Council on American-Islamic Relations don't want to talk about any of that.

Mustafaa Carroll, executive director of CAIR's Houston chapter, told the *Austin Chronicle* that sharia is an essential part of a practicing Muslim's life—just as Christians and Jews have their own religious guidelines to follow. "Sharia is getting married, getting buried," Carroll said. "It is the Islamic principles that Muslims live by."

That's true as far as it goes. But, as we've already seen, sharia law is *central* to Islam. Orthodox Muslims and Islamic State jihadists alike believe that man-made law is un-Islamic. Democracy itself is un-Islamic—a man's vote cannot supersede God's law. Sharia does not respect individual rights, as the West has understood the concept for centuries. Sharia is incompatible with our Constitution and the principles of equality and liberty embodied in our Declaration of Independence.

Needless to say, Carroll and his fellow activists have been working hard to downplay those differences. They're also successfully lobbying against legislation that would prevent state courts from using sharia in their proceedings. A Texas anti-sharia bill failed again in 2015—the third time in three years. The liberal Texas press portrayed the legislation's Republican sponsors—Representatives Jeff Leach and Molly White—as bigoted kooks because they had the nerve to ask members of the Muslim community to publicly announce their allegiance to America and our laws.

The threat is real, and it must be stopped. But how?

In our ongoing struggle with the barbarity that appears tragically inherent in Islam, we need to return to first principles and restore the integrity of our nation's heritage.

Easier said than done, I realize. Our leaders have failed us. Our media is against us. Our Constitution is being eroded away and our culture is becoming ever more secular. Many of us have forgotten who we are as a people and a country. We've forgotten God.

Our enemies have turned many of our strengths into weaknesses. Americans are the most tolerant and charitable people on the face of the earth. We have welcomed millions of refugees from across the globe in the course of our history. That was fine and noble when America had a strong assimilationist ethic. But the past thirty years have seen a shift from assimilation into the melting pot toward a divisive and dangerous form of multiculturalism that encourages ethnic separation.

The United States has had a strange immigration policy since 9/11. Our Muslim population has doubled to more than 2 million between 2001 and 2010. We're accepting thousands of Syrians displaced by the civil war and Democratic lawmakers want the Obama administration to open the gates even wider. In May 2015, a group of fourteen U.S. senators wrote a letter to the president urging the resettlement of as many as 65,000 more Syrian refugees, despite the fact that the FBI says there is no way it can possibly screen the hundreds of people who've entered the country from that war-torn country already.

If our experience with Somalian refugees is any indication, taking in tens of thousands of Syrians would be a recipe for disaster. Since 1991, more than 100,000 Somalis have resettled in the United States. Almost all of them are Muslim and the vast majority of them have planted roots in the Cedar-Riverside neighborhood of Minneapolis, which has become known as "Little Mogadishu." Not coincidentally, Minneapolis has become a hotbed of jihadi recruitment, with at least forty young men having traveled from Minnesota to join the Islamic State.

A sane immigration and resettlement policy would take careful account of who these newcomers are, and where they've come from.

I think an excellent way to approach America's Muslim

population—especially immigrants and refugees—would be to emulate George Washington.

In 1783, the year our fledgling nation finally won its independence from King George III, General Washington wrote a letter welcoming Irish Catholic immigrants who had recently landed in New York City. Remember, many Americans of the founding generation considered Catholics to be wholly undesirable citizens. They were subjects of the pope, not cut out for freedom in a young republic—or so the opinion went. John Adams summed up the sentiment in a letter to his daughter-in-law, Louisa: "Liberty and Popery cannot live together."

Washington disagreed. "The bosom of America," he wrote on December 2, 1783, "is open to receive not only the Opulent and respectable Stranger, but the oppressed and persecuted of all Nations and Religions; whom we shall welcome to a participation of all our rights and privileges, if by decency and propriety of conduct they appear to merit the enjoyment."

In a private letter a few months later to Tench Tilghman, Washington asked his former aide-de-camp if he could hire a bricklayer and a house joiner to work on his estate at Mount Vernon. "I would not confine you to Palatines (Germans)," he wrote. "If they are good workmen, they may be of Assia [sic], Africa, or Europe. They may be Mahometans, Jews, or Christians of any Sect—or they may be Atheists."

But perhaps the statement most relevant to our challenge right now is President Washington's August 1790 letter to the Hebrew Congregation of Newport, Rhode Island. "The Citizens of the United States of America have a right to applaud themselves for having given to mankind examples of an enlarged and liberal policy: a policy worthy of imitation. All possess alike liberty of conscience and immunities of citizenship," he wrote.

"It is now no more that toleration is of, as if it were the indulgence of one class of people, that another enjoyed the exercise of their inherent natural rights," the president continued. "For, happily, the Government of the United States, which gives to bigotry no sanction, to persecution no assistance, requires only that they who live under its protection should demean themselves as good citizens, in giving it on all occasions their effectual support."

Understand what Washington was saying: The United States is the first nation on earth to embrace true religious liberty. Your rights as an immigrant or as a citizen do not depend on your profession of a particular faith or creed. Everyone has a God-given liberty of conscience.

But also notice that in each of those letters, Washington adds a crucial condition: newcomers enjoy all of our rights "if by decency and propriety of conduct they *appear to merit* the enjoyment"; we will pay little mind to where they come from or what they believe if they are "good workmen"; and they may practice their religion freely as long as they "demean themselves as good citizens" and give the country "*on all occasions their effectual support*" (emphasis added).

President George W. Bush seemed to echo Washington in an April 30, 2002, speech in San Jose, California, promoting "compassionate conservatism." "America rejects bigotry," he said. "We reject every act of hatred against people of Arab background or Muslim faith. America values and welcomes peaceful people of all faiths—Christian, Jewish, Muslim, Sikh, Hindu and many others. Every faith is practiced and protected here, because we are one country. Every immigrant can be fully and equally American because we're one country. Race and color should not divide us, because America is one country."

The question facing us now is whether America is still one country.

We remember the 2,997 innocent lives taken in service of

that awful mission on 9/11, but many people may not realize how much else the nineteen hijackers stole from our culture and Western civilization that day.

Countless historical documents, records, and irreplaceable artworks were lost forever when the twin towers fell. Nineteenth- and twentieth-century paintings, drawings, and sculptures by the likes of Pablo Picasso, Roy Lichtenstein, and Auguste Rodin were obliterated. Five World Trade Center was home to the Lower Manhattan Cultural Council, the Broadway Theatre Archive, and a collection of forty thousand negatives of photos by Jacques Lowe that recorded John F. Kennedy's presidency. Underground archives below Six World Trade Center housed millions of objects and artifacts of New York dating back to the eighteenth and nineteenth centuries. The tiny Church of St. Nicholas, a Greek Orthodox parish crushed by debris from tower two, contained relics of fourth- and sixth-century saints and icons dating from nineteenth-century Russia.

The list goes on and on. All of that art, architecture, culture, and history turned to rubble and ash in the name of jihad.

If we are not careful, jihad will take from us much more than physical artifacts—it will destroy our entire way of life.

4. WE CANNOT REFORM ISLAM—ONLY MUSLIMS CAN DO THAT

One of the greatest mistakes the United States made in the aftermath of 9/11 was to adopt the idea that the lessons of history did not apply in the war against radical Islam.

Our leaders believed without a shadow of a doubt that the Muslims of the Middle East—men, women, and children who had known nothing but despotism and dictatorship—desperately wanted everything that Americans have and enjoy. As one enthusiastic Iraqi put it shortly after the fall of Baghdad in 2003: "Democracy, whiskey, sexy."

President George W. Bush gave this idealistic worldview a more elegant spin in his 2004 State of the Union address: "[I]t is mistaken, and condescending, to assume that whole cultures and great religions are incompatible with liberty and self-government. I believe that God has planted in every human heart the desire to live in freedom."

As we've learned at tremendous cost in lives and treasure, the more condescending view was to assume that most Iraqis' understanding of freedom was the same as ours. It's just not true. The Islamic State believes in freedom. But it's the freedom that comes with submission to Allah and his laws.

As long as we harbor misunderstandings about what is and what is not "true Islam," we'll get nowhere. For years, we've heard talk about the need for an Islamic reformation like the Protestant Reformation of five hundred years ago. If we were to go back in time and tell Martin Luther that papal indulgences had nothing to do with Christianity, we'd look like idiots. For good and for ill, indulgences were an integral part of European Christian life in the early 1500s. That's how the vast majority of Christians understood their lives and their world.

We tend to downplay how difficult—and how bloody—the Reformation turned out to be. Protestantism unleashed roughly two centuries of religious warfare, decimated large swaths of continental Europe, displaced millions of people, and ultimately led to the full flowering of individualism and liberal democracy in the New World.

Would an Islamic reformation play out in much the same way? Who knows? It's safe to say, however, that any reforms would be incredibly difficult. As the late, great political scientist James Q. Wilson observed in 2004, the prospect of reshaping the Islamic world along similar lines as the Protestant Reformation is "highly doubtful."

"There is neither a papacy nor a priesthood against which to rebel; nor are mosques comparable to churches in the Catholic sense of dispensing sacraments," Wilson wrote. "There will never be a Muslim Martin Luther or a hereditary Islamic ruler who, by embracing a rival faith, can thereby create an opportunity for lay rule."

Never? I know that many would-be reformers—Muslim and non-Muslim alike—hope Wilson is wrong.

Ayaan Hirsi Ali, the ex-Muslim who has written heroically about her life growing up in Somalia and her escape to freedom in the Netherlands and the United States, argues that, as recently as the mid-nineteenth and early twentieth centuries, parts of the Muslim world made a steady transition into modernity. "By the end of World War II," she wrote, "the central features of sharia had been replaced in many Muslim countries by laws based on European models. . . . At the same time, Islam itself was increasingly being reinterpreted as part of a long continuum in man's attempts to achieve social justice, even being used at times to validate socialist doctrines of redistribution and other efforts to remake society."

Liberal Islamic convert Thomas J. Haidon has argued, "Any genuine movement for Islamic reform must first seek to acknowledge that aspects particular to Islam and our understanding of Islam are problematic, and hence they need critical re-evaluation." The biggest stumbling block is the view that Islam is simply impervious to change because it is "the essence of perfection: the undisputed word of God, and the comprehensive tradition of the Prophet Muhammad."

But, Haidon says, "Unless reformist organizations develop effective, grass roots strategies to achieve goals that are firmly rooted in theological principles . . . the reformist discourse will prove to be nothing but rhetoric."

If there is a glimmer of hope in the unrepentant barbarism

of the Islamic State, it is that their "management of savagery" as they call it is beginning to offend Muslims, even the hard-core Islamists. A case in point is a gentleman by the name of Abd al-Rauf Kara, a hardened Libyan Salafist who is neither a friend to democracy nor a peacemaker. He's the head of Islamist militias that have helped create chaos in the country in the months after the U.S. compound in Benghazi was attacked. But he's finding that Daesh, as the Islamic State is known locally, is too brutal even for him. "Daesh now has a 70-kilometer stretch of the coast," says Kara. "It is a key stretch for launching people-smuggler boats, and Europe should be worried that Daesh can disguise their people as migrants." This is hardly a reformation, but it may be an encouraging sign that more and more Muslims will stand up to oppose the Islamic supremacist ideology that threatens the free world.

I believe that only when Muslims themselves decide they need a reformation will there be a real chance at one. But it isn't for you or me to say. I'm not a Muslim. I cannot tell a Muslim how he or she needs to resolve the deep—and perhaps irreconcilable—conflicts between their faith and freedom.

What I can do—what we all can do—is cast a harsh, bright light on the Muslim Brotherhood and other seemingly mainstream groups that are working to undermine our country's institutions from within. We can support serious scholars attempting genuine reform—devout Muslims such as Abdullahi Ahmed An-Na'im, Khaleel Mohammed, Ahmed Mansour, and Kassim Ahmad, who are making arguments rooted in the Quran but not smothered by it. We can highlight and support the work of American Muslims such as Nonie Darwish, Wafa Sultan, Asra Nomani, Irshad Manji, and Zuhdi Jasser, who founded the Phoenix-based American Islamic Forum for Democracy.

But in the end, Islam will either reform itself or it will destroy itself. If it's the latter, then our job is to trust in God, speak without fear, and make sure America isn't destroyed along with it.

EPILOGUE

During the Second World War, many people, including many of those at the highest levels of our government, claimed ignorance to the holocaust under way. They had heard rumors and whispers, of course, but they could hide behind the fact that they didn't know *for sure* what was going on.

This time there is no place to hide from the eternal eyes of judgment.

This time we do know for sure.

A few years ago, when I went to Auschwitz, I talked to a woman named Paulina. She was one of the righteous among the nations, the term used to refer to non-Jews who risked their lives to come to the aid of the Jewish people during the Holocaust.

"How do I do it?" I asked her. "How do I water the seed of righteousness in others? What do I do?"

She said to me, "Remember, the righteous didn't suddenly become righteous. They just refused to go over the cliff with everyone else."

The world is going over the cliff today. We all know it. But we don't have to go with it. We can come to the aid of Muslims being tortured in the Middle East for not being "pure" enough. We can come to the aid of women being raped and butchered. We can come to the aid of homosexuals being thrown off the tops of buildings. We can defend children being murdered for such "crimes" as eating during Ramadan.

And we can stand with Christians who are being systematically abused, silenced, and exterminated by those claiming to adhere to the "religion of peace."

As I write this, in places like Iraq and Syria, Christians are being tortured with a special kind of zeal. Killing them has become a high priority. If you live in a house with the mark of the Nazarene—which means that those inside worship Jesus of Nazareth—you are very likely to be killed.

Yet, in parts of the Middle East, even inside the caliphate, that symbol is becoming a unifying one—for Christians and non-Christians alike. I recently talked with someone who'd just returned from Egypt. He said that many people are being converted away from the Islamists because of how the Christians are handling their plight. These persecuted Christians are unsettling the butchers of ISIS. The Islamists did not expect the followers of Christ to remain so calm, so determined. They cannot understand why they haven't broken their will. The answer is simple: They refuse to go over the cliff.

In decades to come, future generations will look back on these times and tell these stories of courage as well as those of cowardice. Of those who saw what was going on, and did nothing.

I want my posterity to tell the story of a righteous family that stood against all odds and said, "I am with the Nazarene. I am with the Jew, the homosexual, the atheist, or the Muslim who just wasn't Muslim enough."

I want you to be among the righteous too. You may not know what to do but just sharing this book and doing your own research to verify the truth of it will help do your part. We produced this book in paperback to keep your costs down so you could share it with a friend, but also so that you could put it in your back pocket or purse and refer to it when you begin to hear the lies being told by the politicians, or the mainstream media, the willfully blind and the ignorant.

God will not hold us blameless. Silence in the face of evil is evil itself. Not to stand is to stand. Not to speak is to speak.

So stand. Raise your hand and demand to be counted.

I will not go over the cliff with the rest of humanity. "Never again" is now.

All lives matter.

NOTES

INTRODUCTION: JEFFERSON'S QURAN
PAGE 1: "it's the largest library in the world" "Fascinating Facts," Library of Congress, accessed June 10, 2015, http://www.loc.gov/about/fascinating-facts/. • PAGE 2: "one of the first English translations of the Quran" Denise A. Spellberg, *Thomas Jefferson's Qur'an: Islam and the Founders* (New York: Knopf Doubleday, 2013), p. 85. • "only Founding Father to have a basic understanding of Arabic" Alexandra Méav Jerome, "The Jefferson Qur'an," Oxford Islamic Studies Online, accessed June 10, 2015, http://www.oxfordislamicstudies.com/Public/focus /essay1009_jefferson.html. • "championed the creation of an Oriental languages department" Alexandra Méav Jerome, "The Jefferson Qur'an," Oxford Islamic Studies Online, accessed June 10, 2015, http://www.oxfordislamicstudies.com /Public/focus/essay1009_jefferson.html. • PAGE 3: "neither had undergone a reformation" Denise A. Spellberg, *Thomas Jefferson's Qur'an: Islam and the Founders* (New York: Knopf Doubleday, 2013), p. 105. • PAGE 4: " 'founded on the Laws of their Prophet' " "American Commissioners to John Jay, 28 March 1786," Founders Online, National Archives, accessed June 10, 2015, http://founders .archives.gov/documents/Jefferson/01-09-02-0315. • " 'sure to go to Paradise' " "American Commissioners to John Jay, 28 March 1786," Founders Online, National Archives, accessed June 10, 2015, http://founders.archives.gov/documents /Jefferson/01-09-02-0315. • PAGE 6: " 'they were almost always successful' " "American Commissioners to John Jay, 28 March 1786," Founders Online, National Archives, accessed June 10, 2015, http://founders.archives.gov/documents /Jefferson/01-09-02-0315. • PAGE 9: "subjected to American courts" Center for Security Policy, "Poll of U.S. Muslims Reveals Ominous Levels of Support for Islamic Supremacists' Doctrine of Shariah, Jihad," June 23, 2015. http://www .centerforsecuritypolicy.org/2015/06/23/nationwide-poll-of-us-muslims-shows -thousands-support-shariah-jihad. • PAGE 12: " 'so small that they could not be defined as stones' " Amnesty International, "Iran: Death by Stoning, a Grotesque and Unacceptable Penalty," press release, January 15, 2008, https://www.amnesty .org/press-releases/2008/01/iran-death-stoning-grotesque-and-unacceptable-pen alty-20080115/. • " 'up to 74 lashes' " *Islamic Penal Code of the Islamic Republic of Iran—Book Five*, Iran Human Rights Documentation Center, July 18,2013, http:// iranhrdc.org/english/human-rights-documents/iranian-codes/1000000351-islamic -penal-code-of-the-islamic-republic-of-iran-book-five.html#21. • " 'increasingly

implemented in public' " Amnesty International, "Amnesty International Report 2014/15," accessed June 10, 2015, https://www.amnesty.org/en/countries/middle -east-and-north-africa/iran/report-iran/. • **"Even crucifixion is not off-limits"** Jacob Siegel, "Islamic Extremists Now Crucifying People in Syria—and Tweeting Out the Pictures," *The Daily Beast,* April 30, 2014, http://www.thedailybeast.com /articles/2014/04/30/islamic-extremists-now-crucifying-people-in-syria-and-tweet ing-out-the-pictures.html.

PART ONE: ISLAM 101

CHAPTER ONE: ISLAM AND END TIMES
PAGE 19: " **'would be conquerors of Constantinople'** " Muslim ibn al-Hajjah, *Sahih Muslim,* Hadith 6924, trans. Abdul Hamid Siddiqui, The Only Quran, accessed June 10, 2015, http://www.theonlyquran.com/hadith/Sahih-Muslim/?volume =41&chapter=9. • **PAGE 20:** " **'slaughtering your people on your streets'** " "Gruesome Islamic State Video Announces Death of Peter Kassig," The Clarion Project, November 16, 2014, http://www.clarionproject.org/news/gruesome-islamic-state -video-announces-death-peter-kassig. • **PAGE 21: "open road to Istanbul and Europe beyond"** William McCants, "ISIS Fantasies of an Apocalyptic Showdown in Northern Syria," *Markaz* (blog), Brookings, October 3, 2014, http://www.brookings .edu/blogs/markaz/posts/2014/10/03-isis-apocalyptic-showdown-syria-mccants. • **"picture of St. Peter's Square at the Vatican"** Umberto Bacchi, "Isis Magazine *Dabiq* Threatens 'Rome Crusaders' Flying Islamic State Flag at Vatican on Front Cover," *International Business Times,* October 13, 2014, http://www.ibtimes.co.uk /isis-magazine-dabiq-threatens-rome-crusaders-flying-islamic-state-flag-vatican -front-cover-1469712. •" **'Islamic State is Islamic. Very Islamic.'** " Graeme Wood, "What ISIS Really Wants," *The Atlantic,* March 2015, http://www.theatlantic.com /features/archive/2015/02/what-isis-really-wants/384980/. • **PAGE 22:** " **'and in the shades of black smoke'** " Quran 56:42–43. • " **'He knows best what they are doing'** " Quran 39:68–70. • **PAGE 23:** " **'and hair all over his body'** " "The Dajjāl's Physical Features," The Dajjāl: Knowing the False Messiah, accessed June 10, 2015, http://www.authentic-translations.com/dajjal/texts/Dajjal-4.pdf. • **"on the road between Iraq and Syria"** Anne Speckhard, "End Times Brewing: An Apocalyptic View on al-Baghdadi's Declaration of a Caliphate in Iraq and the Flow of Foreign Fighters Coming from the West," *The Blog* (blog), *The Huffington Post* (UK), June 30, 2014), http://www.huffingtonpost.co.uk/anne-speckhard/isis-iraq_b_5541693 .html. • **"Seventy thousand Jews will be seduced"** Tom Porter, "Isis Uses Picture of 'Cyclops Baby' to Recruit Fighters for Apocalyptic Battle," *International Business Times,* September 14, 2013, http://www.ibtimes.co.uk/isis-use-picture -cyclops-baby-recruit-fighters-apocalyptic-battle-1465323. • **"on social media of supposedly one-eyed babies"** Fitry Yhanis, Twitter post, August 19, 2014, 10:17 a.m., https://twitter.com/xfitryyuhanisx/status/501734749719646209. • **"actual real-life children born with one eye"** Tom Porter, "Isis Uses Picture of 'Cyclops Baby' to Recruit Fighters for Apocalyptic Battle," *International Business Times,* September 14, 2013, http://www.ibtimes.co.uk/isis-use-picture-cyclops-baby-recruit-fighters -apocalyptic-battle-1465323. • **PAGE 24: "Sunnis make up 85 to 90 percent"** "Sunnis and Shia: Islam's Ancient Schism," BBC News, June 20, 2014, http://www.bbc .com/news/world-middle-east-16047709. • **"in the Shia tradition, continues to this day"** Bernd Kaussler, "Is the End Nigh for the Islamic Republic?" *Current Trends in Islamist Ideology* 13 (January 2012): 69–90, http://www.hudson.org/content /researchattachments/attachment/1271/kaussler.pdf. • " **'What! Is he still alive?'** "

Muhammad Baqir As-Sadr, *An Inquiry Concerning Al-Mahdi* (Self-published and printed by CreateSpace, 2014). • **PAGE 25: "almost exclusively (90–95 percent) Shia"** "The World Fact Book: Iran" Central Intelligence Agency, accessed June 11, 2015, https://www.cia.gov/library/publications/the-world-factbook/geos/ir.html. • " **'he will behead the Western leaders'** " Reza Kahlili, "Leading Iranian Ayatollah: Islamic Messiah 'Will Behead Western Leaders,' " *The Daily Caller,* March 16, 2014, http://dailycaller.com/2014/03/16/leading-iranian-ayatollah-islamic-messiah-will -behead-western-leaders/. • **PAGE 26: " 'beads like pearls would scatter from it' "** "Translation of Sahih Muslim, Book 41: The Book Pertaining to the Turmoil and Portents of the Last Hour," University of Southern California Center for Muslim-Jewish Engagement, accessed June 11, 2015, http://www.usc.edu/org/cmje /religious-texts/hadith/muslim/041-smt.php. • " **'their blood on Jesus's lance' "** Muslim ibn al-Hajjah, *Sahih Muslim,* Hadith 6924, trans. Abdul Hamid Siddiqui, *The Only Quran,* accessed June 10, 2015, http://www.theonlyquran.com/hadith /Sahih-Muslim/?volume=41&chapter=9. • **PAGE 27: " 'to be hopeful about these developments' "** Bill Kristol, interview by Chris Wallace, *Fox News Sunday with Chris Wallace,* Fox News, February 13, 2011. • " **'that doesn't make them Kobe Bryant' "** David Remnick, "Going the Distance: On and Off the Road with Barack Obama," *The New Yorker,* January 27, 2014, http://www.newyorker.com /magazine/2014/01/27/going-the-distance-2?currentPage=all. • **PAGE 29: " 'Iraq is not for the Iraqis' "** Michael Weiss and Hassan Hassan, *Isis: Inside the Army of Terror* (New York: Regan Arts, 2015), p. 1. • " **'attacking the remaining targets and opposing the authorities' "** Michael Weiss and Hassan Hassan, *Isis: Inside the Army of Terror* (New York: Regan Arts, 2015), p. 1, 41. • **PAGE 30: "frightening (others) and masquerading' "** Michael Weiss and Hassan Hassan, *Isis: Inside the Army of Terror* (New York: Regan Arts, 2015), p. 1, 41. • " **'during their weddings' "** Rory McCarthy and Qais al-Bashir, "Suicide Bomb Attack Kills 22 at Mosque Wedding," *The Guardian,* January 21, 2005, http:// www.theguardian.com/world/2005/jan/22/iraq.rorymccarthy. • " **'they beheaded captives"** Ted Thornhill, "Raped, Tortured, Forced to Watch Beheadings, Then Beaten When They Tried to Kill Themselves: Yazidi Girls Reveal the Hell They Endured During ISIS Captivity," *Daily Mail,* October 1, 2014, http://www .dailymail.co.uk/news/article-2776268/Raped-tortured-forced-watch-beheadings -beaten-tried-kill-Yazidi-girls-reveal-hell-endured-witnessed-ISIS-captivity.html. • " **'abducted children to train as suicide bombers' "** John Hall, "ISIS Are Forcing Captured Yazidi Children to Train as Islamist Soldiers and Brainwashing Mentally Handicapped Boys into Becoming Suicide Bombers, Iraqi Politician Reveals," *Daily Mail,* May 13, 2015, http://www.dailymail.co.uk/news/article-3079975 /ISIS-forcing-captured-Yazidi-children-train-Islamist-soldiers-brainwashing-men tally-handicapped-boys-suicide-bombers-Iraqi-politician-reveals.html. • **"enslaved and raped by ISIS fighters"** Sameer N. Yacoub, "Iraqi Official: Hundreds of Yazidi Women Held Captive by Islamic State," *The Huffington Post,* August 8, 2014, http:// www.huffingtonpost.com/2014/08/08/yazidi-women-captive_n_5662805.html. • **PAGE 31: "Caliphate will be ruled from Jerusalem"** Mytheos Holt, "Egyptian Cleric Claims Muslim Brotherhood Presidential Candidate Will Make Jerusalem 'the Capital of the Caliphate,' " *TheBlaze,* May 7, 2012, http://www.theblaze.com /stories/2012/05/07/egyptian-cleric-claims-muslim-brotherhood-presidential-can didate-will-make-jerusalem-the-capital-of-the-caliphate/.

CHAPTER 2: FROM REVELATION TO EMPIRE

PAGE 32: "had been transformed into something else entirely" "The Life of Muhammad," PBS, accessed June 11, 2015, http://www.pbs.org/muhammad/timeline _html.shtml. • **PAGE 33: "have been subjected to death threats"** Tom Holland, "When I Questioned the History of Muhammad," *The Wall Street Journal*, January 9, 2015, http://www.wsj.com/articles/when-i-questioned-the-history-of -muhammad-1420821462. • **PAGE 34: "and then to others in his tribe"** "The Life of Muhammad," PBS, accessed June 11, 2015, http://www.pbs.org/muhammad /timeline_html.shtml. • **"whose name shall be Ahmed"** Quran 61: 6. • **PAGE 36: "a result of trickery by the Devil"** Quran 22: 52. • **" 'Allah is All-Knower, All-Wise' "** Quran 22:52. • **PAGE 37: "those convinced of the divinity of his message"** "The Life of Muhammad," PBS, accessed June 11, 2015, http://www.pbs.org/muhammad /timeline_html.shtml. • **"tone of his message changed dramatically"** Ira M. Lapidus, *A History of Islamic Societies*, 2nd Ed. (New York: Cambridge University Press, 2002). • **"those who wronged them and treated them badly"** "The Founding of the Community" Sacred Texts, accessed June 11, 2015, http://www.sacred-texts.com /isl/isl/isl12.htm. • **PAGE 38: " 'does not like the *Mufsidun* (mischief-makers)' "** Quran 5:64. • **" 'then surely he is one of them' "** Quran 5:51. • **" 'they have been performing' "** Quran 5:63 • **PAGE 39: " 'until the way lays down its burdens' "** Quran 47: 3–4. • **PAGE 41: "and subsequent dynasties after Ali's death"** Council on Foreign Relations, "The Struggle Between Sunni and Shia Muslims Explained," *Newsweek*, December 14, 2014, http://www.newsweek.com/struggle-between -sunni-and-shia-muslims-explained-291419. • **"or Shia—the 'party of Ali' "** "Sunnis and Shia: Islam's Ancient Schism," *BBC News*, June 20, 2015, http://www.bbc .com/news/world-middle-east-16047709. • **"complete written document until years after Muhammad's death"** *Encyclopedia Britannica Online*, "Qur'an," accessed June 12, 2015, http://www.britannica.com/EBchecked/topic/487666/Quran/261599 /Compilation. • **PAGE 42: "nearly 180 years after the prophet's death"** *Encyclopedia Britannica Online*, "Hadith," accessed June 12, 2015, http://www.britannica .com/EBchecked/topic/251132/Hadith/68899/The-compilations. • **PAGE 43: "from fines to amputation to hanging or beheading"** Nina Rastogi, "Decapitation and the Muslim World," *Slate*, February 20, 2009, http://www.slate.com/articles /news_and_politics/explainer/2009/02/decapitation_and_the_muslim_world.html. • **" 'will be a great torment' "** Quran 16:06. • **" 'who reverts from Islam and leaves the Muslims' "** Muhammad al-Bukhari, *Sahih al-Bukhari* 4:52, Hadith 260. • **PAGE 45: "at the Battle of Tours in 732"** *Encyclopedia Britannica Online*, "Battle of Tours," accessed June 12, 2015, http://www.britannica.com/EBchecked /topic/600883/Battle-of-Tours. • **" 'how disease spreads and how it can be healed'"** Barack Obama, "Remarks by the President on a New Beginning," (lecture, Cairo University, Cairo, Egypt, June 4, 2009). • **PAGE 46: " 'network of commerce and communications' "** Bernard Lewis, *What Went Wrong: The Clash Between Islam and Modernity in the Middle East* (New York: Oxford University Press, 2002), 6.

CHAPTER THREE: WAHHABISM AND SALAFISM

PAGE 48: " 'power merely through preaching' " Sayyid Qutb, *Milestones* (Kazi Publications, Lahore, Pakistan, 1964). • **"Not if the Mamluks had anything to say about it"** "Napoleon at War: Campaigns and Battles: The Egyptian Campaign," PBS, accessed June 12, 2015, http://www.pbs.org/empires/napoleon/n_war/campaign /page_3.html. • **PAGE 49: " 'forty centuries look down on you' "** "Napoleon at War: Campaigns and Battles: The Egyptian Campaign," PBS, accessed June 12, 2015, http://www.pbs.org/empires/napoleon/n_war/campaign/page_3.html. • **"ten thou-**

sand Mamluk warriors bearing sabers on horseback" Paul Strathern, *Napoleon in Egypt* (New York: Bantam, 2007), 107. • **PAGE 51: "were 'sorcerers' who believed in devil worship"** Dore Gold, *Hatred's Kingdom* (Washington, D.C.: Regnery, 2012), 25. • **"the faith practiced by Muhammad and his followers"** As'ad AbuKhalil and Mahmoud Haddad, "Revival and Renewal" *Oxford Islamic Studies Online,* accessed June 12, 2015, http://www.oxfordislamicstudies.com/article/opr/t236 /e0682. • **" 'perform jihad against the unbelievers' "** Dore Gold, *Hatred's Kingdom* (Washington, D.C.: Regnery, 2012), 20. • **PAGE 52: "more interested in amassing harems of beautiful women and material wealth"** Bernard Lewis, "Ottoman Observers of Ottoman Decline," *Islamic Studies* 1, no. 1, (March 1962): 71–87. • **PAGE 53: "the 'sick man of Europe'—the Ottoman Empire"** "The Real Sick Man of Europe," *The Economist,* May 19, 2005, http://www.economist.com/node/3987219. • **PAGE 54: "committed by the 'Jewish traitor' Atatürk"** Nick Danforth, "The Myth of the Caliphate: The Political History of an Idea," *Foreign Affairs,* November 19, 2014, https://www.foreignaffairs.com/articles/middle-east/2014–11–19/myth -caliphate?cid=rss-foreign_affairs_report-the_myth_of_the_caliphate-000000. • **PAGE 55: "Austrian Jew who launched the modern Zionist movement"** *Encyclopedia Britannica Online,* "Theodore Herzl," accessed June 12, 2015, *Encyclopedia Britannica Online.* • **"during the Palestinian riots of 1929"** "A History of Conflict: 1929–1936: Arab Discontent," BBC News, accessed June 13, 2015, http://news.bbc .co.uk/2/shared/spl/hi/middle_east/03/v3_ip_timeline/html/1929_36.stm. • **PAGE 56: "richest and most powerful family in the Muslim world"** Note: The Saudis have used the billions of dollars in oil money to advance the worldwide Salafist movement, based in Madrassas (religious schools) from one end of the Muslim World to the other. In so doing, they created the monster that attacked us on 9/11 and that now, in the form of ISIS, threatens to kill its creator, like Dr. Frankenstein's monster. • **"symbolized the unity of the Islamic faithful"** Gilles Kepel, *Jihad: The Trail of Political Islam,* trans. Anthony F. Roberts (Cambridge, MA: Belknap Press, 2002), 27. • **PAGE 57: " 'the loftiest of our wishes,' al-Banna proclaimed"** Gilles Kepel, *Jihad: The Trail of Political Islam,* trans. Anthony F. Roberts (Cambridge, MA: Belknap Press, 2002), 30. • **PAGE 58: " 'system to other countries,' Husseini proclaimed"** Alan Dershowitz, *The Case for Israel* (Hoboken, NJ: John Wiley and Sons, 2003), 54. • **PAGE 59: " 'what the prophet did thirteen centuries ago' "** Gilbert Achcar, *The Arabs and the Holocaust,* trans. G.M. Goshgarian (New York: Picador 2011), 157. • **" 'eliminate the scourge that Jews represent in the world' "** Gilbert Achcar, *The Arabs and the Holocaust,* trans. G.M. Goshgarian (New York: Picador 2011), 157. • **PAGE 60: "a young student named Osama bin Laden"** Bruce Riedel, "The 9/11 Attacks' Spiritual Father," *The Daily Beast,* September 11, 2011, http:// www.thedailybeast.com/articles/2011/09/11/abdullah-azzam-spiritual-father-of -9–11-attacks-ideas-live-on.html. • **PAGE 61: " 'she shows all this and does not hide it"** Robert Siegel, "Sayyid Qutb's America: Al Qaeda Inspiration Denounced U.S. Greed, Sexuality," NPR, May 6, 2003, http://www.npr.org/templates/story/story .php?storyId=1253796.

CHAPTER FOUR: REESTABLISHING THE CALIPHATE
PAGE 66: " 'You haven't changed a bit' " National Commission on Terrorist Attacks, *The 9/11 Commission Report: Final Report of the National Commission on Terrorist Attacks upon the United States* (New York: W.W. Norton & Company, 2004), 139. • **" 'Why do you call him a killer?' "** Thomas Harding, "Blast Survivor Tells of Massoud Assassination," *The Telegraph,* October 26, 2001, http://www.telegraph .co.uk/news/worldnews/asia/afghanistan/1360632/Blast-survivor-tells-of-Massoud

-assassination.html. • **PAGE 69: " 'would develop in the future,' he wrote"** Yassin Musharbash, "The Future of Terrorism: What al-Qaida Really Wants," *Der Spiegel,* August 22, 2005, http://www.spiegel.de/international/the-future-of-terrorism-what -al-qaida-really-wants-a-369448.html. • **" 'became a closer and easier target"** Yassin Musharbash, "The Future of Terrorism: What al-Qaida Really Wants," *Der Spiegel,* August 22, 2005, http://www.spiegel.de/international/the-future-of -terrorism-what-al-qaida-really-wants-a-369448.html. • **"and bases established in other Arabic states"** Yassin Musharbash, "The Future of Terrorism: What al-Qaida Really Wants," *Der Spiegel,* August 22, 2005, http://www.spiegel.de/international /the-future-of-terrorism-what-al-qaida-really-wants-a-369448.html. • **PAGE 72: "against the apostate rulers and their removal"** Brigitte Gabriel, *They Must Be Stopped: Why We Must Defeat Radical Islam and How We Can Do It* (New York: St. Martin's Press, 2008), 123. • **"dubbed it 'the *Mein Kampf* of jihad' "** David Ignatius, "The Manual That Chillingly Foreshadows the Islamic State," *The Washington Post,* September 25, 2014, http://www.washingtonpost.com/opinions /david-ignatius-the-mein-kampf-of-jihad/2014/09/25/4adbfc1a-44e8–11e4–9a15 –137aa0153527_story.html. • **"would lose its 'aura of invincibility' "** Abu Bakr Naji, *The Management of Savagery: The Most Critical Stage Through Which the Umma Will Pass,* trans. William McCants (Cambridge, MA: John M. Olin Institute for Strategic Studies at Harvard University, 2006), https://azelin.files.wordpress .com/2010/08/abu-bakr-naji-the-management-of-savagery-the-most-critical-stage -through-which-the-umma-will-pass.pdf. • **" 'will lead to an increase in savagery' "** Abu Bakr Naji, *The Management of Savagery: The Most Critical Stage Through Which the Umma Will Pass,* trans. William McCants (Cambridge, MA: John M. Olin Institute for Strategic Studies at Harvard University, 2006), https://azelin .files.wordpress.com/2010/08/abu-bakr-naji-the-management-of-savagery-the -most-critical-stage-through-which-the-umma-will-pass.pdf. • **PAGE 73: " 'knew the effect of rough violence in times of need' "** Abu Bakr Naji, *The Management of Savagery: The Most Critical Stage Through Which the Umma Will Pass,* trans. William McCants (Cambridge, MA: John M. Olin Institute for Strategic Studies at Harvard University, 2006), https://azelin.files.wordpress.com/2010/08/abu-bakr -naji-the-management-of-savagery-the-most-critical-stage-through-which-the -umma-will-pass.pdf. • **" 'such that death is a heartbeat away' "** Abu Bakr Naji, *The Management of Savagery: The Most Critical Stage Through Which the Umma Will Pass,* trans. William McCants (Cambridge, MA: John M. Olin Institute for Strategic Studies at Harvard University, 2006), https://azelin.files.wordpress .com/2010/08/abu-bakr-naji-the-management-of-savagery-the-most-critical-stage -through-which-the-umma-will-pass.pdf. • **" 'the most sparing of the spilling of blood' "** Abu Bakr Naji, *The Management of Savagery: The Most Critical Stage Through Which the Umma Will Pass,* trans. William McCants (Cambridge, MA: John M. Olin Institute for Strategic Studies at Harvard University, 2006), https:// azelin.files.wordpress.com/2010/08/abu-bakr-naji-the-management-of-savagery -the-most-critical-stage-through-which-the-umma-will-pass.pdf. • **"responsible for the deaths of twice that many people"** Lawrence Wright, "The Master Plan," *The New Yorker,* September 11, 2006, http://www.newyorker.com/maga zine/2006/09/11/the-master-plan. • **PAGE 75: " 'just the train we board to reach our destination' "** Andrew C. McCarthy, *Spring Fever: The Illusion of Islamic Democracy* (New York: Encounter, 2013), 3. • **" 'make them slaves to Allah,' explained Abu Abdullah"** Brigitte Gabriel, *They Must Be Stopped: Why We Must Defeat Radical Islam and How We Can Do It* (New York: St. Martin's Press, 2008). • **" 'religious duty imposed by the Holy Law"** Bernard Lewis, "Communism and

Islam," *International Affairs* 30, no. 1 (January 1954), 1–12. • **PAGE 76: " 'and we only fill in the blanks' "** Andrew C. McCarthy, *The Grand Jihad: How Islam and the Left Sabotage America* (New York: Encounter, 2010), 88. • **"groups such as Jabhat al-Nusra and the Yarmouk Brigade"** Patrick Cockburn, "How the US Helped ISIS Grow Into a Monster," *Mother Jones,* August 21, 2014, http://www.motherjones.com/politics/2014/08/how-us-helped-isis-grow-monster-iraq-syria-assad. • **"administration saw little danger in the growing menace"** David Remnick, "Going the Distance: On and Off the Road with Barack Obama," *The New Yorker,* January 27, 2014, http://www.newyorker.com/magazine/2014/01/27/going-the-distance-2?currentPage=all. • **PAGE 77: "and dozens of other jihadi groups pledge allegiance"** Patrick Cockburn, "How the US Helped ISIS Grow Into a Monster," *Mother Jones,* August 21, 2014, http://www.motherjones.com/politics/2014/08/how-us-helped-isis-grow-monster-iraq-syria-assad. • **PAGE 78: " 'self-recruited and can spring up anywhere' "** Patrick Cockburn, "How the US Helped ISIS Grow Into a Monster," *Mother Jones,* August 21, 2014, http://www.motherjones.com/politics/2014/08/how-us-helped-isis-grow-monster-iraq-syria-assad. • **PAGE 79: "only effective fighting force against the Islamic State"** Frederik Pleitgen, "'We Will Destroy ISIS': Iranian Militia Vows to Fight Terror Group," CNN, April 22, 2015, http://www.cnn.com/2015/04/22/middleeast/iran-fighting-isis/. • **"in Bahrain and Yemen to foment instability"** Yara Bayoumy and Mohammed Ghobari, "Iranian Support Seen Crucial for Yemen's Houthis," Reuters, December 15, 2014, http://www.reuters.com/article/2014/12/15/us-yemen-houthis-iran-insight-idUSKBN0JT17A20141215. • **" 'keep things in perspective and in the categories' "** Damien Cave, "For Congress: Telling Sunni from Shiite," The *New York Times,* December 17, 2006, http://www.nytimes.com/2006/12/17/weekinreview/17cave.html?_r=2&. • **PAGE 80: " 'off-the-shelf' atomic weapons from Pakistan"** Tom Harnden and Christina Lamb, "Saudis 'to Get Nuclear Weapons,' " *The Sunday Times,* May 17, 2015, http://www.thesundaytimes.co.uk/sto/news/world_news/Middle_East/article1557090.ece. • **" 'every single Sunni there is a Daesh' "** Anne Barnard and Tim Arango, "Using Violence and Persuasion, ISIS Makes Political Gains," *The New York Times,* June 3, 2015, http://www.nytimes.com/2015/06/04/world/isis-making-political-gains.html?emc=edit_th_20150604&nl=todaysheadlines&nlid=55829462&_r=1&referrer. • **"an Arabic term that means 'cute little Daesh' "** Anne Barnard and Tim Arango, "Using Violence and Persuasion, ISIS Makes Political Gains," *The New York Times,* June 3, 2015, http://www.nytimes.com/2015/06/04/world/isis-making-political-gains.html?emc=edit_th_20150604&nl=todaysheadlines&nlid=55829462&_r=1&referrer.

PART TWO: THIRTEEN DEADLY LIES

INTRODUCTION TO PART TWO

PAGE 85: "headline 'Is the Bible more violent than the Quran?' " Barbara Bradley Hagerty, "Is the Bible More Violent Than the Quran?" NPR, March 18, 2010, http://www.npr.org/templates/story/story.php?storyId=124494788. • **PAGE 87: " 'which is aberrant, undeveloped, inferior' "** Edward Said, "Arabs, Islam, and the Dogmas of the West," *The New York Times Book Review,* October 31, 1976. • **"assigned as reading in at least 868 courses in American colleges"** Joshua Muravchik, "Enough Said: The False Scholarship of Edward Said," *World Affairs,* March/April 2013, http://www.worldaffairsjournal.org/article/enough-said-false-scholarship-edward-said. • **" 'an imperialist, and almost totally ethnocentric' "** Joshua Muravchik, "Enough Said: The False Scholarship of Edward Said," *World Affairs,* March/April

2013, http://www.worldaffairsjournal.org/article/enough-said-false-scholarship
-edward-said. • **PAGE 89: "the 25,000 global incidents . . . we've endured"** "List of
Islamic Terrorist Attacks for the Last 30 Days," Islam: The Politically Incorrect Truth,
accessed June 16, 2015, http://www.thereligionofpeace.com/index.html#Attacks.

LIE #1: ISLAM IS A RELIGION OF PEACE, AND ISLAMIC TERRORISTS AREN'T REALLY MUSLIMS

PAGE 92: " 'Islam is a religion that preaches peace' " Barack Obama, interview by
Steve Kroft, *60 Minutes*, CBS, September 28, 2014, http://www.cbsnews.com/news
/president-obama-60-minutes/. • **" 'that's not what the Koran says' "** Yehuda
Remer, "Howard Dean: 'I Stopped Calling These People Muslim Terrorists' and
'ISIS Is a Cult,' " TruthRevolt, January 7, 2015, http://www.truthrevolt.org/news
/howard-dean-i-stopped-calling-these-people-muslim-terrorists-and-isis-cult. •
"repeated by . . . sports stars" Shawna Thomas, "Kareem Abdul-Jabbar on *Meet the
Press:* 'Islam Is a Religion of Peace,' " NBC, January 25, 2015, http://www.nbcnews
.com/storyline/middle-east-unrest/kareem-abdul-jabbar-meet-press-islam-reli
gion-peace-n293201. • **"repeated by . . . the pope"** Josephine McKenna, "Pope
Challenges Muslims to Condemn Violence," *USA Today,* December 23, 2014, http://
www.usatoday.com/story/news/world/2014/12/23/pope-francis-muslim-christian
-middle-east-christmas/20816259/. • **"and even terrorists themselves"** Daniel
Greenfield, "Sydney Hostage Taker: 'Islam Is the Religion of Peace,' " *FrontPage
Mag,* December 15, 2014, http://www.frontpagemag.com/2014/dgreenfield/sydney
-hostage-taker-islam-is-the-religion-of-peace/. • **PAGE 93: " 'Islam is peace' "** The
White House, Office of the Press Secretary, " 'Islam Is Peace,' Says President," press
release, September 17, 2001, http://georgewbush-whitehouse.archives.gov/news
/releases/2001/09/20010917-11.html. • **" 'benevolence that is at the heart of
Islam' "** "Rice Welcomes Muslim Generosity as Reflection of Ramadan Spirit," US
Embassy in Chad, October 25, 2005, http://ndjamena.usembassy.gov/rice_welcomes
_muslim_generosity_as_reflection_of_ramadan_spirit_10/25/2005.html. • **"Holder
explained in his testimony"** *Oversight of the US Department of Justice Hearing
Before the Committee on the Judiciary, US House of Representatives,* 111th Cong.
(2010) (statement of Eric Holder, Attorney General of the United States), http://
judiciary.house.gov/_files/hearings/pdf/Holder100513.pdf. • **"who have 'distorted'
the Islamic faith"** David Lauter, "Hillary Clinton Warns US 'Can't Close Our Eyes'
to Muslim Extremism," *Los Angeles Times,* January 21, 2015, http://www.latimes
.com/nation/politics/politicsnow/la-pn-hillary-terrorism-20150121-story.html. •
"believe that Islam is a 'peaceful religion' " Jon Cohen and Jennifer Agiesta, "Americans Support Goal of Improved Relations with Muslim World," *Washington Post,*
April 6, 2009, http://www.washingtonpost.com/wp-dyn/content/article/2009/04/05
/AR2009040501586.html?hpid=topnews. • **"52 percent of Americans now believe
that Islam encourages violence"** "Americans Think Islam Needs to Clean Up Its
Act," Rasmussen Reports, January 13, 2015, http://www.rasmussenreports.com
/public_content/politics/general_politics/january_2015/americans_think_islam
_needs_to_clean_up_its_act. • **PAGE 94: " 'In brief, Islam = Submission' "** Daniel
Pipes, " 'Islam' Does Not Mean 'Peace,' " *Lion's Den* (blog), *Daniel Pipes Middle East
Forum,* October 18, 2014, http://www.danielpipes.org/blog/2005/10/islam-does
-not-mean-peace. • **"and a cofounder of the terrorist group Al-Muhajiroun"**
Alan Travis, "Extremist Islamist Groups to Be Banned Under New Terror Laws,"
The Guardian, January 11, 2010, http://www.theguardian.com/politics/2010/jan/11
/islam4uk-al-muhajiroun-ban-laws. • **justifying the attack by al-Qaeda-linked
terrorists"** Catherine E. Shoichet and Josh Levs, "Al-Qaeda Branch Claims Charlie

Hebdo Attack Was Years in the Making," CNN, January 21, 2015, http://www.cnn
.com/2015/01/14/europe/charlie-hebdo-france-attacks/. • **"killed twelve journalists and a Paris policeman"** Ray Sanchez, Ed Payne, and Ashley Fantz, "French
Cartoonists Killed in Paris Took a Profane Aim at the World," CNN, January
9, 2015, http://www.cnn.com/2015/01/07/world/france-magazine-attack-victims/.
• **" 'and not based on people's desires' "** Anjem Choudary, "People Know the
Consequences: Opposing View," *USA Today*, January 8, 2015, http://www.usatoday
.com/story/opinion/2015/01/07/islam-allah-muslims-shariah-anjem-choudary-edi
torials-debates/21417461/. • **"Christians speak about 'surrendering' to God's will"**
Rick Warren, "Surrender: Let Go and Let God Work," Daily Hope with Rick Warren, May 21, 2014, http://rickwarren.org/devotional/english/surrender-let-go-and
-let-god-work_993. • **PAGE 95: " 'surrender their livelihoods and follow him' "**
Rosemary Pennington, "What Is the Meaning of the Word 'Islam'?" Muslim Voices,
October 1, 2008, http://muslimvoices.org/word-islam-meaning/. • **" 'as if he has
saved all of mankind' "** "TRANSCRIPT: Remarks of President Obama in Cairo,"
Fox News, June 4, 2009, http://www.foxnews.com/politics/2009/06/04/transcript
-remarks-president-obama-cairo/. • **" 'to exceed the limits . . . in the land!' "**
Quran 5:32. • **PAGE 96: " 'refers to various types of evil' "** Ibn Kathir, "The Punishment of Those Who Cause Mischief in the Land," Quran Tafsir Ibn Kathir, accessed June 17, 2015, http://www.qtafsir.com/index.php?option=com_content&ta
sk=view&id=784&Itemid=60. • **" 'and feel themselves subdued' "** Quran 9: 29. •
PAGE 98: " 'feeble indeed is the plot of Shaitan (Satan)' " "Full Text: bin Laden's
'Letter to America,' " *The Guardian*, November 24, 2002, http://www.theguard
ian.com/world/2002/nov/24/theobserver. • **PAGE 99: " 'Islam is not a religion
of peace' "** Ayaan Hirsi Ali, "Islam Is Not a Religion of Peace: Ayaan Hirsi Ali,"
Salon, April 4, 2015, http://www.salon.com/2015/04/04/islam_is_not_a_religion
_of_peace_ayaan_hirsi_ali/. • **PAGE 100: " 'which he has made known to them' "**
"Transcript: al-Baghdadi's Latest Message," Inside the Jihad, May 14, 2015, http://
insidethejihad.com/2015/05/transcript-al-baghdadis-latest-message/. • **" 'Islam is
the religion of war' "** Robert Spencer, "Islamic State Caliph: 'Islam Is The Religion
of War,' " *Jihad Watch*, May 14, 2015, http://www.jihadwatch.org/2015/05/islamic
-state-caliph-islam-is-the-religion-of-war.

LIE #2: ISLAM IS NOT THAT MUCH DIFFERENT THAN CHRISTIANITY OR JUDAISM

PAGE 101: " 'religions have been violent, including Christianity' " Lisette Thooft,
"Karen Armstrong: 'There Is Nothing in the Islam That Is More Violent Than Christianity," *Nieuwwij*, January 18, 2015, http://www.nieuwwij.nl/english/karen-armstrong
-nothing-islam-violent-christianity/. •**" 'less violent than those in the Bible' "** Barbara Bradley Hagerty, "Is the Bible More Violent Than the Quran?" NPR, March 18,
2010, http://www.npr.org/templates/story/story.php?storyId=124494788. • **PAGE
102: " 'civilization and heritage that we all share'"** Garry Gutting, "How Does
Islam Relate to Christianity and Judaism?" *The Stone* (blog), *The New York Times*,
September 25, 2014, http://opinionator.blogs.nytimes.com/2014/09/25/why-do
-shiites-and-sunnis-fight/?_r=1. • **"as a literal or figurative father of the religion"**
"Religions: Judaism: Abraham," BBC, accessed June 17, 2015, http://www.bbc.co.uk
/religion/religions/judaism/history/abraham_1.shtml. • **"is descended from Abraham as well"** Dr. Mona Siddiqui, "Religions: Islam: Ibrahim—The Muslim View of
Abraham," BBC, accessed June 17, 2015, http://www.bbc.co.uk/religion/religions
/islam/history/ibrahim.shtml. • **" 'the entire assembly is to stone him' "** Lev. 24:13.
• **PAGE 103: " 'My kingdom is not of this world' "** John 18: 36. • **" 'to God what**

is God's' " Mark 12: 17. • " 'including a full program for government' " Robert Spencer, *Religion of Peace? Why Christianity Is and Islam Isn't* (Washington, D.C.: Regnery, 2007), 165. • **PAGE 104:** " 'and Islam became a state' " Robert Spencer, *Religion of Peace? Why Christianity Is and Islam Isn't* (Washington, D.C.: Regnery, 2007), 165. • " 'must be the ruling ideology of the state' " Robert Spencer, *Religion of Peace? Why Christianity Is and Islam Isn't* (Washington, D.C.: Regnery, 2007), 166. • **"broad support in the Muslim world today"** The Pew Forum on Religion and Public Life, *The World's Muslims: Religion, Politics, and Society* (Washington, D.C.: Pew Research Center, 2013), chap. 1, http://www.pewforum.org/2013/04/30 /the-worlds-muslims-religion-politics-society-beliefs-about-sharia/. • " **'from lashes to banishment to death'** " The Pew Forum on Religion and Public Life, *The World's Muslims: Religion, Politics, and Society* (Washington, D.C.: Pew Research Center, 2013), app. B, http://www.pewforum.org/2013/04/30/the-worlds-muslims-religion -politics-society-appb/. • **PAGE 105: "Percentage supporting by country"** The Pew Forum on Religion and Public Life, *The World's Muslims: Religion, Politics, and Society* (Washington, D.C.: Pew Research Center, 2013), chap. 1, http://www .pewforum.org/2013/04/30/the-worlds-muslims-religion-politics-society-beliefs -about-sharia/#how-should-sharia-be-applied. • **"Even in Russia, 26 percent of Muslims"** The Pew Forum on Religion and Public Life, *The World's Muslims: Religion, Politics, and Society* (Washington, D.C.: Pew Research Center, 2013), chap. 1, http://www.pewforum.org/2013/04/30/the-worlds-muslims-religion-politics -society-beliefs-about-sharia/#how-should-sharia-be-applied. • **PAGE 106: "Nearly everyone in the crowd raised a hand"** Michael W. Chapman, "Norway Islamic Leader: 'Every Muslim' Wants 'Death Penalty for Homosexuals,' " CNS News, February 3, 2015, http://cnsnews.com/blog/michael-w-chapman/norway-islamic -leader-every-muslim-wants-death-penalty-homosexuals. • **"declared that homosexuals should be stoned"** Sam Greenhill, "All Homosexuals Should Be Stoned to Death, Says Muslim Preacher of Hate," *Daily Mail*, March 20, 2009, http:// www.dailymail.co.uk/news/article-1163510/All-homosexuals-stoned-death-says -Muslim-preacher-hate.html#ixzz3an7ys8L8. • **"famously reminded at audience at the National Prayer Breakfast"** Ross Douthat, "Obama the Theologian," *The New York Times*, February 7, 2015, http://www.nytimes.com/2015/02/08/opinion /sunday/ross-douthat-obama-the-theologian.html. • **PAGE 107:** " **'medieval Christendom's conflict with Europe'** " Ross Douthat, "Obama the Theologian," *New York Times*, February 7, 2015, http://www.nytimes.com/2015/02/08/opinion/sunday /ross-douthat-obama-the-theologian.html?rref=collection%2Fcolumn%2Fross -douthat. • **"since the eighth century A.D."** *Encyclopedia Britannica Online*, "Reconquista," accessed June 17, 2015, http://www.britannica.com/EBchecked /topic/493710/Reconquista. • " **'could have escaped conquest by Muslim armies'** " *Encyclopedia Britannica Online*, "Crusades: The Results of the Crusades," accessed June 17, 2015, http://www.britannica.com/EBchecked/topic/144695/Crusades /235543/The-results-of-the-Crusades. • **"held back from seizing Vienna in 1683"** Walter Leitsch, "1683: The Siege of Vienna," *History Today* 33, no. 7 (July 1983), http://www.historytoday.com/walter-leitsch/1683-siege-vienna.

LIE #3: "JIHAD IS A PEACEFUL, INTERNAL STRUGGLE, NOT A WAR AGAINST INFIDELS."
PAGE 108: " **'to do good works and help to reform society'** " John L. Esposito, *What Everyone Needs to Know About Islam* (New York: Oxford University Press, 2011), 117. • " **'it is about taking personal responsibility'** " "About the MyJihad Campaign," MyJihad, accessed June 17, 2015, http://myjihad.org/about/. • " **'Muslims strive to**

attain this every day' " Alex Seitz-Wald, "Can 'Jihad' Survive Pam Geller?" *Salon,* January 9, 2013, http://www.salon.com/2013/01/09/can_jihad_be_rebranded/. • **PAGE 109: " 'against oppressors if that's the only way'** " Brian Handwerk, "What Does 'Jihad' Really Mean to Muslims?" *National Geographic,* October 24, 2003, http://news.nationalgeographic.com/news/2003/10/1023_031023_jihad.html. • **" 'about taking personal responsibility . . .'** " "About the MyJihad Campaign," MyJihad, accessed June 17, 2015, http://myjihad.org/about/. • **PAGE 110: " 'lavishly Saudi-funded Prince Alwaleed bin Talal Center"** Caryle Murphy, "Saudi Gives $20 Million to Georgetown," *Washington Post,* December 13, 2005, http://www.washingtonpost.com/wp-dyn/content/article/2005/12/12/AR2005121200591 .html. • **"to do good works and help to reform society'** " John L. Esposito, *What Everyone Needs to Know About Islam* (New York: Oxford University Press, 2011), 117. • **" 'commitment to peace and social justice'** " John L. Esposito, letter to Judge Leonie Brinkema, July 2, 2008, http://www.investigativeproject.org /documents/misc/144.pdf. • **"designated Palestinian terrorist organization"** Elaine Silvestrini, "Al-Arian Admits His Role in Jihad," *Tampa Tribune,* April 18, 2006. • **" 'democracy, pluralism, and human rights'** " John L. Esposito, "Islam and the Power of Democracy," *Boston Review,* April 1, 2003, http://bostonreview.net/forum /islam-and-challenge-democracy/john-l-esposito-practice-and-theory. • **PAGE 111: " 'be at the hands of the believers'** " "Sheikh Yousuf Al-Qaradhawi: Allah Imposed Hitler on the Jews to Punish Them—'Allah Willing the Next Time Will Be at the Hand of the Believers,' " The Middle East Research Institute, February 3, 2009, http://www .memri.org/report/en/0/0/0/0/0/0/0/3062.htm. • **" 'most important action for the sake of mankind'** " "Jihad in the Hadith" Peace with Realism, accessed June 17, 2015, http://www.peacewithrealism.org/jihad/jihad03.htm. • **PAGE 112: " 'arms must be taken up in a just war'** " Kabir Helminski, "Does the Quran Really Sanction Violence Against 'Unbelievers'?" *The Blog* (blog), *Huffington Post,* September 24, 2010, http://www.huffingtonpost.com/kabir-helminski/does-the-quran -really-adv_b_722114.html. • **" 'and it is the lesser Jihad'** " *Reliance of the Traveller,* Revised Edition (Beltsville: Amana, 1988), 599, http://www.islamicbulletin.org /free_downloads/resources/reliance2_complete.pdf. • **PAGE 113: " 'fight the idolaters utterly'** " *Reliance of the Traveller,* Revised Edition (Beltsville: Amana, 1988), 617, http://www.islamicbulletin.org/free_downloads/resources/reliance2_complete .pdf. • **" 'their final reckoning is with Allah'** " Muslim ibn al-Hajjah, *Sahih Muslim,* Hadith 01: 33, University of Southern California Center for Muslim-Jewish Engagement, accessed June 17, 2015, http://www.usc.edu/org/cmje/religious-texts/hadith /muslim/001-smt.php#001.0033. • **" 'perform the prayer, and pay zakat'** " Muslim ibn al-Hajjah, *Sahih Muslim,* Hadith 01: 33, University of Southern California Center for Muslim-Jewish Engagement, accessed June 17, 2015, http://www.usc.edu /org/cmje/religious-texts/hadith/muslim/001-smt.php#001.0033. • **PAGE 114: " 'establish their religion among their own people'** " Ibn Khaldun, *The Muqaddimah: An Introduction* (Princeton, NJ: Princeton University Press, 1969), ch. 3, http://www.muslimphilosophy.com/ik/Muqaddimah/Chapter3/Ch_3_31.htm. • **PAGE 115: " 'and all means of land and sea fighting'** " Hasan al-Banna, *Kitabul Jihad,* in *Milestones,* ed. A.B. al-Mehri (Birmingham, England: Maktabah, 2006), 220. • **" 'non-Muslims must accept either Islam or death'** " Maulana Waris Mazhari, "A Critique of the Doctrine of Offensive Jihad," trans. Yoginder Sikand, *The American Muslim,* May 8, 2010, http://theamericanmuslim.org/tam.php/features/articles/a _critique_of_the_doctrine_of_offensive_jihad. • **PAGE 116: " 'who is attacking religion and life'** " World Islamic Front, "Jihad Against Jews and Crusaders," statement, accessed June 17, 2015, http://fas.org/irp/world/para/docs/980223-fatwa

.htm. • **PAGE 117:** " 'who have no means of defending themselves' " Muhammad Hussein Fadlallah, "The Many Meanings of Jihad to 2 Prominent Muslims," *The Washington Post,* July 28, 2007, http://www.washingtonpost.com/wp-dyn/content/article/2007/07/27/AR2007072701863.html. • **PAGE 118: "some 60 million throughout the Muslim world"** David Schenker, "Qaradawi and the Struggle for Sunni Islam," The Washington Institute for Near East Policy, October 16, 2013, http://www.washingtoninstitute.org/policy-analysis/view/qaradawi-and-the-struggle-for-sunni-islam. • " 'who controlled the necks and minds of men' " Al Mutarjim, "Al-Qaradawi: '[Moderate Muslims] Accept Offensive Jihad, and Attacking the Infidels in Their Land,' " *Translating Jihad* (blog), June 2, 2011, https://web.archive.org/web/20110607045544/http://www.translatingjihad.com/2011/06/al-qaradawi-moderate-muslims-accept.html.

LIE #4: "MUSLIMS DON'T ACTUALLY SEEK TO LIVE UNDER SHARIA, LET ALONE IMPOSE IT ON OTHERS; THERE ARE SO MANY DIFFERENT INTERPRETATIONS OF IT ANYWAY."

PAGE 120: " 'This leads to many different interpretations' " "The GOP and the Sharia Myth," Chicago Office of the Council on American Islamic Relations, June 23, 2011, http://www.cairchicago.org/blog/2011/06/the-gop-and-the-sharia-myth/. • " 'incorporated into political systems relatively easily"** Toni Johnson and Mohammed Aly Sergie, "Islam: Governing Under Sharia," Council on Foreign Relations, July 25, 2014, http://www.cfr.org/religion/islam-governing-under-sharia/p8034. • **PAGE 121: "imposed on 'any unwilling persons' "** Qasim Rashid, "Shariah Law: The Five Things Every Non-Muslim (and Muslim) Should Know," *The Blog* (blog), *Huffington Post,* November 4, 2011, http://www.huffingtonpost.com/qasim-rashid/shariah-law-the-five-things-every-non-muslim_b_1068569.html. • **"it governs and dictates everything"** Clare Lopez, ed., *Sharia: The Threat to America: An Exercise in Competitive Analysis* (Washington, D.C.: Center for Security Policy, 2010), 57. • **PAGE 122:** " 'it would be doomed from the start' " Imran Ahsan Khan Nyazee, *Theories of Islamic Law: The Methodology of Ijtihad* (Islamabad: International Institute of Islamic and The Islamic Research Institute, 1994). • **"widespread support for the adoption of sharia law"** The Pew Forum on Religion and Public Life, *The World's Muslims: Religion, Politics, and Society* (Washington, D.C.: Pew Research Center, 2013), overview, http://www.pewforum.org/2013/04/30/the-worlds-muslims-religion-politics-society-overview/. • **PAGE 123:** " 'thus defines the Muslim's belief in God"** Feisal Abdul Rauf, *Islam: A Sacred Law: What Every Muslim Should Know About the Shari'ah* (Brattleboro, VT: Qibla Books, 2000), 58. • **PAGE 124:** " 'referring to His law for judgment' "** Islamic State, "This Is the Promise of Allah," Al-Hayat Media Center, accessed June 17, 2015, http://gtrp.haverford.edu/aqsi/aqsi-statement/816. • **PAGE 125:** " 'establish the Shari'a of Allah on earth' "** Raymond Ibrahim, "An Analysis of Al-Qa'ida's Worldview: Reciprocal Treatment or Religious Observation?" Middle East Forum, accessed June 17, 2015, http://www.meforum.org/2043/an-analysis-of-al-qaidas-worldview. • " 'goals of Islam and the true religion' "** "Bylaws of the International Muslim Brotherhood," The Investigative Project on Terrorism, accessed June 17, 2015, http://www.investigativeproject.org/documents/misc/673.pdf. • **"goal of installing Islamic law worldwide"** Richard C. Martin, Said Amir Arjomand, Marcia Harmansen, Abdulkader Tayob, and Rochelle Davis, eds., *Encyclopedia of Islam and the Muslim World* (New York: Macmillan, 2003), 371. • **PAGE 126:** " 'naturally bound to be world revolution' "** Syed Abul 'Ala Maududi, "Jihad in Islam," (speech, Town Hall, Lahore, Pakistan, April 13, 1939), http://muhammadanism.com/Terrorism/jihah_in_islam/jihad_in_islam.pdf.

LIE #5: "AMERICA IS SAFE FROM SHARIA LAW"

PAGE 127: " 'legislation that actually undermines our courts' " Abed Awad, "The True Story of Sharia in American Courts," *The Nation,* June 13, 2012, http://www .thenation.com/article/168378/true-story-sharia-american-courts#. • " 'Islamic law is encroaching on our courts' " "Nothing to Fear: Debunking the Mythical 'Sharia Threat' to Our Judicial System," American Civil Liberties Union, accessed June 17, 2015, https://www.aclu.org/report/nothing-fear-debunking-mythical-sharia-threat -our-judicial-system. PAGE 128: • "judicial system enjoyed by people of other creeds' " "Nothing to Fear: Debunking the Mythical 'Sharia Threat' to Our Judicial System," American Civil Liberties Union, accessed June 17, 2015, https://www.aclu .org/report/nothing-fear-debunking-mythical-sharia-threat-our-judicial-system. • " 'commercial disputes and negligence matters' " Abed Awad, "The True Story of Sharia in American Courts," *The Nation,* June 13, 2012, http://www.thenation .com/article/168378/true-story-sharia-american-courts#. • PAGE 129: " 'It will suit every age and time' " Stephen Coughlin, *Catastrophic Failure: Blindfolding America in the Face of Jihad* (self-published and printed by CreateSpace, 2015), 56. • " 'to succeed in the solution of their problems' " Stephen Coughlin, *Catastrophic Failure: Blindfolding America in the Face of Jihad* (self-published and printed by CreateSpace, 2015), 57. • PAGE 130: " 'complete lack of Islamic alternatives' " "Decisions and Recommendations of the Fifth Conference of the Assembly of Muslim Journalists in America," Assembly of Muslim Journalists in America, accessed June 18, 2015, http://www.amjaonline.org/en/declarations/20-declarations/53-deci sions-and-recommendations-of-amja-s-fifth-annual-convention. • " 'enable them to judge by Islamic Law' " "Decisions and Recommendations of the Fifth Conference of the Assembly of Muslim Journalists in America," Assembly of Muslim Journalists in America, accessed June 18, 2015, http://www.amjaonline.org/en /declarations/20-declarations/53-decisions-and-recommendations-of-amja-s-fifth -annual-convention. • " 'in his heart hate the man-made law' " Stephen Coughlin, *Catastrophic Failure: Blindfolding America in the Face of Jihad* (self-published and printed by CreateSpace, 2015), 58–59. • PAGE 131: "Fortunately this decision was reversed on appeal" Maxim Lott, "Advocates of Anti-Sharia Measures Alarmed by Judge's Ruling," Fox News, August 5, 2010, http://www.foxnews.com/us/2010/08/05 /advocates-anti-shariah-measures-alarmed-judges-ruling/. • " 'erred by looking to Islamic law' " Marriage of Obaidi, 227 P. 3d 787 (Wash. Ct. App. 2010), http://leg .mt.gov/bills/2015/Minutes/Senate/Exhibits/jus27a06.pdf. • " 'appeared to defer' to the sharia court" Center for Security Policy, *Sharia in American Courts: The Expanding Incursion of Islamic Law in the US Legal System* (Washington, D.C.: Center for Security Policy Press, 2014). • PAGE 132: "established itself as a sharia court in Irving" "North Texas Islamic Tribunal Using Sharia Law to Settle Disputes," KTUL ABC News, February 16, 2015, http://www.ktul.com/story/28063464/north -texas-islamic-tribunal-using-sharia-law-to-settle-disputes. • " 'He will never do it' " Wilson Garrett, "Sharia Law in Texas? Don't Miss the Incredible Interview," Glenn Beck, February 9, 2015, http://www.glennbeck.com/2015/02/09/sharia-law -in-texas-dont-miss-this-incredible-interview/. • "only passed by a 5–4 vote" Avi Selk, "Irving City Council Backs State Bill Muslims Say Targets Them," *The Dallas Morning News,* Mach 19, 2015, http://www.dallasnews.com/news/metro/20150319 -dispute-on-islam-roils-irving.ece. • " 'more than eighty sharia courts in 2009' " Divya Talwar, "Growing Use of Sharia by UK Muslims," BBC News, January 16, 2012, http://www.bbc.co.uk/news/mobile/uk-16522447. • "custody of children to violent spouses" Jane Corbin, "Are Sharia Councils Failing Vulnerable Women?" BBC News, April 7, 2013, http://www.bbc.com/news/uk-22044724. • "Muslim leaders looking to set up their own courts" "North Texas Islamic Tribunal Using Sharia Law to Settle Disputes," KTUL ABC News, February 16, 2015, http://www.ktul.com /story/28063464/north-texas-islamic-tribunal-using-sharia-law-to-settle-disputes. • " 'that we stop protecting our own,' she said" Dina Samir Shehata, "Anti-Sharia Bill Dead, but Sentiment Alive," *The Austin Chronicle,* May 22, 2015, http://www .austinchronicle.com/news/2015–05–22/anti-sharia-bill-dead-but-sentiment-alive/.

LIE #6: THE CALIPHATE IS A FANCIFUL DREAM
PAGE 134: " 'Robert Welch and the John Birch Society' " William Kristol, "Stand for Freedom," *The Weekly Standard,* February 14, 2011, http://www.weeklystandard .com/articles/stand-freedom_541404.html. • " 'a feckless delusion that is never going to happen' " Brendan Bordelon, "Flashback: Top Obama Advisor Claimed Terrorist Caliphate 'Absurd,' 'Never Going to Happen,' " *The Daily* Caller, August 12, 2014. • " 'No, I don't believe that at all' " "CNN's Acosta to Earnest: Do You Believe ISIS Has Established a Caliphate? Earnest: No" Real Clear Politics, May 21, 2015, http://www.realclearpolitics.com/video/2015/05/21/cnns_acosta_to_earnest_do _you_believe_isis_has_established_a_caliphate_earnest_no.html. • **"what *US News and World Reports* . . .** militants' 'caliphate' " Paul D. Shinkman, "War of Words: Ramadi a Propaganda Coup for ISIS," *US News and World Reports,* May 18, 2015, isis-takeover-in-ramadi-a-worrisome-victory-in-the-propaganda-war. • **PAGE 135: "as well as other outlets . . . militants' 'caliphate' "** Patrick Cockburn, "Life Under ISIS: The Everyday Reality of Living in the Islamic 'Caliphate' with Its 7th Century Laws, Very Modern Methods, and Merciless Violence," *The Independent,* March 15, 2015, http://www.independent.co.uk/news/world/middle-east/life-under-isis-the -everyday-reality-of-living-in-the-islamic-caliphate-with-its-7th-century-laws -very-modern-methods-and-merciless-violence-10109655.html. • " **'true message and governing system of Islam' "** Stephen Coughlin, *Catastrophic Failure: Blindfolding America in the Face of Jihad* (self-published and printed by CreateSpace, 2015), 151. • " **'extend its power to the entire planet' "** Stephen Coughlin, *Catastrophic Failure: Blindfolding America in the Face of Jihad* (self-published and printed by CreateSpace, 2015), 153. • **PAGE 136:** " **'are sinful for if they do not try to establish' "** Islamic State, "This Is the Promise of Allah," Al-Hayat Media Center, accessed June 18, 2015, http://gtrp.haverford.edu/aqsi/aqsi-statement/816. • " **'the most rigid interpretation of the Koran"** Elisabeth Bumiller, "21st-Century Warnings of a Threat Rooted in the 7th," *The New York Times,* December 12, 2005, http://www .nytimes.com/2005/12/12/politics/21stcentury-warnings-of-a-threat-rooted-in-the -7th.html. • " **'legitimate governments in Europe, Africa, and Asia' "** Elisabeth Bumiller, "21st-Century Warnings of a Threat Rooted in the 7th," *The New York Times,* December 12, 2005, http://www.nytimes.com/2005/12/12/politics/21stcentury -warnings-of-a-threat-rooted-in-the-7th.html. • " **'intend to do from their own words' "** Elisabeth Bumiller, "21st-Century Warnings of a Threat Rooted in the 7th," *The New York Times,* December 12, 2005, http://www.nytimes.com/2005/12/12 /politics/21stcentury-warnings-of-a-threat-rooted-in-the-7th.html. • **PAGE 137:** " **'is exaggerating the magnitude of the threat' "** Elisabeth Bumiller, "21st-Century Warnings of a Threat Rooted in the 7th," *The New York Times,* December 12, 2005, http://www.nytimes.com/2005/12/12/politics/21stcentury-warnings-of-a-threat -rooted-in-the-7th.html. • " **'It's a silly threat' "** Elisabeth Bumiller, "21st-Century Warnings of a Threat Rooted in the 7th," *The New York Times,* December 12, 2005, http://www.nytimes.com/2005/12/12/politics/21stcentury-warnings-of-a-threat -rooted-in-the-7th.html. • **and a justice system operated on sharia law"** Hannah Fairfield, Tim Wallace, and Derek Watkins, "How ISIS Expands," *The New York Times,* accessed June 18, 2015, http://www.nytimes.com/interactive/2015/05/21

/world/middleeast/how-isis-expands.html?smid=tw-nytimes&_r=0. • **PAGE 138:** " **'by nature, they will like the strong horse'** " "Transcript of Bin Laden Videotape," NPR, December 13, 2001, http://www.npr.org/news/specials/response /investigation/011213.binladen.transcript.html. • **"creation of an Islamic Caliphate sometime between 2013 and 2016"** Yassin Musharbash, "The Future of Terrorism: What Al-Qaeda Really Wants," *Der Spiegel,* August 12, 2005 http://www.spiegel .de/international/the-future-of-terrorism-what-al-qaida-really-wants-a-369448 .html. • **"ensuring its 'definitive victory'** " Yassin Musharbash, "The Future of Terrorism: What Al-Qaeda Really Wants," *Der Spiegel,* August 12, 2005, http:// www.spiegel.de/international/the-future-of-terrorism-what-al-qaida-really-wants -a-369448.html.

LIE #7: "ISLAM IS TOLERANT TOWARD NON-MUSLIMS."

PAGE 140: " **'Islam has a proud tradition of tolerance'** " Barack Obama, "Remarks by the President on a New Beginning," (lecture, Cairo University, Cairo, Egypt, June 4, 2009). • " **'strongest advocate of human rights anywhere on Earth'** " "You're Gonna Serve Somebody," Beliefnet, accessed June 18, 2015, http://www.beliefnet .com/Entertainment/Music/2001/04/Youre-Gonna-Serve-Somebody.aspx?p=4. • " **'compel a single human being to change his faith'** " Sayyid Qutb, *In the Shade of the Qur'an,* vol. 8, p. 244, http://ia600803.us.archive.org/27/items/InTheShade OfTheQuranSayyidQutb/Volume_8_surah_9.pdf. • **PAGE 141: "Christians were legitimate targets for death"** "Islamic State's Position on Christians," BBC News, February 27, 2015, http://www.bbc.com/news/world-middle-east-31648888. • **its main enemies deserving of Jihad"** "Islamic State's Position on Christians," BBC News, February 27, 2015, http://www.bbc.com/news/world-middle-east-31648888. • **PAGE 142:** " **'They have to willingly choose it'** " Juan Cole, "Top Ten Ways Islamic Law Forbids Terrorism," *Informed Comment* (blog), April 9, 2015, http://www .juancole.com/2015/04/ways-islamic-forbids-terrorism.html. • **PAGE 143:** " **'how an informed Muslim is to regard Christians and Jews'** " Stephen Coughlin, *Catastrophic Failure: Blindfolding America in the Face of Jihad* (self-published and printed by CreateSpace, 2015), 75–76. • **PAGE 144: "first group of people to be canonized by Pope Francis"** "Pope Canonises 800 Italian Ottoman Victims of Otranto," BBC News, May 12, 2013, http://www.bbc.com/news/world-europe-22499327. • **"enslavement of millions of Hindus . . . 1.5 million Christian Armenians killed"** Koenraad Elst, "Was There an Islamic 'Genocide' of Hindus?" The Koenraad Elst Site, accessed June 18, 2015, http://koenraadelst.bharatvani.org/articles/irin /genocide.html. • **"dhimmi can also mean 'guilty'** " Robert Spencer, *The Politically Incorrect Guide to Islam (and the Crusades)* (Washington, D.C.: Regnery, 2005), 49. • **PAGE 145:** " **'acknowledge their position as second class citizens'** " Hugh Kennedy, *The Great Arab Conquests: How the Spread of Islam Changed the World We Live In* (Boston: Da Capo, 2008), 50. • **"and wearing distinctive clothing items"** Bill Siegel, *The Control Factor* (Lanham, MD: University Press of America, 2012), 16. • " **'when the structure of caliphal finance collapsed'** " Hugh Kennedy, *Was Islam Spread by the Sword,* (New Haven: MacMillan Center, 2008) http://rps.macmillan .yale.edu/sites/default/files/files/kennedy.pdf. • **"quotes almost directly from verse 9:29"** Eliott C. McLaughlin, "ISIS Executes More Christians in Libya, Video Shows," CNN, April 20, 2015, http://www.cnn.com/2015/04/19/africa/libya-isis-executions -ethiopian-christians/. • " **'they will have nothing but the sword'** " "Iraqi Christians Flee After ISIS Issue Mosul Ultimatum," BBC News, July 18, 2014, http://www.bbc .com/news/world-middle-east-28381455. • **PAGE 146: "could be bought for $172"** Johnlee Varghese, "Shocking: ISIS Official 'Slave' Price List Shows Yazidi, Christian Girls Aged '1 to 9' Being Sold for $172," *International Business Times,* November 5,

2014, http://www.ibtimes.co.in/shocking-isis-official-slave-price-list-shows-yazidi
-christian-girls-aged-1-9-being-sold-613160. • **"justify this practice by citing
sharia law"** Steve Hopkins, "Full Horror of the Yazidis Who Didn't Escape Mount
Sinjar: UN Confirms 5,000 Men Were Executed and 7,000 Women Are Now Kept as
Sex Slaves," *Daily Mail,* October 14, 2014, http://www.dailymail.co.uk/news/article
-2792552/full-horror-yazidis-didn-t-escape-mount-sinjar-confirms-5–000-men
-executed-7–000-women-kept-sex-slaves.html.

LIE #8: "ADDRESSING FRUSTRATION, POVERTY, AND JOBLESSNESS IN THE MUSLIM WORLD—MAYBE EVEN CLIMATE CHANGE—WILL END TERRORISM."

PAGE 147: " **'and express themselves through strong civil societies' "** Barack Obama,
"President Obama: Our Fight Against Violent Extremism," *Los Angeles Times,*
February 17, 2015, http://www.latimes.com/opinion/op-ed/la-oe-obama-terrorism
-conference-20150218-story.html. • **" 'because hope is an answer to terror' "**
George W. Bush, "Remarks at the International Conference on Financing for
Development," (speech, Monterey, Mexico, March 22, 2002), https://www.un.org
/ffd/statements/usaE.htm. • " **'[such as] lack of opportunity for jobs' "** Marie Harf,
interview by Chris Matthews, *Hardball,* MSNBC, February 17, 2015. • **PAGE 148:**
" 'descended into civil war in the heart of the Middle East' " Barack Obama,
"Remarks by the President at the United States Coast Guard Academy Com-
mencement," (speech, United States Coast Guard Academy, New London, Con-
necticut, May 20, 2015), https://www.whitehouse.gov/the-press-office/2015/05/20
/remarks-president-united-states-coast-guard-academy-commencement. • **PAGE
149:** " **'poverty and ignorance, helplessness and despair' "** Joshua Keating, "Was
State Senator Obama Right That Poverty Causes Terrorism?" *The World* (blog),
Slate, September 13, 2013, http://www.slate.com/blogs/the_world_/2013/09/11
/obama_s_initial_response_to_9_11_as_a_state_senator_he_argued_that_violent
.html. • **" 'grappling with crushing poverty and deadly insurgencies' "** Peter
Baker, "Obama Says Al Qaeda in Yemen Planned Bombing Plot, and He Vows Retri-
bution," *The New York Times,* January 2, 2010, http://www.nytimes.com/2010/01/03
/us/politics/03address.html?_r=1. • **" 'have job opportunities for these people' "**
Marie Harf, interview by Chris Matthews, *Hardball,* MSNBC, February 17, 2015. •
" 'misunderstanding of the U.S. before they are radicalized' " "Tore's 'Open Borders' Rant: 'Muslim Poverty Is What Threatens Our Security,' " Real Clear Politics,
May 6, 2013, http://www.realclearpolitics.com/video/2013/05/06/toures_open_bor
ders_message_muslim_poverty_is_what_threatens_our_security.html. • **" 'all of
this might have been avoided' "** Jim Geraghty, " 'Lord, If Only I Could Have Talked
to Hitler, All of This Might Have Been Avoided,' " *The Campaign Spot* (blog), *National Review,* May 15, 2008, http://www.nationalreview.com/campaign-spot/9625
/lord-if-only-i-could-have-talked-hitler-all-might-have-been-avoided-jim-geraghty.
• **PAGE 151: "by some estimates, was worth $300 million"** Dan Ackman, "The
Cost of Being Osama bin Laden," *Forbes,* September 14, 2001, http://www.forbes
.com/2001/09/14/0914ladenmoney.html. • **"positive indicators for possible terrorist activities"** "Youth, Wealth, and Education Found to Be Risk Factors for
Violent Radicalisation," Queen Mary University of London, March 19, 2014,
http://www.qmul.ac.uk/media/news/items/smd/125815.html. • **"many came from
middle—or upper-class backgrounds"** Marlena Telvick, "Al Qaeda Today: The
New Face of Global Jihad," *Frontline,* PBS, January 25, 2005, http://www.pbs
.org/wgbh/pages/frontline/shows/front/etc/today.html. • **PAGE 152: " 'Two were
the sons of millionaires' "** J. Victoroff, ed., *Tangled Roots: Social and Psychological*

Factors in the Genesis of Terrorism (Amsterdam: IOS Press, 2006), 150. • " 'no significant relationship' between economic conditions and terrorism" Alvin Powell, "Freedom Squelches Terrorist Violence," *Harvard Gazette,* November 4, 2004, http://news.harvard.edu/gazette/2004/11.04/05-terror.html. • " 'both of domestic and foreign origin' " Alvin Powell, "Freedom Squelches Terrorist Violence," *Harvard Gazette,* November 4, 2004, http://news.harvard.edu/gazette/2004/11.04/05 -terror.html. • **PAGE 153:** " 'No, you have to do it where it's fisabilillah' " "Government Exhibit 101-E2-T: United States v. James Cromitie et al.," Investigative Project on Terrorism, accessed June 18, 2015, http://www.investigativeproject.org/documents /case_docs/1433.pdf. • **"jihadist to obtain a heavenly reward"** Shaykh' Abdul-Qadir Ibn 'Abdil-'Aziz, *Jihad and the Effects of Intention Upon It* (At-Tibyan Publications, 2012), https://thejihadproject.files.wordpress.com/2012/05/effectso fintention.pdf. • " 'then he is not from my Ummah' " Shaykh' Abdul-Qadir Ibn 'Abdil-'Aziz, *Jihad and the Effects of Intention Upon It* (At-Tibyan Publications, 2012), https://thejihadproject.files.wordpress.com/2012/05/effectsofintention.pdf. • **"wounds from 'foreign domination' "** Mark LeVine, "Why Charlie Hebdo Attack Is Not About Islam," *Al Jazeera,* January 10, 2015, http://www.aljazeera.com /indepth/opinion/2015/01/charlie-hebdo-islam-cartoon-terr-20151106726681265 .html. • " 'upon the correct intentions of the one performing' " Shaykh' Abdul-Qadir Ibn 'Abdil-'Aziz, *Jihad and the Effects of Intention Upon It* (At-Tibyan Publications, 2012), https://thejihadproject.files.wordpress.com/2012/05/effectsofintention.pdf.

LIE #9: "CRITICS OF ISLAM ARE BIGOTS"
PAGE 155: " 'negative stereotypes of Islam wherever they appear' " Barack Obama, "Remarks by the President on a New Beginning," (lecture, Cairo University, Cairo, Egypt, June 4, 2009). • " 'Everyone needs to do their part' " Council on American-Islamic Relations, "CAIR to Hold Instagram Contest for Apple Watch During May 22–25 ICNA-MAS Convention in Baltimore," press release, May 20, 2015, http://www.cair.com/press-center/press-releases/12992-cair-to-hold-instagram -contest-for-apple-watch-during-may-23–25-icna-mas-convention-in-baltimore .html. • **"under arrest for 'suspicion of religious/racial harassment' "** Lizzie Parry, "Arrested for Quoting Winston Churchill: European Election Candidate Accused of Religious and Racial Harassment After He Repeats Wartime Prime Minister's Words on Islam During Campaign Speech," *Daily Mail,* April 28, 2014, http:// dailym.ai/1CSsexY. • **PAGE 156: "jailed for several hours before being released"** "British Politician Arrested After Speech Quoting Churchill's Take on Islam," Fox News, April 29, 2014, http://www.foxnews.com/world/2014/04/29/british-politician -arrested-after-speech-quoting-churchills-take-on-islam/. • " 'a militant and proselytizing faith" Benjamin Weingarten, "If You Quote Winston Churchill on This Topic, You Could Go to Jail in Modern-Day Great Britain," TheBlaze, April 27, 2014, http://www.theblaze.com/blog/2014/04/27/if-you-quote-winston-churchill-on-this -topic-you-could-go-to-jail-in-modern-day-great-britain/. • **PAGE 157:** " 'those claiming Islam as a motivation for their actions' " Council on American-Islamic Relations, "About," Islamophobia Monitor, accessed June 18, 2015, http://www .islamophobia.org/about.html. • **"And, of course, me"** Steve Rendall and Isabel Macdonald, "The Dirty Dozen: Who's Who Among America's Leading Islamophobes," Fairness and Accuracy in Reporting, October 1, 2008, http://fair.org /article/the-dirty-dozen/. • **"And, of course, me again"** Olivia Kittel, "Right-Wing Media's Worst Islamophobic Rhetoric," Media Matters, January 1, 2015, http:// mediamatters.org/research/2015/01/11/right-wing-medias-worst-islamophobic -rhetoric/202087. • " 'UK's leading independent race equality think tank' "

"About Us," Runnymede, accessed June 19, 2015, http://www.runnymedetrust.org/about.html. • " 'fear or dislike of all or most Muslims' " Dr. Johannes Kandel, *Islamophobia: On the Career of a Controversial Term* (Bonn, Germany: Friedrich Ebert Foundation, 2006), http://www.fes.de/BerlinerAkademiegespraeche/publika tionen/islamundpolitik/documents/Islamophobia.pdf. • **PAGE 158: "case against the Holy Land Foundation"** jatrahan, "FBI: CAIR Is a Front Group and Holy Land Foundation Tapped Hamas Clerics for Fundraisers," *Crime Blog* (blog), *The Dallas Morning News,* October 7, 2008, http://crimeblog.dallasnews.com/2008/10/fbi-cair-is-a-front-group-and.html/. • **"which gave money to Hamas"** "Council on American-Islamic Relations (CAIR) Links to Holy Land Foundation," Anti-Defamation League, July 15, 2010, http://archive.adl.org/israel/cair/links2.html#.VYMYv9jbKP-. • **" 'promotes prejudice against or hatred of Muslims' "** Council on American-Islamic Relations, "About," Islamophobia Monitor, accessed June 18, 2015, http://www.islamophobia.org/about.html. • **" 'as deadly to men as that of Muhammad' "** Alexis de Tocqueville, "Letter to Arthur de Gobineau," October 22, 1843, Olivier Zunz and Alan S. Kahn, eds., *The Tocqueville Reader: A Life in Letters and Politics,* (Blackwell, 2002), p. 229. • **" 'against all who deny that Mahomet is the prophet of God' "** Andrew G. Bostom, "John Quincy Adams Knew Jihad," *FrontPage Mag,* September 29, 2004, http://archive.frontpagemag.com/readArticle.aspx?ARTID=11283. • **PAGE 159: " 'while we have kept on developing' "** George S. Patton, *War as I Knew It* (Boston: Houghton Mifflin Harcourt, 1995), 49. • **" 'It's more than just a fringe element' "** Jeff Poor, "Bill Maher: Comparing Violence of Islam to Christianity 'Liberal Bullsh•t,' " *The Daily Caller,* April 20, 2013, http://dailycaller.com/2013/04/20/bill-maher-violence-islam-christianity-liberal-bullshit/. • **"to Christianity was 'liberal bullshit' "** Jeff Poor, "Bill Maher: Comparing Violence of Islam to Christianity 'Liberal Bullsh•t,' " *The Daily Caller,* April 20, 2013, http://dailycaller.com/2013/04/20/bill-maher-violence-islam-christianity-liberal-bullshit/. • **" 'proof of an aggressive intent' "** "Christopher Hitchens: Most Provocative Quotes" *The Telegraph,* April 13, 2011, http://www.telegraph.co.uk/culture/tvandradio/8448250/Christopher-Hitchens-most-provocative-quotes.html.

LIE #10: "ISLAM RESPECTS THE RIGHTS OF WOMEN."

PAGE 161: " 'contemporary international human rights documents' " Ghena Krayem and Haisam Farache, "Grim Picture of Sharia Hides It's Useful Aspects," *The Sydney Morning Herald,* February 18, 2008, http://www.smh.com.au/news/opinion/grim-picture-of-sharia-hides-its-useful-aspects/2008/02/17/1203190646668.html?page=f ullpage#contentSwap1. • **" 'the religion and society in general' "** "Beliefs and Daily Lives of Muslims," *Frontline,* PBS, accessed June 19, 2015, http://www.pbs.org/wgbh/pages/frontline/teach/muslims/beliefs.html. • **PAGE 162: " 'practices alien to the religion itself' "** Ghena Krayem and Haisam Farache, "Grim Picture of Sharia Hides It's Useful Aspects," *The Sydney Morning Herald,* February 18, 2008, http://www.smh.com.au/news/opinion/grim-picture-of-sharia-hides-its-useful-aspects/2008/02/17/1203190646668.html?page=fullpage#contentSwap1. • **" 'which may reflect male-dominated societies' "** "Beliefs and Daily Lives of Muslims," *Frontline,* PBS, accessed June 19, 2015, http://www.pbs.org/wgbh/pages/frontline/teach/muslims/beliefs.html. • **PAGE 164: " 'but we have had lots of improvements' "** Mike Celizic, "Beyond the Veil: Lives of Women in Iran," *Today News,* NBC, September 13, 2007, http://www.today.com/news/beyond-veil-lives-women-iran-2D80555320. • **PAGE 165: "Expose her head"** Mike Celizic, "Beyond the Veil: Lives of Women in Iran," *Today News,* NBC, September 13, 2007, http://www.today.com/news/beyond-veil-lives-women-iran-2D80555320. • **"Apply for a passport**

without her husband's permission" "Official Laws Against Women in Iran," Women's Forum Against Fundamentalism in Iran, accessed June 19, 2015, http://www.wfafi.org/laws.pdf. • **"Sing any way she chooses"** Sam Wilkin, "Iran Eases Ban on Women Attending Sports Matches," *Huffington Post,* April 4, 2015, http://www.huffingtonpost.com/2015/04/04/iran-women-sports_n_7003726.html. • **"husbands can divorce for any reason"** Mike Celizic, "Beyond the Veil: Lives of Women in Iran," *Today News,* NBC, September 13, 2007, http://www.today.com/news/beyond-veil-lives-women-iran-2D80555320. • **"Commit adultery—and live"** Mike Celizic, "Beyond the Veil: Lives of Women in Iran," *Today News,* NBC, September 13, 2007, http://www.today.com/news/beyond-veil-lives-women-iran-2D80555320. • **"Inherit an equal share as her brother"** Mike Celizic, "Beyond the Veil: Lives of Women in Iran," *Today News,* NBC, September 13, 2007, http://www.today.com/news/beyond-veil-lives-women-iran-2D80555320. • **"Watch men play sports"** Golnaz Esfandiari, "Men's Sports, Shorts Not for Women in Iran," Radio Free Europe/Radio Liberty, June 19, 2015, http://www.rferl.org/content/iran-women-banned-sports-stadiums/25434040.html. • **"(with a few exceptions)"** Sam Wilkin, "Iran Eases Ban on Women Attending Sports Matches," *Huffington Post,* April 4, 2015, http://www.huffingtonpost.com/2015/04/04/iran-women-sports_n_7003726.html. • **"Marry a non-Islamic man"** Mike Celizic, "Beyond the Veil: Lives of Women in Iran," *Today News,* NBC, September 13, 2007, http://www.today.com/news/beyond-veil-lives-women-iran-2D80555320. • **"Publicly socialize with men"** Max Fisher, "The Latest Tings You Can't Do in Iran: Go to Coffee Shops, Eat Chicken on TV," *The Atlantic,* July 19, 2012, http://www.theatlantic.com/international/archive/2012/07/the-latest-things-you-cant-do-in-iran-go-to-coffee-shops-eat-chicken-on-tv/259962/. • **"Sit in the front of a bus"** Margaret Hartmann, "For Iranian Women, Cars Represent Both Limitations and Freedoms," *Jezebel,* October 8, 2008, http://jezebel.com/5060696/for-iranian-women-cars-represent-both-limitations-and-freedoms. • **"Run for president"** Gissou Nia, "Why Iranian Women Can't Have Any of It," Iran Human Rights Documentation Center, accessed June 19, 2015, http://www.iranhrdc.org/english/news/in-the-news/1000000312-why-iranian-women-can%E2%80%99t-have-any-of-it.html. • **"or go to school without her husband's permission"** "Under the Islamic Rule," Alliance of Iranian Women, June 19, 2015, http://allianceofiranianwomen.org/. • **"Attend her father's funeral without her husband's permission"** "Official Laws Against Women in Iran," Women's Forum Against Fundamentalism in Iran, accessed June 19, 2015, http://www.wfafi.org/laws.pdf. • **"(countless numbers have been tortured for doing so"** "Official Laws Against Women in Iran," Women's Forum Against Fundamentalism in Iran, accessed June 19, 2015, http://www.wfafi.org/laws.pdf. • **"unsanctioned interviews with foreign media"** Elsie Auerbach, "Women Get the Short End of the Stick in Iran and Can't Even Protest," *Human Rights Now* (blog), Amnesty International, March 30, 2015, http://blog.amnestyusa.org/middle-east/women-get-the-short-end-of-the-stick-in-iran-and-cant-even-protest/. • **"should her husband decide to have another life"** "Under the Islamic Rule," Alliance of Iranian Women, June 19, 2015, http://allianceofiranianwomen.org/. • **"object to having acid thrown in her face"** Elsie Auerbach, "Women Get the Short End of the Stick in Iran and Can't Even Protest," *Human Rights Now* (blog), Amnesty International, March 30, 2015, http://blog.amnestyusa.org/middle-east/women-get-the-short-end-of-the-stick-in-iran-and-cant-even-protest/. • **"Choose not to have children (law pending)"** Elsie Auerbach, "Women Get the Short End of the Stick in Iran and Can't Even Protest," *Human Rights Now* (blog), Amnesty International, March 30, 2015, http://blog.amnestyusa.org/middle-east/women-get-the-short-end-of-the-stick-in-iran-and-cant

-even-protest/. • **PAGE 166: "Have sex outside of marriage"** "Iran Bans Women's Magazine for Promoting Cohabitation," Newsmax, April 27, 2015, http://www.newsmax.com/World/GlobalTalk/Iran-Womens-Magazine-Cohabitation/2015/04/27/id/640897/. • **"computer science, English literature, or business"** Fariba Sahraei, "Iranian University Bans on Women Causes Consternation," BBC News, September 22, 2012, http://www.bbc.com/news/world-middle-east-19665615. • "other Islamic countries like, say, Saudi Arabia" "Twelve Things Women in Saudi Arabia Can't Do," *The Week,* June 10, 2015, http://www.theweek.co.uk/60339/twelve-things-women-in-saudi-arabia-cant-do. • **"dubbing Tehran . . . the 'next Aspen' "** Laurence Cornet, "Could Tehran (Yes, Tehran) Be the Next Aspen?" *Vogue,* January 28, 2015, http://www.vogue.com/9003569/skiing-in-tehran-iran/. • **"not even allowed to ski unaccompanied"** Rachel Shukert, *"Vogue* Anoints Tehran the New Aspen," *The Scroll* (blog), *Tablet,* February 2, 2015, http://www.tabletmag.com/scroll/188716/vogue-anoints-tehran-the-new-aspen. • **PAGE 167: " 'will not be a whip, a stick, or a board' "** Steven Stalinsky and Y. Yehoshua, *Muslim Clerics on the Religious Rulings of Wife-Beating,* (Washington, D.C.: Middle East Media Research Institute, March 22, 2004), http://www.memri.org/report/en/0/0/0/0/0/0/1091.htm. • **"at least half responded 'yes' "** The Pew Forum on Religion and Public Life, *The World's Muslims: Religion, Politics, and Society* (Washington, D.C.: Pew Research Center, 2013), chap. 4, http://www.pewforum.org/2013/04/30/the-worlds-muslims-religion-politics-society-women-in-society/#wives-role. • **"have to witness the actual penetration"** Lisa Beyer, "The Women of Islam," *Time,* November 25, 2001, http://content.time.com/time/world/article/0,8599,185647,00.html. • **" 'hand or stick or pull her by the ears' "** Rick Dewsbury, " 'Pull Her by the Ear, Beat Her by Hand or Stick': How the Islamic Guide to a Happy Marriage Advises Husbands to Treat Their Wives," *Daily Mail,* March 24, 2012, http://www.dailymail.co.uk/news/article-2119846/Muslim-guide-marriage-tells-husbands-beat-hand-stick.html. • **PAGE 168: "temporary sex slaves for ISIS fighters"** "ISIS Kills More Than 150 Women, Girls for Refusing 'Jihad Marriage,' " Al Arabiya, December 17, 2014, http://english.alarabiya.net/en/News/middle-east/2014/12/17/. • **"strangling each other to commit assisted suicide"** Chris Hughes, "ISIS Sex Slaves: Captured Iraqi Women Strangling Each Other and Killing Themselves to Escape Rape," *Mirror,* December 22, 2014, http://www.mirror.co.uk/news/world-news/isis-sex-slaves-captured-iraqi-4857970. • **"to undergo female genital mutilation"** "UN: ISIS Orders Female Genital Mutilation," Al Arabiya, July 24, 2014, http://english.alarabiya.net/en/News/middle-east/2014/07/24/. • **" 'Eventually, they took all the girls' "** Fariba Sahraei, "Iranian University Bans on Women Causes Consternation," BBC News, September 22, 2012, http://www.bbc.com/news/world-middle-east-19665615. • **PAGE 169: "complete with Quranic citations"** "Islamic State (ISIS) Releases Pamphlet on Female Slaves," The Middle East Research Institute, December 4, 2014, http://www.memrijttm.org/islamic-state-isis-releases-pamphlet-on-female-slaves.html.

LIE #11: "IRAN CAN BE TRUSTED WITH A NUCLEAR WEAPON."

PAGE 170: " 'contradict our fundamental religious and ethical convictions' " Jim Sciutto, Jennifer Rizzo, and Tom Cohen, "Rouhani: Nuclear Weapons Have No Place in Iran's Security," CNN, September 25, 2013, http://www.cnn.com/2013/09/24/world/un-general-assembly-tuesday/. • **" 'the entire world will be safer' "** Louis Charbonneau and Arshad Mohammed, "Kerry Says Iran, World Powers Closer Than Ever to Historic Nuclear Deal," Reuters, April 27, 2015, http://www.reuters.com/article/2015/04/27/us-iran-nuclear-idUSKBN0NI0B920150427. • **"en-**

gaging in 'aggressive personal diplomacy' with clerics" Michael R. Gordon and Jeff Zeleny, "Obama Envisions New Iran Approach," *The New York Times,* November 2, 2007, http://www.nytimes.com/2007/11/02/us/politics/02obama.html?_r=1&. • **PAGE 166: "as 'naïve' on foreign policy"** "Clinton: Obama Is 'Naïve' on Foreign Policy," NBC, July 24, 2007, http://www.nbcnews.com/id/19933710/ns/politics-the _debates/t/clinton-obama-naive-foreign-policy/#.VYQ9udjbJMs. • **PAGE 171: "calling for 'a more serious, substantive' discussion"** Joby Warrick and Jason Rezaian, "Rouhani, Obama Sound Positive, but Progress Likely to Take Time," *The Washington Post,* June 17, 2013, http://www.washingtonpost.com/world/national -security/rouhani-obama-sound-positive-but-progress-likely-to-take-time/2013 /06/17/dd42d330-d793-11e2-a016-92547bf094cc_story.html. • **" 'based on transparency, accountability, verification' "** Dale Armbruster, "Kerry on Iran: 'The Deal Is What They Said It Was,' " NBC, April 12, 2015, http://www.nbcnews.com/story line/iran-nuclear-talks/kerry-iran-deal-what-we-said-it-was-n340176. • **" 'should be the possibility of getting a deal' "** James S. Robbins, "Iran's Nuclear Weapons Fatwa Is a Myth," *World Report* (blog), *US News and World Report,* February 18, 2015, http://www.usnews.com/opinion/blogs/world-report/2015/02/18/irans-nuclear -weapons-fatwa-is-a-myth. • **PAGE 172: "no evidence of any fatwa of this sort"** James S. Robbins, "Iran's Nuclear Weapons Fatwa Is a Myth," *World Report* (blog), *US News and World Report,* February 18, 2015, http://www.usnews.com /opinion/blogs/world-report/2015/02/18/irans-nuclear-weapons-fatwa-is-a-myth. • **" 'amended and changed by circumstances' "** James S. Robbins, "Iran's Nuclear Weapons Fatwa Is a Myth," *World Report* (blog), *US News and World Report,* February 18, 2015, http://www.usnews.com/opinion/blogs/world-report/2015/02/18 /irans-nuclear-weapons-fatwa-is-a-myth. • **" 'disrupt the dreams of America and Israel' "** Reza Kahlili, "Islamic World Must Have Nuclear Weapons, Says Iran," *The Daily Caller,* June 10, 2012, http://dailycaller.com/2012/06/10/islamic-world-must -have-nuclear-weapons-says-iran/. • **PAGE 173: "the bottom of the mural: 'death to the USA' "** Homa Katouzian and Hossein Shahidi, eds., *Iran in the 21st Century: Politics, Economics & Conflict* (New York: Routledge, 2007), 83. • **during a speech to a frenzied crowd in Iran"** *The Situation Room with Wolf Blitzer,* "Amid Nuke Talks, Ayatollah Says, 'Death to America,' " CNN, March 23, 2015, http://www.cnn .com/videos/world/2015/03/23/tsr-acosta-iran-ayatollah-nuke-talks.cnn. • **"nuclear Iran is a far greater threat than ISIS"** Louis Charbonnau and Michelle Nichols, "Israel PM Tries to Shift Focus from Islamic State to Iran at UN," Reuters, September 29, 2014, http://www.reuters.com/article/2014/09/30/us-un-assembly-israel -idUSKCN0HO1U220140930. • **PAGE 174: " 'a thousand times more dangerous and destructive' "** "Nuclear Iran 1,000 Times More Dangerous Than ISIS— Netanyahu," RT News, May 28, 2015, http://rt.com/news/262309-netanyahu-isis -iran-nuclear/. • **" 'it was the Iranian king who saved the Jews"** Robert Mackey, "In a Dance Remix of Netanyahu's Speech, Two Words Echo: 'Iran—Haman,' " *The New York Times,* March 6, 2015, http://www.nytimes.com/2015/03/07/world/middleeast /in-a-dance-remix-of-netanyahus-speech-two-words-echo-iran-haman.html?_r=0. • **" 'all of us should mobilize to kill' "** Joshua Teitelbaum and Michael Segall, *The Iranian Leadership's Continuing Declarations of Intent to Destroy Israel* (Jerusalem: Jerusalem Center for Public Affairs, 2012), 6, http://jcpa.org/wp-content/uploads /2012/05/IransIntent2012b.pdf#page=6. • **" 'to erase Israel from the map of the region' "** Joshua Teitelbaum and Michael Segall, *The Iranian Leadership's Continuing Declarations of Intent to Destroy Israel* (Jerusalem: Jerusalem Center for Public Affairs, 2012), 6, http://jcpa.org/wp-content/uploads/2012/05/IransIntent2012b .pdf#page=6. • **" 'Zionist regime's death sentence' "** Joshua Teitelbaum and Michael

Segall, *The Iranian Leadership's Continuing Declarations of Intent to Destroy Israel* (Jerusalem: Jerusalem Center for Public Affairs, 2012), 6, http://jcpa.org/wp-con tent/uploads/2012/05/IransIntent2012b.pdf#page=6. • **PAGE 175: " 'Israel in its entirety with a big holocaust' "** "Senior Iranian Official Mohammad Hassan Rahimian: Our Missiles Can Cause 'Big Holocaust' in Israel," The Middle East Media Research Institute TV Monitor Project, January 12, 2010, http://www.memritv.org /clip/en/2342.htm. • **" 'not even have time to pack their suitcases' "** "Cash: Olympics 2020 Held in Egypt and Palestine Is Free!" *Daily Aftab,* September 3, 2011, http://aftabnews.ir/vdcefx8zzjh8xwi.b9bj.html. • **" 'a cancerous tumor and it will be removed' "** Dudi Cohen, "Khamenei: Zionist Regime Is a Cancer," *Ynetnews,* February 3, 2012, http://www.ynetnews.com/articles/0,7340,L-4184838,00.html. • **" 'no intention of going to war with Israel' "** "Mr. Rafsanjani! So We Have Our War?" *Vatan,* accessed June 19,2015, http://www.magiran.com/npview.asp?ID =2720716. • **" 'this generation will be witness to its destruction' "** "Representative of the Supreme Leader of the Qods Force: The Destruction of the Zionist Regime, and the Present Generation Will See the Destruction of Israel Soon," Fars News, accessed June 19, 2015, http://www.farsnews.com/newstext.php?nn=13920511000792. • **" 'has no cure but to be annihilated' "** Daniel Politi, "Iran's Khamenei: No Cure for Barbaric Israel but Annihilation," *Slate,* November 9, 2014, http://www.slate .com/blogs/the_slatest/2014/11/09/iran_s_khamenei_israel_must_be_annihilated .html. • **" 'Islamic nations awakening for your defeat' "** "Not Safe Anywhere in Israel: Palestine Will Not Calm," Fars News, Accessed June 19, 2015, http://www.fars news.com/newstext.php?nn=13930503000516. • **PAGE 176: " 'no such thing as the Zionist regime on Planet Earth' "** "Iranian Regime Escalates Threats to Annihilate Israel," The Middle East Media Research Institute, December 17, 2014, http://www .memri.org/report/en/print8337.htm. • **" 'not be quiet so long as Israel exists in it' "** "Iranian Regime Escalates Threats to Annihilate Israel," The Middle East Media Research Institute, December 17, 2014, http://www.memri.org/report/en/print8337 .html. • **" 'totally deleted from the region's geopolitics' "** Reuters, "Iran Vows to Retaliate After Israeli Strike Kills Iranian General," *Huffington Post,* January 20, 2015, http://www.huffingtonpost.com/2015/01/20/israel-iranian-general-killed_n _6507146.html. • **"destruction of Israel can bring about the end times"** "The Emergence of the Middle East Should Be Changed," Iranian Students' News Agency, June 19, 2015, http://bit.ly/1HzJXQ0. • **PAGE 177: " 'there is a Jew behind me; come and kill him' "** Muslim ibn al-Hajjah, *Sahih Muslim,* Hadith 041: 6985, University of Southern California Center for Muslim-Jewish Engagement, accessed June 20, 2015, http://www.usc.edu/org/cmje/religious-texts/hadith/muslim/041 -smt.php#041.6985. • **" 'a new beginning, a rebirth and a resurrection' "** Stoyan Zaimov, "Iranian President Ahmadinejad Tells UN Jesus Christ and 'Ultimate Savior' Are Coming," *The Christian Post,* September 27, 2012, http://m.christianpost .com/news/iranian-president-ahmadinejad-tells-un-jesus-christ-and-ultimate-savior -are-coming-82336/. • **" 'prelude to the appearance of the Mahdi' "** Miriam Karouny, "Apocalyptic Prophesies Drive Both Sides to Syrian Battle for the End of Time," Reuters, April 1, 2014, http://www.reuters.com/article/2014/04/01/us-syria -crisis-prophecy-insight-idUSBREA3013420140401. • **PAGE 178: "Islamic prophecy speaks of armies with 'yellow flags' "** Miriam Karouny, "Apocalyptic Prophesies Drive Both Sides to Syrian Battle for the End of Time," Reuters, April 1, 2014, http://www.reuters.com/article/2014/04/01/us-syria-crisis-prophecy-insight-idUS BREA3013420140401. • **"later killed by a car bomb"** "Iran Car Explosion Kills Nuclear Scientist in Tehran," BBC News, January 11, 2012, http://www.bbc.com /news/world-middle-east-16501566. • **" 'depends on what you are doing in Na-**

tanz' " Saeed Ghasseminejad, "Iran's Apocalyptic Policy Makers," *The Blogs: Saeed Ghasseminejad* (blog), *The Times of Israel,* June 10, 2013, http://blogs.timesofisrael .com/a-military-strategy-for-apocalypse-soon/. • " 'and IRGC is the instrument to do it' " Saeed Ghasseminejad, "Iran's Apocalyptic Policy Makers," *The Blogs: Saeed Ghasseminejad* (blog), *The Times of Israel,* June 10, 2013, http://blogs.time sofisrael.com/a-military-strategy-for-apocalypse-soon/.

LIE #12: "THE MUSLIM BROTHERHOOD IS A MODERATE, MAINSTREAM ISLAMIC GROUP."
PAGE 179: " 'a betterment of the political order' " Josh Gerstein, "DNI Clapper Retreats from 'Secular' Claim on the Muslim Brotherhood," *Under the Radar* (blog), *Politico,* February 10, 2011, http://www.politico.com/blogs/joshgerstein/0211/DNI_Clapper _Egypts_Muslim_Brotherhood_largely_secular.html. • " 'Allahu-Akbar! Allahu-Akbar!' " Richard P. Mitchell, *The Society of Muslim Brothers* (New York: Oxford University Press, 1969), 193–94. • **"Jihadist luminaries such as Sayyid Qutb and Ayman Zawahiri"** "The Muslim Brotherhood: Understanding Its Roots and Impacts," Foundation for Defense of Democracies, accessed June 20, 2015, http://www.defenddemocracy.org/the-muslim-brotherhood-understanding-its -roots-and-impact/. • **"even vocal backing of the Obama administration"** Arshad Mohammed, "Egypt Summons US Ambassador over Muslim Brotherhood," Yahoo! News, June 8, 2015, http://news.yahoo.com/egypt-summons-u-ambassador-over -muslim-brotherhood-001016590.html, and Spencer Case, "How Obama Sided with the Muslim Brotherhood," *National Review,* July 3, 2014, http://www.national review.com/article/381947/how-obama-sided-muslim-brotherhood-spencer-case. • **PAGE 180: "then Muslim Brotherhood ruler Mohammed Morsi in Cairo"** Nick Meo, "US Secretary of State Hillary Clinton Meets Egypt's Muslim Brotherhood President Mohammed Morsi in Historic First," *The Telegraph,* July 14, 2014, http:// www.telegraph.co.uk/news/worldnews/africaandindianocean/egypt/9400749/US -Secretary-of-State-Hillary-Clinton-meets-Egypts-Muslim-Brotherhood-president -Mohammed-Morsi-in-historic-first.html. • **"sentenced to death for his part in the uprising"** Sharif Tarek, "Egypt's Ousted President Morsi Sentenced to Death," *Los Angeles Times,* May 16, 2015, http://www.latimes.com/world/middleeast/la-fg -egypt-court-sentences-morsi-to-death-20150516-story.html. • **"invited Brother-hood members to his Cairo speech"** Marc Ambinder, " 'Brotherhood' Invited to Obama Speech by US," *The Atlantic,* June 3, 2009, http://www.theatlantic.com /politics/archive/2009/06/-brotherhood-invited-to-obama-speech-by-us/18693/. • **"eighty bankers boxes' worth of documents"** Mohamed Akram, David Reaboi, and Frank J. Gaffney, Jr., *An Explanatory Memorandum: From the Archives of the Muslim Brotherhood in America* (Washington, D.C.: Center for Security Policy, 2013), introduction. • **PAGE 181:** " 'made victorious over all other religions' " Mohamed Akram, David Reaboi, and Frank J. Gaffney, Jr., *An Explanatory Memo-randum: From the Archives of the Muslim Brotherhood in America* (Washington, D.C.: Center for Security Policy, 2013). • **"evidence in a 2007 terrorism-financing trial"** Government Exhibit 003–0085, United States v. Holy Land Foundation et al., 3:04-CR-240-G. • **PAGE 182:** " 'against the Zio-American arrogance and tyranny"** Jeffrey Goldberg, "What the Muslim Brotherhood Stands For," *The At-lantic,* January 31, 2011, http://www.theatlantic.com/international/archive/2011/01 /what-the-muslim-brotherhood-stands-for/70502/. • " 'pursues death just as the enemy pursues life' " "The Muslim Brotherhood: On the Record," The Washington Institute for Near East Policy, February 4, 2011, http://www.washingtoninstitute .org/policy-analysis/view/the-muslim-brotherhood-on-the-record. • " 'not through

the sword but through dawa' " Andrew C. McCarthy, *The Grand Jihad: How Islam and the Left Sabotage America* (New York: Encounter, 2010), 84. • **"pushing sharia into Western societies bit by bit"** "A Short Course Part 3: 'Civilization Jihad'—the Muslim Brotherhood's Potent Weapon," Sharia: The Threat to America, Center for Security Policy, accessed June 20, 2015, http://shariahthethreat.org/a-short-course -1-what-is-shariah/a-short-course-3-civilization-jihad/. • **"colonizing positively the United States of America"** Pamela Geller, "Tariq Ramadan Openly Calls for a Muslim Colonization of the US," Pamela Geller: Atlas Shrugs, August 3, 2011, http://pamelageller.com/2011/08/tariq-ramadan-openly-calls-for-a-muslim-colo nization-of-the-us.html/. • **PAGE 183: "among the world's top 'thinkers' "** Bruce Crumley, "The 2004 *Time* 100: Tariq Ramadan," *Time,* April 26, 2004, http://content .time.com/time/specials/packages/article/0,28804,1970858_1970909_1971700,00. html. • **" 'most important intellectuals in the world' "** Paul Donnelly, "Tariq Ramadan: The Muslim Martin Luther?" *Salon,* February 15, 2002, http://www .salon.com/2002/02/15/ramadan_2/. • **"and the 'Muslim Martin Luther' "** Paul Donnelly, "Tariq Ramadan: The Muslim Martin Luther?" *Salon,* February 15, 2002, http://www.salon.com/2002/02/15/ramadan_2/. • **"immense barrier in our quest for an Islamic state"** Andrew C. McCarthy, *The Grand Jihad: How Islam and the Left Sabotage America* (New York: Encounter, 2010), 95. • **"haranguing people who don't dress modestly enough"** David A. Graham, "Why the Muslim 'No-Go Zone' Myth Won't Die," *The Atlantic,* January 20, 2015, http://www.theatlantic .com/international/archive/2015/01/paris-mayor-to-sue-fox-over-no-go-zone-com ments/384656/. • **PAGE 184: " 'and obligatory to lie if the goal is obligatory' "** *Reliance of the Traveller,* Revised Edition (Beltsville: Amana, 1988), 745. http://www .islamicbulletin.org/free_downloads/resources/reliance2_complete.pdf • **" 'not just for Muslims, but for all Egyptians' "** Essam el-Errian, "What the Muslim Brothers Want," *The New York Times,* February 9, 2011, http://www.nytimes.com/2011/02/10 /opinion/10erian.html?_r=1. • **"Coptic Christians were massacred and persecuted"** Mike Giglio and Sophia Jones, "Christians Under Attack," *The Daily Beast,* August 15, 2013, http://www.thedailybeast.com/articles/2013/08/15/christians-under -attack.html. • **"The Muslim Community Association (MCA), and others"** "A Short Course Part 12: The Muslim Brotherhood in America," Sharia: The Threat to America, Center for Security Policy, accessed June 21, 2015, http://shariahthethreat .org/a-short-course-1-what-is-shariah/a-short-course-12-the-muslim-brother hood-in-america/. • **PAGE 185: "and the Islamic Society of North America (ISNA)"** "A Short Course Part 12: The Muslim Brotherhood in America," Sharia: The Threat to America, Center for Security Policy, accessed June 21, 2015, http:// shariahthethreat.org/a-short-course-1-what-is-shariah/a-short-course-12-the -muslim-brotherhood-in-america/. • **" 'groups like ISIS, al-Qaeda, Boko Haram, and the Muslim Brotherhood' "** Stephen Coughlin, *Catastrophic Failure: Blind-folding America in the Face of Jihad* (self-published and printed by CreateSpace, 2015), 18. • **" 'are addressed with a keen sense of urgency' "** Stephen Coughlin, *Catastrophic Failure: Blindfolding America in the Face of Jihad* (self-published and printed by CreateSpace, 2015), 21–22. • **"deemed 'biased, false, and highly of-fensive' would be removed"** Stephen Coughlin, *Catastrophic Failure: Blindfolding America in the Face of Jihad* (self-published and printed by CreateSpace, 2015), 21–22. • **PAGE 186: "meet with the brotherhood, over the objections of congress"** Stephen Coughlin, *Catastrophic Failure: Blindfolding America in the Face of Jihad* (self-published and printed by CreateSpace, 2015), 21–22. • **"Muslim 145 times, and Islam 322 times"** National Commission on Terrorist Attacks, *The 9/11 Commission Report: Final Report of the National Commission on Terrorist Attacks upon* *the United States* (New York: W.W. Norton & Company, 2004). • **"Instead, they refer to 'violent extremism' in general"** US Department of Justice, *Federal Bureau of Investigation: Counterterrorism Analytical Lexicon* (Washington, D.C., 2009), http://cryptome.org/fbi-ct-lexicon.pdf, and Office of the Director of National Intelligence, *The National Intelligence Strategy* (Washington, D.C., August 2009), http://www.dni.gov/files/documents/Newsroom/Reports%20and%20Pubs/2009_NIS.pdf.

LIE #13: "ISLAM RESPECTS FREEDOM OF SPEECH."
PAGE 187: " **'obliges Muslims to attain a higher standard of wisdom'"** Qasim Rashid, "Islam Backs Free Speech: Column," *USA Today,* January 9, 2015, http://www.usatoday.com/story/opinion/2015/01/09/free-speech-islam-charlie-hebdo-column/21458257/. • " **'free to be a bigot or even an idiot'** " William Saletan, "Muslims for Free Speech," *Slate,* October 3, 2012, http://www.slate.com/articles/news_and_politics/frame_game/2012/10/muslims_for_free_speech_can_islam_tolerate_innocence_of_muslims_.html. • " **'never shy away from ever defending this right'** " William Saletan, "Muslims for Free Speech," *Slate,* October 3, 2012, http://www.slate.com/articles/news_and_politics/frame_game/2012/10/muslims_for_free_speech_can_islam_tolerate_innocence_of_muslims_.html. • **PAGE 188: "inaugural Muhammad art exhibit and contest"** Sasha Goldstein, "Garland Shooting Suspect Elton Simpson Tied to Previous Terror Probe, Authorities Say as Search of Phoenix Apartment Continues," *New York Daily News,* May 5, 2015, http://www.nydailynews.com/news/crime/garland-shooter-elton-simpson-tied-previous-terror-probe-article-1.2209345. • **"a jihad-inspired act of mass murder"** Catherine Shoichet and Michael Pearson, "Garland, Texas, Shooting Suspect Linked Himself to ISIS in Tweets," CNN, May 4, 2015, http://www.cnn.com/2015/05/04/us/garland-mohammed-drawing-contest-shooting/. • **PAGE 189:** " **'jihad against freedom will only grow more virulent'** " Bob Price, "$10,000 Muhammad Art and Cartoon Contest to Be Held at Site of 'Stand with the Prophet' Conference in Texas," Breitbart, February 11, 2015, http://www.breitbart.com/texas/2015/02/11/10000-muhammad-art-and-cartoon-contest-to-be-held-at-site-of-stand-with-the-prophet-conference-in-texas/. • **"on Fox News that she 'knew the consequences'** " Jeff Poor, "Muslim Leader: Geller Should Be Tried and Executed," Breitbart, May 7, 2014, http://www.breitbart.com/video/2015/05/07/muslim-leader-geller-should-be-tried-and-executed/. • **"not just Jihadists, believe is a grave insult"** Eric Weiner, "Why Cartoons of the Prophet Insult Muslims," NPR, February 8, 2006, http://www.npr.org/templates/story/story.php?storyId=5196323. • **PAGE 190:** " **'motivated by anything other than hate is simply hogwash'** " The Editorial Board, "Free Speech vs. Hate Speech," *The New York Times,* May 6, 2015, http://www.nytimes.com/2015/05/07/opinion/free-speech-vs-hate-speech.html?_r=0. • **"Chris Matthews mused on MSNBC"** Josh Feldman, " 'When You Provoke People . . . ': Matthews, Guest Tackle 'Causality' of Texas Shooting," *Mediaite,* May 4, 2015, http://www.mediaite.com/tv/when-you-provoke-people-matthews-guest-tackle-causality-of-tx-shooting/. • " **'as provocative as hosting a "Muhammad Drawing Contest"** James Taranto, " 'Free Speech Aside': In Defense of Provocation," *The Wall Street Journal,* May 4, 2015, http://www.wsj.com/articles/free-speech-aside-1430760333. • " **'bought into an ideology that is sick'** " Jeff Poor, "CNN's Cuomo to Pamela Geller: 'N-Word Gets Treated Same Way Depictions of Mohammed Does,' " Breitbart, May 29, 2015, http://www.breitbart.com/video/2015/05/29/cnns-cuomo-to-pamela-geller-n-word-gets-treated-same-way-depictions-of-mohammed-does/. • **PAGE 191:** " **'because it's offensive, not because legally I can't'** " Billy Hallowell, " 'Snap Out of It: CNN Host Likens Drawing the Prophet Muhammad to Saying the

N-Word," The Blaze, May 28, 2015, http://www.theblaze.com/stories/2015/05/28 /snap-out-of-it-cnn-host-likens-drawing-the-prophet-muhammad-to-saying-the -n-word/. • " **'exercise of that right includes using good judgment' "** Erik Wemple, "Fox News's Greta Van Susteren Scolds Pamela Geller," Washington Post, May 6, 2015, http://www.washingtonpost.com/blogs/erik-wemple/wp/2015/05/06/fox -newss-greta-van-susteren-scolds-pamela-geller/. • **"riots throughout Europe and the Middle East"** "Rewind: Danish Newspaper Satirizes Islam," 60 Minutes: Overtime, CBS, January 8, 2015, http://www.cbsnews.com/news/danish-newspaper-sati rizes-islam/. • **"including the New York Sun,** the Philadelphia Inquirer" Julie Bosman, "Protesters at Philadelphia Paper Ask It to Apologize for Cartoon," The New York Times, February 7, 2006, http://www.nytimes.com/2006/02/07/national /07philly.html?_r=0. • **"and the left-wing Harper's** magazine" "Harper's Publishes Mo Cartoons," Michelle Malkin, May 17, 2006, http://michellemalkin.com/2006 /05/17/harpers-publishes-mo-cartoons/. • " **'our readers' culture when it didn't add anything to the story' "** Joel Brinkley and Ian Fisher, "US Says It Also Finds Cartoons of Muhammad Offensive," The New York Times, February 4, 2006, http:// www.nytimes.com/2006/02/04/politics/04mideast.html?adxnnl=1&adxnnlx =1434928110-nHwdubAJz2/crUhBIQmuHA. • **PAGE 192:** " **'look at with whom you're expressing solidarity' "** Brian Knowlton, "Syria and Iran Fuel the Riots," The New York Times, February 8, 2006, http://www.nytimes.com/2006/02/08/world /americas/08iht-policy-5751544.html. • **PAGE 193:** " **'cartoonists union to draw Muhammad as they see him' "** Jytte Klausen, The Cartoons That Shook the World (New Haven, CT: Yale University Press, 2009). Note: Ironically, Yale University Press decided at the eleventh hour to exclude from publication the very cartoons that the book was written about. In a press release, YUP Director John Donatich explained, "On behalf of the Yale Press, the university consulted a number of senior academics, diplomats, and national security experts. The overwhelming judgment of the experts with the most insight about the threats of violence was that there existed an appreciable chance of violence occurring if either the cartoons or other depictions of the Prophet Muhammad were printed in a book about the cartoons published by Yale University Press." (See "Statement by John Donatich," Sept. 9, 2009. http:// yalepress.yale.edu/yupbooks/KlausenStatement.asp). • **"Many were forced into hiding"** Creg Margason, "Artist Goes Into Hiding After Denmark Terror Attacks," Fox News, February 16, 2015, http://fox59.com/2015/02/16/denmark-terror-attacks -artist-goes-into-hiding/. • **"Many were forced into hiding"** Peter McGraw and Joel Warner, "The Danish Cartoon Crisis of 2005 and 2006: 10 Thinks You Didn't Know About the Original Muhammad Controversy," The Blog (blog), The Huffington Post, September 25, 2012, http://www.huffingtonpost.com/peter-mcgraw-and-joel-war ner/muhammad-cartoons_b_1907545.html. • **"still require twenty-four-hour police protection"** Daily Mail, "Controversial Cartoonist 'under police protection' after posting derogatory picture of Prophet Muhammad," January 12 2015, http:// www.dailymail.co.uk/news/article-2907565/Controversial-cartoonist-Larry-Picker ing-claims-police-protection-posting-derogatory-picture-Prophet-Mohammed .html. • " **'trumping the fundamental right of free speech' "** Daniel Pipes, "Naser Khader and Flemming Rose: Reflections on the Danish Cartoon Controversy," Middle East Quarterly 14, no. 4 (Fall 2007), http://www.meforum.org/1758/naser -khader-and-flemming-rose-reflections-on. • " **'it shows that violence works' "** Teis Jensen, "Danish Newspaper Says Won't Print Prophet Cartoon," Reuters, January 9, 2015, http://ca.reuters.com/article/topNews/idCAKBN0KI0WD20150109. • **PAGE 194: "no ban on using Muhammad's image in Islam"** Christiane Gruber, "The Koran Does Not Forbid Images of the Prophet," Newsweek, January 9, 2015, http://www.newsweek.com/koran-does-not-forbid-images-prophet-298298. • " 'to act otherwise than with justice' " Qasim Rashid, "Islam Backs Free Speech: Column," *USA Today,* January 9, 2015, http://www.usatoday.com/story/opinion/2015/01/09/free-speech-islam-charlie-hebdo-column/21458257/. • " 'but refraining from doing so' " Council on American-Islamic Relations, "US Muslims Condemn Paris Terror Attack, Defend Free Speech," press release, January 7, 2015, https://www.cair.com/press-center/press-releases/12797-american-muslims-condemn-paris-terror-attack-defend-free-speech.html • "invoking the war in Iraq—'represented Christianity' " "Paris," Russell Brand, January 10, 2015, http://www.russellbrand.com/paris/. • PAGE 195: " 'and his miracles are described in every detail' " "Product Description: Muhammad: Messenger of Allah, Revised Edition," Islamic Bookstore.com, accessed June 21, 2015, http://www.islamicbookstore.com/b12199.html. • "what must be done with those who disrespect Muhammad" Qadi 'Iyad Ibn Musa al-Yahsubi, *Ash Shifa (Muhammad: Messenger of Allah)* (Norwich, England: Diwan Press, 2010). • " 'a clear statement or allusion' " Qadi 'Iyad Ibn Musa al-Yahsubi, "Muhammad: Messenger of Allah: Part Four, Section One," trans. Aisha Abdarrahman Bewley, Masud, accessed June 21, 2015, http://www.masud.co.uk/ISLAM/misc/alshifa/pt4ch1sec1.htm. • "through Muhammad's daughter Fatima" *Encyclopaedia Britannica Online,* "Al-Husayn ibn Ali," accessed June 21, 2015, http://www.britannica.com/biography/al-Husayn-ibn-Ali-Muslim-leader-and-martyr. • " 'Whoever curses my Companions, beat him' " Qadi 'Iyad Ibn Musa al-Yahsubi, "Muhammad: Messenger of Allah: Part Four, Section Two," trans. Aisha Abdarrahman Bewley, Masud, accessed June 21, 2015, http://www.masud.co.uk/ISLAM/misc/alshifa/pt4ch1sec2.htm. • PAGE 196: " 'in any manner that might cause disrespect for them' " John McManus, "Have Pictures of Muhammad always been forgiven?" BBC News, January 15, 2015, http://www.bbc.com/news/magazine-30814555. • " 'depict him in any shape, any way or form' " Emma Graham-Harrison, "Drawing the Prophet: Islam's Hidden History of Muhammad Images," *The Guardian,* January 10, 2015, http://www.theguardian.com/world/2015/jan/10/drawing-prophet-islam-muhammad-images. • "would be murdered like Theo van Gogh" Ed Pilkington, "South Park Censored After Threat of Fatwa Over Muhammad Episode," *The Guardian,* April 22, 2010, http://www.theguardian.com/tv-and-radio/2010/apr/22/south-park-censored-fatwa-muhammad. • "documentary on the mistreatment of women in Islamic societies" "Gunman Kills Dutch Film Director," BBC News, November 2, 2004, http://news.bbc.co.uk/2/hi/europe/3974179.stm. • " 'encourage Muslims to kill whoever does that' " Tim Lister, "Security Brief: Radical Islamic Web Site Takes on *South Park,*" *This Just In* (blog), CNN, April 19, 2010, http://news.blogs.cnn.com/2010/04/19/security-brief-radical-islamic-web-site-takes-on-south-park/?hpt=T2. • "The executives feared similar reprisals" Jake Tapper and Dan Morris, "Secrets of *South Park,*" ABC News, September 22, 2006, http://abcnews.go.com/Nightline/Entertainment/Story?id=2479197&page=1. • PAGE 197: " 'we couldn't just show a simple image' " Jake Tapper and Dan Morris, "Secrets of *South Park,*" ABC News, September 22, 2006, http://abcnews.go.com/Nightline/Entertainment/Story?id=2479197&page=1. • " 'refused to broadcast an image of Mohammad on their network' " Jake Tapper and Dan Morris, "Secrets of *South Park,*" ABC News, September 22, 2006, http://abcnews.go.com/Nightline/Entertainment/Story?id=2479197&page=1. • " 'We're afraid of getting blown up' " Jake Tapper and Dan Morris, "Secrets of *South Park,*" ABC News, September 22, 2006, http://abcnews.go.com/Nightline/Entertainment/Story?id=2479197&page=1. • "but with a catch" Yusuf al-Qarawadi, "Freedom of Expression from an Islamic Perspective," On Islam, January 8, 2015, http://www

.onislam.net/english/ask-the-scholar/shariah-based-systems/imamate-and-politi
cal-systems/174717-freedom-of-expression-from-an-islamic-perspective.
html?Political_Systems. • " **'dignity should not be transgressed upon'** " Yusuf
al-Qarawadi, "Freedom of Expression from an Islamic Perspective," On Islam, January 8, 2015, http://www.onislam.net/english/ask-the-scholar/shariah-based-systems
/imamate-and-political-systems/174717-freedom-of-expression-from-an
-islamic-perspective.html?Political_Systems. • " **'punishments for such transgressions vary from fines to death'** " Angelina Theodorou, "Which Countries Still
Outlaw Apostasy and Blasphemy?" *Fact Tank,* Pew Research Center, May 26, 2014,
http://www.pewresearch.org/fact-tank/2014/05/28/which-countries-still-outlaw
-apostasy-and-blasphemy/. • **"Qatar, Afghanistan, Pakistan, and Iran"** Angelina
Theodorou, "Which Countries Still Outlaw Apostasy and Blasphemy?" *Fact Tank,*
Pew Research Center, May 26, 2014, http://www.pewresearch.org/fact
-tank/2014/05/28/which-countries-still-outlaw-apostasy-and-blasphemy/. • **PAGE
198: "blogger in Tunisia was jailed for 'insulting Islam' "** Amnesty International,
"Tunisia: Blogger Jailed for 'Insulting Islam' Must Be Released," press release,
March 12, 2013, https://www.amnesty.org/en/press-releases/2013/03/tunisia-blog
ger-jailed-insulting-islam-must-be-released/. • **"song that was considered offensive
to the Muslim faith"** Syed Raza Hassan and Katharine Houreld, "Ballooning Pakistan Blasphemy Charges Engulf Television Stations," Reuters, May 20, 2014, http://
in.reuters.com/article/2014/05/20/pakistan-blasphemy-tv-stations-idINKBN0E00
Y420140520. • " **'have been hurt for any reason can file a case'** " Syed Raza Hassan
and Katharine Houreld, "Ballooning Pakistan Blasphemy Charges Engulf Television
Stations," Reuters, May 20, 2014, http://in.reuters.com/article/2014/05/20/pakistan
-blasphemy-tv-stations-idINKBN0E00Y420140520. • **"enact laws to counter it, including deterrent punishment'** " Patrick Poole, "Largest Islamic Body in the World
Calls for More Anti-Free Speech Laws in Wake of *Charlie Hebdo* Attack," *PJ Tattler*
(blog), PJ Media, January 12, 2015, http://pjmedia.com/tatler/2015/01/12/organiza
tion-of-islamic-cooperation-calls-for-more-speech-codes-defamation-laws-in
-wake-of-charlie-hebdo-attack/. • " **'imminent violence based on religion or belief'** " United Nations Human Rights Council, Resolution 16/18, "Combatting Intolerance, Negative Stereotyping and Stigmatization of, and Discrimination,
Incitement to Violence and Violence Against, Persons Based on Religion or Belief,"
April 12, 2011, http://www2.ohchr.org/english/bodies/hrcouncil/docs/16session/A
.HRC.RES.16.18_en.pdf. • " **'must be followed by sustained commitment'** " Secretary of State Hillary Rodham Clinton, "Adoption of Resolution at Human Rights
Council Combatting Discrimination and Violence," press release, March 24, 2011,
https://geneva.usmission.gov/2011/03/24/adoption-of-resolution-at-human-rights
-council-combating-discrimination-and-violence/. • **PAGE 199: " 'old-fashioned
techniques of peer pressure and shaming'** " Andrew C. McCarthy, "Coercing
Conformity," *National Review,* December 28, 2013, http://www.nationalreview.com
/article/367132/coercing-conformity-andrew-c-mccarthy. • **"he said, 'then we still
have a problem'** " "Ekmeleddin Ihsano?lu, Secretary-General of the Organization
of Islamic Cooperation," *The Interview,* France 24, October 5, 2012, http://www.france
24.com/en/20121004-ekmeleddin-ihsanoglu-secretary-general-organisation
-islamic-cooperation-ioc-protests-arab-world-anti-islam-film-syria/. • **"would lead
to demonstrations and violence"** "Ekmeleddin Ihsano?lu, Secretary-General of the
Organization of Islamic Cooperation," The Interview, France 24, October 5, 2012,
http://www.france24.com/en/20121004-ekmeleddin-ihsanoglu-secretary-general
-organisation-islamic-cooperation-ioc-protests-arab-world-anti-islam-film-syria/.
• " **'suppress speech that casts Islam in a bad light'** " Jeremy Rabkin, "Islam and

Free Speech," *The American Spectator,* March, 2009, http://spectator.org/articles
/42095/islam-and-free-speech. • **PAGE 200: "58 percent of US Muslims surveyed
replied 'No' "** Andrew J. Bostom, "Sixty Percent of US Muslims Reject Freedom of
Expression," *American Thinker,* November 1, 2012, http://www.americanthinker
.com/blog/2012/11/sixty_percent_of_us_muslims_reject_freedom_of_expression
.html#ixzz3c7nuG0N8.

PART THREE: WHAT CAN BE DONE
PAGE 203: " 'the favorable moment for helping them to another step' " "Jefferson
Quotes and Family Letters: Extract of Thomas Jefferson to Thomas Cooper," Monticello, accessed June 22, 2015, http://tjrs.monticello.org/letter/1701. • **"to mock the
Court's decision"** Michael Lucchese, "ISIS 'Celebrates' SCOTUS Decision by Toss-
ing 4 Accused Gay Men Off Roof," *Breitbart.com,* June 30, 2015. http://www
.breitbart.com/national-security/2015/06/30/isis-celebrates-scotus-decision-by
-tossing-4-accused-gay-men-off-roof. • **"drowning those inside"** Joe Tacopino,
"ISIS slowly drowns prisoners in a cage," *New York Post,* http://nypost.com/2015
/06/24/new-video-shows-isis-slowly-drowning-prisoners-in-a-cage. • **"record their
heads being blown off"** Sharona Schwartz, "Islamic State's Latest Execution Video
May Be Its Most Horrifying Yet," *TheBlaze,* June 23, 2015, http://www.theblaze.com
/stories/2015/06/23/islamic-state-groups-latest-video-of-executions-may-be-its
-worst-yet. • **PAGE 204: "enemies are 'people who have perverted Islam' "**
"Obama: We Are at War with People Who Perverted Islam," *USA Today,* February
18, 2015, http://www.usatoday.com/videos/news/nation/2015/02/18/23638083/. •
" 'trying, in effect, to hijack Islam itself' " George W. Bush, "George W. Bush Ad-
dresses Muslims in the Aftermath of the 9/11 Attacks," Berkley Center for Religion,
Peace & World Affairs, Georgetown University, September 20, 2001, http://berkley
center.georgetown.edu/quotes/george-w-bush-addresses-muslims-in-the-after
math-of-the-9-11-attacks. • **PAGE 205: "and as 'a war against evil, not against
Islam' "** See, for example: George W. Bush and King Abdullah of Jordan "Remarks
by President George W. Bush and His Majesty King Abdullah of Jordan," (speech,
The Oval Office, Washington, D.C., September 28, 2001), and The White House, Office of the Press Secretary, "President Bush, President Havel Discuss Iraq, NATO,"
press release, November 20, 2002, http://georgewbush-whitehouse.archives.gov
/news/releases/2002/11/20021120-1.html. • **" 'majority of Muslims reject that interpretation of Islam' "** Jeremy Diamond, "Why Obama Won't Call Terror Fight a
War on Radical Islam," CNN, February 1, 2015, http://www.cnn.com/2015/02/01
/politics/obama-radical-islam-terrorism-war/. • **PAGE 206: " 'worthless to us even
if they are worth billions of dollars' "** Kareem Shaheen, "ISIS Fighters Destroy
Ancient Artifacts at Mosul Museum," *The Guardian,* February 26, 2015, http://www
.theguardian.com/world/2015/feb/26/isis-fighters-destroy-ancient-artefacts-mosul
-museum-iraq. • **"ISIS vandals demolished the ruins of Hatra"** Chris Johnston,
"ISIS Militants Destroy Remains of Hatra in Northern Iraq," *The Guardian,* March 7,
2015, http://www.theguardian.com/world/2015/mar/07/isis-militants-destroy-hatra
-iraq. • **PAGE 207: "before leveling the entire place with explosives"** Kareem
Shaheen, "Outcry over ISIS Destruction of Ancient Assyrian Site of Nimrud," *The
Guardian,* March 6, 2015, http://www.theguardian.com/world/2015/mar/06/isis
-destroys-ancient-assyrian-site-of-nimrud. • **" 'what they can't sell they destroy' "**
Loveday Morris, "Islamic State Isn't Just Destroying Ancient Artifacts—It's Selling
Them," *Washington Post,* June 8, 2015, http://www.washingtonpost.com/world
/middle_east/islamic-state-isnt-just-destroying-ancient-artifacts—its-selling-them
/2015/06/08/ca5ea964-08a2-11e5-951e-8e15090d64ae_story.html. • **"slaughtered**

thousands of Christians in Nigeria" Mark Anderson, "Nigeria Suffers Highest Number of Civilian Deaths in African War Zones," *The Guardian,* January 23, 2015, http://www.theguardian.com/global-development/2015/jan/23/boko-haram-nigeria -civilian-death-toll-highest-acled-african-war-zones, and Stoyan Zaimov, "Boko Haram Hacks to Death Dozens, Including Scores of Christians; Continues Forcing Young Girls to Carry Out Suicide Bombings," *Christian Post,* May 28, 2015, http:// www.christianpost.com/news/boko-haram-hacks-to-death-dozens-including -scores-of-christians-continues-forcing-young-girls-to-carry-out-suicide-bombings -139674/. • **"as young as nine or ten years old as sexual slaves"** Catrina Stewart, "Nigeria's Abducted Schoolgirls: We'll Send Them as Slaves, Pledges Boko Haram Terror Leader," *The Independent,* May 6, 2014, http://www.independent.co.uk/news /world/africa/nigerias-abducted-schoolgirls-boko-haram-leader-pledges-to-sell -them-in-the-marketplace-9324496.html. • **" 'took slaves himself during [the] Badr war' "** Ryan Mauro, "Efforts Mount to Gloss Over Islamist Ideology of Boko Haram," The Clarion Project, May 15, 2014, http://www.clarionproject.org/analysis /efforts-mount-gloss-over-islamist-ideology-boko-haram#. • **PAGE 208: " 'by tongue and teeth' "** Anonymous, "Al-Qaeda Manual," in *Voices of Terror: Manifestoes, Writings and Manuals of Al Qaeda, Hamas, and Other Terrorists from Around the World and Throughout the Ages,* ed. Walter Laqueur (New York: Reed Press, 2004). • **" 'underestimate it and back foolish schemes to counter it' "** Graeme Wood, "What ISIS Really Wants," *The Atlantic,* March 2015, http://www.theatlantic .com/features/archive/2015/02/what-isis-really-wants/384980/. • **" 'to an organization that has decisively eclipsed it' "** Graeme Wood, "What ISIS Really Wants," *The Atlantic,* March 2015, http://www.theatlantic.com/features/archive/2015/02/what -isis-really-wants/384980/. • **PAGE 209: " 'and ultimately to bringing about the apocalypse"** Graeme Wood, "What ISIS Really Wants," *The Atlantic,* March 2015, http://www.theatlantic.com/features/archive/2015/02/what-isis-really-wants /384980/. • **"one in four think highly of Hezbollah"** Global Attitudes Project, *Muslim Publics Share Concerns About Extremist Groups* (Washington, D.C.: Pew Research Center, September 10, 2013), http://www.pewglobal.org/files/2013/09/Pew -Global-Attitudes-Project-Extremism-Report-Final-9–10–135.pdf. • **"aren't the least bit worried about Islamic extremism"** Global Attitudes Project, *Muslim Publics Share Concerns About Extremist Groups* (Washington, D.C.: Pew Research Center, September 10, 2013), http://www.pewglobal.org/files/2013/09/Pew-Global -Attitudes-Project-Extremism-Report-Final-9–10–135.pdf. • **PAGE 210: "and al-Qaeda 'comes from nowhere' "** Ryan Mauro, "Efforts Mount to Gloss Over Islamist Ideology of Boko Haram," The Clarion Project, May 15, 2014, http://www .clarionproject.org/analysis/efforts-mount-gloss-over-islamist-ideology-boko-haram#. • **" 'We do not even understand the idea' "** Eric Schmit, "In Battle to Defang ISIS, US Targets Its Psychology," *The New York Times,* December 28, 2014, http://www.ny times.com/2014/12/29/us/politics/in-battle-to-defang-isis-us-targets-its-psychol ogy-.html?_r=0. • **" 'for me it's about avoiding failure' "** Eric Schmit, "In Battle to Defang ISIS, US Targets Its Psychology," *The New York Times,* December 28, 2014, http://www.nytimes.com/2014/12/29/us/politics/in-battle-to-defang-isis-us-targets -its-psychology-.html?_r=0. • **PAGE 211: " 'Islam is the religion of war' "** Robert Spencer, "Islamic State Caliph: 'Islam Is the Religion of War,' " Jihad Watch, May 14, 2015, http://www.jihadwatch.org/2015/05/islamic-state-caliph-islam-is-the-religion -of-war. • **" 'until Allah is worshiped alone' "** Robert Spencer, "Islamic State Caliph: 'Islam Is the Religion of War,' " Jihad Watch, May 14, 2015, http://www.jihad watch.org/2015/05/islamic-state-caliph-islam-is-the-religion-of-war. • **" 'never for a day grew tired of war' "** Robert Spencer, "Islamic State Caliph: 'Islam Is the Reli-

gion of War,' " Jihad Watch, May 14, 2015, http://www.jihadwatch.org/2015/05
/islamic-state-caliph-islam-is-the-religion-of-war. • **PAGE 213: "laid the blame for
a shoot-out . . . on the free-speech event's organizer"** John Hinderaker, "Blaming
Pamela Geller," *Powerline,* May 5, 2015, http://www.powerlineblog.com/archives
/2015/05/blaming-pamela-geller.php, and Carol Brown, "Media Piling on Pamela
Geller," *American Thinker,* May 6, 2015, http://www.americanthinker.com/blog
/2015/05/media_piling_on_pamela_geller_.html. • **"publishing U.S. secrets in the
fight against al-Qaeda"** Gabriel Schoenfield, "Has the *New York Times* Violated the
Espionage Act," *Commentary,* March 1, 2006, https://www.commentarymagazine
.com/article/has-the-%e2%80%9cnew-york-times%e2%80%9d-violated-the-espio
nage-act/. • **"amounted to a tragic case of 'workplace violence' "** Michael Daly,
"Nidal Hasan's Murders Termed 'Workplace Violence' by US," *The Daily Beast,* August 6, 2013, http://www.thedailybeast.com/articles/2013/08/06/nidal-hasan-s-murders
-termed-workplace-violence-by-u-s.html. • **"shouts of 'Allahu Akbar' as he
gunned down his victims"** Ewan MacAskill, "Fort Hood Gunman Shouted 'Allahu
Akbar' as He Opened Fire," *The Guardian,* November 6, 2009, http://www.theguard
ian.com/world/2009/nov/06/fort-hood-shooter-alive. • **"correspondence Hasan
carried on with Anwar al-Awlaki"** David Johnston and Scott Shane, "US Knew of
Suspects Tie to Radical Cleric," *New York Times,* November 9, 2009, http://www.ny
times.com/2009/11/10/us/10inquire.html. • **PAGE 214: "he was 'on the wrong side'
in the U.S. Army"** David Usborne, "Fort Hood Gunman, Nidal Hasan, Was on
'Wrong Side' in War Against Muslims," *The Independent,* August 6, 2013, http://
www.independent.co.uk/news/world/americas/fort-hood-gunman-nidal-hasan
-was-on-wrong-side-in-war-against-muslims-8748840.html. • **"considered himself
a 'Soldier of Allah' "** Peter Selvin, "Apartment's Detritus Offers Glimpse into Suspect's Life," *The Washington Post,* November 12, 2009, http://www.washingtonpost
.com/wp-dyn/content/article/2009/11/11/AR2009111125063.html?hpid=topnews. •
" 'this includes my oath of US citizenship' " Catherine Herridge and Pamela
Browne, "Hasan Sends Writings to Fox News Ahead of Fort Hood Shooting Trial,"
Fox News, August 1, 2013, http://www.foxnews.com/politics/2013/08/01/hasan
-sends-writings-ahead-fort-hood-shooting-trial/. • **"even I was shocked by the
media's response"** Wilson, "Glenn: 'After What I Have Learned This Week I'm a
Changed Person," Glenn Beck, April 19, 2013, http://www.glennbeck.com/2013
/04/19/glenn-%E2%80%9Cafter-what-i-have-learned-this-week-im-a-changed
-person-%E2%80%9D/. • **" 'could this be homegrown terror' "** Scott Whitlock,
"ABC speculates: Could this be 'Homegrown Terror?' Newsbusters, John Hall, April
16, 2013, http://newsbusters.org/blogs/scott-whitlock/2013/04/16/abc-speculates
-was-boston-homegrown-terror-features-mark-potok-extre. • **PAGE 215: " 'promised victory and we will surely get it' "** Eric Levenson, "Here's the Note Dzhokhar
Tsarnaev Wrote Inside the Boat Where He Was Captured," Boston.com, March 10,
2015, http://www.boston.com/news/local/massachusetts/2015/03/10/here-the-note
-dzhokhar-tsarnaev-wrote-inside-the-boat-where-was-captured/h7xFrSTXKT6L4
Euc8N5bEN/story.html. • **"were 'lone wolves' . . . not connected with any terrorist group"** David Crary, Denise Lavoie, Eileen Sullivan, and Lara Jakes, " 'Boston
Suspects Were Lone Wolves Motivated by Radical Islam,' " *The Times of Israel,* April
23, 2013, http://www.timesofisrael.com/boston-suspects-motivated-by-anti-us-views
-radical-islam/. • **"at least thirty US citizens involved in a 'lone wolf' terrorist
plot"** Brian Bennett, "White House Steps Up Warnings About Terrorism on US
Soil," *Los Angeles Times,* May 18, 2015, http://www.latimes.com/nation/la-na-terror
-threat-20150518-story.html#page=1. • **" 'who may strike with little or no warning' "** Brian Bennett, "White House Steps Up Warnings About Terrorism on US

Soil," *Los Angeles Times,* May 18, 2015, http://www.latimes.com/nation/la-na-terror-threat-20150518-story.html#page=1. • **PAGE 216: " 'anti-Christian images, or any other religious belief' "** Joel Brinkley and Ian Fisher, "US Says It Also Finds Cartoons of Muhammad Offensive," *The New York Times,* February 4, 2006, http://www.nytimes.com/2006/02/04/politics/04mideast.html?adxnnl=1&adxnnlx=143492 8110-nHwdubAJz2/crUhBIQmuHA. • **"his parole in a completely unrelated case"** Evan Perez and Erica E. Phillips, "Alleged Maker of Anti-Muslim Video Jailed in Fraud Case," *The Wall Street Journal,* September 28, 2012, http://www.wsj.com/arti cles/SB10000872396390443328404578022953359653378. • **"wound up spending a year in a federal prison cell"** Steve Gorman, "California Man Behind Anti-Islam Film to Be Freed from Federal Custody," Reuters, September 26, 2013, http://www.reuters.com/article/2013/09/26/us-usa-film-protests-idUSBRE98P0FV20130926, and Victoria Kim, Abby Sewell, and Jessica Garrison, "Jailing of 'Innocence of Muslims' Creator Raises Free Speech Worries," *Los Angeles Times,* October 2, 2012. • **" 'churches are destroyed, or the Holocaust is denied' "** "At UN Debate, US President Urges Dealing Honestly with Tensions Between Arabs and West," UN News Centre, September 25, 2012, http://www.un.org/apps/news/story.asp?NewsID=42998# .VYnaldjbJMt. • **PAGE 217: "sharia law into the fabric of our society and our judicial system"** Ryan Mauro, "Assembly of Muslims Jurists of America," The Clarion Project, January 28, 2014, http://www.clarionproject.org/category/tags/assembly -muslim-jurists-america#. • **" 'first official Shariah law system in the United States' "** Benjamin Gill, "Islamic Shariah Tribunal Begins Operating in Texas," CBN News, February 6, 2015, http://www.cbn.com/cbnnews/us/2015/February/Islamic -Shariah-Tribunal-Begins-Operating-in-Texas/. • **" 'invade the White House or invade Austin' "** Benjamin Gill, "Islamic Shariah Tribunal Begins Operating in Texas," CBN News, February 6, 2015, http://www.cbn.com/cbnnews/us/2015/February /Islamic-Shariah-Tribunal-Begins-Operating-in-Texas/. • **PAGE 218: " 'Islamic principles that Muslims live by' "** Dina Samir Shehata, "Anti-Sharia Bill Dead, but Sentiment Alive," *Austin Chronicle,* May 22, 2015, http://www.austinchronicle.com /news/2015–05–22/anti-sharia-bill-dead-but-sentiment-alive/. • **"announce their allegiance to America and our laws"** Dina Samir Shehata, "Anti-Sharia Bill Dead, but Sentiment Alive," *Austin Chronicle,* May 22, 2015, http://www.austinchronicle .com/news/2015–05–22/anti-sharia-bill-dead-but-sentiment-alive/. • **PAGE 219: "doubled to more than 2 million between 2001 and 2010"** Meghan Neal, "Number of Muslims in the US Doubles Since 9/11," *New York Daily News,* May 3, 2012, http://www.nydailynews.com/news/national/number-muslims-u-s-doubles-9–11 -article-1.1071895. • **"urging the resettlement of as many as 65,000 more Syrian refugees"** Martin Matishak, "Senate Dems Call on Obama to Resettle 65,000 Syrian Refugees," *The Hill,* May 21, 2015, http://thehill.com/policy/defense/242873-senate -dems-call-on-obama-to-resettle-6k-syrian-refugees, and Justin Fishel and Mike Levine, "US Officials Admit Concern over Syrian Refugee Effort," ABC News, February 12, 2015, http://abcnews.go.com/International/officials-fear-syrian-refugees -pose-threat-us/story?id=28930114. • **"having traveled from Minnesota to join the Islamic State"** Jamie Yuccas, "Minneapolis Has Become Recruiting Ground for Islamic Extremists," CBS News, August 27, 2014, http://www.cbsnews.com/news /minneapolis-has-become-recruiting-ground-for-islamic-extremists/. • **PAGE 220: " 'Liberty and Popery cannot live together' "** James H. Hutson, ed., *The Founders on Religion* (Princeton, NJ: Princeton University Press, 2005), 41. • **" 'they appear to merit the enjoyment' "** Steve Coffman, ed., *Words of the Founding Fathers: Selected Quotations of Franklin, Washington, Adams, Jefferson, Madison, and Hamilton, with Sources* (Jefferson, NC: McFarland, 2012), 53. • **" 'of any sect—or they may be**

Atheists' " George Washington, *Writings,* ed. John H. Rhodehamel (New York: Literary Classics of the United States, 1997), 555–56. • **PAGE 221: " 'giving it on all occasions their effectual support' "** George Washington, *Writings,* ed. John H. Rhodehamel (New York: Literary Classics of the United States, 1997), 767. • **" 'because America is one country' "** The White House, Office of the Press Secretary, "President Promotes Compassionate Conservatism," press release, April 30, 2002, http://georgewbush-whitehouse.archives.gov/news/releases/2002/04/20020430–5 .html. • **PAGE 222: " 'Democracy, whiskey, sexy' "** Jim Dwyer, "A Nation at War: In the Field: 101st Airborne; A Bridgehead, and a Thirsty Welcome," *New York Times,* April 3, 2003, http://www.nytimes.com/2003/04/03/world/a-nation-at-war-in-the -field-101st-airborne-a-bridgehead-and-a-thirsty-welcome.html. • **PAGE 223: " 'in every human heart the desire to live in freedom' "** "The President's Public Expression of Religion," *Frontline,* PBS, April 29, 2004, http://www.pbs.org/wgbh/pages /frontline/shows/jesus/president/public.html. • **"as the Protestant Reformation is 'highly doubtful' "** James Q. Wilson, "Islam and Freedom," *Commentary,* December 4, 2004, https://www.commentarymagazine.com/article/islam-and-freedom-1/. • **PAGE 224: " 'thereby create an opportunity for lay rule' "** James Q. Wilson, "Islam and Freedom," *Commentary,* December 4, 2004, https://www.commentarymaga zine.com/article/islam-and-freedom-1/. • **" 'and other efforts to remake society' "** Ayaan Hirsi Ali, *Heretic: Why Islam Needs a Reformation Now* (New York: Harper Collins, 2015), 60. • **" 'comprehensive tradition of the Prophet Muhammad' "** Thomas J. Haidon, "The Islamic Reformation," *FrontPage Mag,* January 18, 2015, http://archive.frontpagemag.com/readArticle.aspx?ARTID=9952. • **" 'will prove to be nothing but rhetoric' "** Thomas J. Haidon, "The Islamic Reformation," *FrontPage Mag,* January 18, 2015, http://archive.frontpagemag.com/readArticle.aspx?ARTID =9952. • **PAGE 225: " 'can disguise their people as migrants' "** Jamie Dettmer, "Meet the Islamic Fanatic Who Wants to Kill ISIS," *The Daily Beast,* June 10, 2015, http://www.thedailybeast.com/articles/2015/06/10/meet-the-islamic-fanatic-who -wants-to-kill-isis.html.